ime

WORLD WITHOUT END?

WORLD WITHOUT END?

Environmental Disaster and the Collapse of Empires

Ian Whyte

I.B. TAURIS
LONDON · NEW YORK

Published in 2008 by I.B.Tauris & Co. Ltd
6 Salem Road, London W2 4BU
175 Fifth Avenue, New York NY 10010
www.ibtauris.com

In the United States of America and Canada distributed
by Palgrave Macmillan, a division of St. Martin's Press,
175 Fifth Avenue, New York NY 10010

ISBN 978 1 84511 055 0

A full CIP record for this book is available from the British Library
A full CIP record is available from the Library of Congress

Library of Congress Catalog Card Number: available

Set in OurType Arnhem by Ewan Smith, London
Printed and bound in the Czech Republic by FINIDR, s.r.o.

CONTENTS

ILLUSTRATIONS

Figures

Table

Plates (between pages 118 and 119)

For Rebecca and Ruth,
who will experience much environmental
change in their lives

CHAPTER 1

Environmental Change and Human Response in Perspective: the Last 12,000 Years

In the last 12,000 years or so – the Holocene or post-glacial period – the physical environment in most parts of the world has undergone profound and sometimes rapid change. Such change has often been due to variations in natural conditions but increasingly, as population has grown and technology has improved, it has been the result of human agency. Paul Crutzen, in a specialist study of the ozone layer, has suggested that we have entered a new geological period, the Anthropocene, in which humans now play a key role in geological and ecological change. Crutzen (2002) puts the opening of the Anthropocene in the late eighteenth century, i.e. with the beginning of the Industrial Revolution, marking the start of the steady rise in levels of atmospheric carbon dioxide which is considered to be a major component of contemporary global warming.

Despite such advances in technology, the impact of *natural* processes on human societies remains a major feature of life on Earth today (in developed as much as in developing countries), a fact demonstrated every week in the media, where news of natural hazards such as earthquakes, volcanic eruptions, hurricanes, floods and droughts repeatedly appears. These events represent relatively rapid, short-term environmental processes focused on specific areas. Often, however, environmental change is less dramatic, more subtle, yet nevertheless highly significant. Measured globally, the scale of environmental fluctuation may not always seem very impressive – a few centimetres rise in sea level or a fraction of a degree increase in average annual temperatures, for instance, may not seem exactly life-threatening – but the consequences can be none the less far-reaching. For example, the variation in global average annual temperatures between the start of the Holocene period some 12,000 years ago and its warmest phase some 7,000 years ago has been around 4°C. This may not sound very great, yet fluctuations within this range have been sufficient to cause major changes in vegetation patterns, agriculture and settlement in many parts of the world. Of course, these are only global averages: temperature changes have sometimes been more pronounced in some key sensitive regions, such as the uplands of north-west Europe. The environment, then, has been not just a scenic backdrop to human activity, as historians have sometimes tended to think, but an important determinant in how societies developed.

Yet environmental changes have not always been slow and gradual. If we take the example of climate again, a modern blockbuster film, *The Day After Tomorrow*, has brought the idea of sudden, dramatic climatic change, albeit in a sensationalised fashion, to a far wider audience than merely the scientific community. The suggestion that climate could suddenly flip over a key threshold into a totally different, and from our point of view much less desirable, mode is not just the stuff of Hollywood films: the speed at which environmental changes can occur may clearly be seen in the real world (if in less dramatic fashion). Some 13,000 years ago conditions had warmed such that ice had probably disappeared entirely from the British Isles (see Plate 1). Within a period of only about 700 years, however, temperatures dropped sufficiently for a major ice cap to build up in the western Scottish Highlands, stretching from Torridon to Loch Lomond, with ice up to 600 metres thick and smaller glaciers occurring as far south as the Lake District (Lowe and Walker 1984) (see Plate 2). The change from ice-free to glacial mode seems to have happened quite rapidly. At the end of this cold snap temperatures rose even faster – perhaps within a decade – causing the ice to melt and leaving the moraines that can clearly be seen in the Scottish glens today (Dansgaard et al. 1989; Hughen et al. 1996). That such a large ice cap could develop, create major depositional landforms and then disappear all within a few centuries – the merest blink of geological time – shows just how rapidly environmental changes can occur.

This sudden cold snap is thought by some scientists to have been caused, paradoxically, by a major inflow of fresh water into the North Atlantic as a result of the collapse of the major continental ice cap in North America (Williams et al. 1998). The meltwater destabilised the North Atlantic ocean circulation, which is driven by salinity and density differences. Currently many climate specialists are concerned that this process could occur again as an indirect result of human action. It has been suggested that if the amount of fresh water entering the North Atlantic from the melting of ice caps (especially in Greenland, and from other sources such as melting permafrost) reaches sufficient levels then salinity changes in the Atlantic Ocean could shut down the Gulf Stream and return western Europe to ice-age conditions, a freeze ironically brought on by global warming! Already there are indications that in parts of the North Atlantic the ocean circulation is weakening compared with the 1970s and 1980s, although it is not clear yet whether this trend is part of a natural cycle or the result of human-induced global warming. It should be said that global environmental conditions are very different today from what they were at the end of the last ice age, so that they may not provide a suitable analogue for the twenty-first century. The fact that climatic conditions can change so fast, however, regardless of cause, is a matter for concern. Three decades ago the Greenland ice cap was seen as being virtually indestructible under any immediately foreseeable climatic conditions. Today reports are suggesting that, if current atmospheric warming trends continue, the ice cap could disappear within the next thousand years. Perhaps this will be scaled down to a century in a few more years?

Because of the scale of human interference, there is scarcely such a thing today as a 'natural environment'. Indeed, many ecosystems which are often considered to be 'natural', such as the acid grasslands and heather moorlands that cover extensive areas of the British uplands, are in fact no more natural than a field of wheat (Simmons 2003). In Britain, probably the nearest countryside that we have to a natural upland habitat is the high plateaux of the Cairngorms with their stony expanses sparsely covered by arctic-alpine plants, mosses and lichens. Yet even here human activity intrudes. The growing popularity of walking, climbing and skiing has brought increasing numbers of people into the area in recent decades. The evidence of their presence is stuffed into crevices in the summit cairns in the form of banana skins and orange peel, optimistically considered to be biodegradable by the visitors who have left them. In fact, in the low mean temperatures of the area this happens only extremely slowly. The patter of not-so-tiny climbing boots affects the vegetation while discarded sandwiches attract gulls into the area which then remain to steal the eggs of true mountain birds such as ravens (Lambert 2001; Watson 1991).

Nor is human interference with, and modification of, the environment a recent phenomenon. When European settlers first began to make serious inroads into the forests of the eastern USA they found not virgin woodlands but ones that had long been altered in terms of their extent and species composition by the activities of the indigenous population. These woodlands had only recently begun to revert to something more closely resembling a natural climax forest after the natives were almost wiped out by smallpox and other diseases introduced by early European explorers (Williams, M. 1989).

In the past it has often been assumed that human impact on the natural environment was relatively limited until recent times. The identification of the start of the Anthropocene with the beginning of the Industrial Revolution would seem to support this assumption. As our knowledge of prehistory becomes more detailed, however, it becomes increasingly evident that human societies have been capable of altering their environment on a significant scale since very early times, sometimes deliberately, sometimes accidentally, sometimes to their benefit but sometimes with disastrous, harmful consequences. The deterministic view that early human societies were the passive playthings of their environments has thus long been challenged. In a number of instances where archaeological and historical evidence has suggested a sudden decline in the population of an area, there are now signs that poor land management may have been a major contributory factor in addition to environmental changes operating independently of human activity. Since the Industrial Revolution the human race has developed ever more powerful means to control or alter natural environments to suit ever more complex and comfortable lifestyles with a belief that science is capable of achieving almost anything. Since the middle of the twentieth century, however, we have become increasingly aware that both our deliberate and inadvertent modifications of the environment are producing impacts that are rebounding on us to the extent that if current trends continue unchecked into the future, the very survival of our species may indeed be under threat.

One obvious direct influence on the physical environment and, at the same time, a major reason why certain kinds of environmental impact appear to have increased dramatically over time, has been the growing size of global population. Some 12,000 years ago the global human population may have been only around a million. The development of agriculture helped take this to around seven million by 6,000 years ago. By 500 BC it has risen to *c*.100 million, by AD 1700 to 600 million and by AD 1900 to 1,550 million. In the 1950s steady growth seemed set to continue. In recent years, however, the rate of increase has slowed down. In 2002 world population grew by *c*.74 million compared with 87 million in 1990. The rate of growth peaked forty years ago at 2.2 per cent per year. Although population is expected to rise to 9.1 billion by 2050 – an increase of almost 50 per cent on 2002 – by this time growth should have levelled off, with fertility at below replacement levels. It should not be assumed, however, that it necessarily needs a large population to produce considerable environmental impact. According to many scientists this is amply demonstrated by the rapid extinction of big-game animals in North America at the start of the Holocene period, probably by a very small population of hunters (Chapter 3), and by the effects of settlement, clearance and cultivation on soils and vegetation in the British uplands during the Bronze Age (Chapter 4).

The ways in which human societies respond to environmental change are as crucial as the nature of the changes themselves (whether those changes are independent of the societies or generated by their activities). Humans have indeed sometimes been passive receptors – even victims – of environmental change. Often their response has been more positive. The choices available to societies faced by environmental change varied. They might decide simply to suffer and endure – perhaps like the Norse Greenlanders facing colder, wetter weather conditions; or like the peasants in Norway and the Alps during the Little Ice Age coming to terms with glaciers advancing over their lands, and blaming it on divine wrath (Chapter 6). Alternatively, they might adapt their lifestyles and technology to meet the changed conditions. Or they might choose simply to migrate to a more favourable area.

Sometimes the response to pressures on resources generated by environmental change can be subtle and hard to detect. People may not even realise that they are responding at all. In Tudor and Stuart England, for instance, over-rapid population growth was regulated by a number of social mechanisms such as a relatively high age of first marriage for women, breastfeeding (which delayed further conceptions), and high rates of female celibacy (Wrigley and Schofield 1989). This distinguished English demographic patterns and social structures from those on the Continent. Even within Britain other approaches to the same problems were possible. The Scots were similar to the English in having a relatively late age at marriage for women and a good deal of female celibacy (Flinn 1976). During the seventeenth century, however, they also appear to have tackled the problem of keeping population pressure in check by accepting a change of diet: from one with a considerable amount of meat and meat products to an equally nutritious but less attractive one based overwhelmingly on cereal consumption (Gibson and Smout 1989). Climatic change, changes within ecosystems, and deliberate and accidental human impacts all have important roles in producing specific outcomes in particular cases of human interaction with the physical environment. Such interactions between so many causal variables are complex and difficult to unravel.

The aim of this book is to look at how environmental change, operating independently or as a result of human management and mismanagement, has impacted on human societies throughout the Holocene period. Equally importantly, it also examines how various

societies have responded to environmental stresses, sometimes suc-
cessfully, sometimes poorly. Following an introductory chapter, which
looks at environmental systems and processes, and at how we can
reconstruct past environments and date the changes in them, the bulk
of the book consists of a range of examples drawn from various periods,
focusing on societies at different stages of technological, economic and
social development and ranging from Palaeolithic hunter-gatherers
to modern developed societies. Examples are drawn from around the
globe. The aim is to highlight the diversity and complexity of human
responses to environmental pressures but sometimes, too, the simil-
arity of responses to environmental changes in different parts of the
world and at widely differing periods. The author's background is
that of a historical geographer whose interests overlap into landscape
and environmental history. In the process I will consider some of the
techniques by which physical and human geographers, environmental
scientists, archaeologists, historians and other specialists establish the
character of past environments and how much reliability we can place
on the reconstructions derived from them. I will try to show that establishing the nature of past environments and how they varied between
regions and changed over time can be difficult and that, despite the
sophistication of modern techniques, the results of research are often
uncertain and ambiguous.

There is no deliberate or overt agenda behind this book, but if you
are looking for any underlying message it is that there is an urgent need
for governments and environmental managers to develop truly sustainable ways of managing resources. These should be based, moreover,
on an understanding of the past as well as an appreciation of the
present and predictions of future trends. Too many current approaches
to environmental management are based on observations going back
for only a handful of years rather than decades or, preferably, centuries.
Lack of a historical perspective on environmental change and human
response can sometimes blind us to the significance of trends that
are in progress today. The recent collapse of the Atlantic cod fishery
may provide a warning of the danger of short-term memory. In 1992

the devastating collapse of cod stocks off the coast of Newfoundland forced the Canadian government to close the fishery with the loss of over 40,000 jobs, devastating fishing communities. The lessons of a previous disaster in the mid-1970s had not been learned. The collapse of this important fishery should, in turn, have rung warning bells with government fisheries departments around the world but, judging from recent policies relating to the North Sea, the warnings have once more been in vain. To take another example, much of our uncertainty about current rates of sea level change is due to a lack of hard data over sufficiently long periods of time (Chapter 8). Understanding how past societies have coped with environmental change can teach us lessons for the future.

CHAPTER 2

Environmental Systems and Processes

The study of environmental changes and how human societies respond to them involves posing only a few basic questions. What changes happened? When and why did they occur? How did people react to them? Answering such questions, however, is harder than asking them. It involves establishing the nature of past environments, how they have varied through time at scales ranging from local to global, and the dating of particular changes before going on to discuss why and how they happened. This can be done using a variety of scientific techniques, some of which will be discussed below.

Establishing how human societies reacted to a particular set of changes throws up another set of problems, for it may also involve the use of a totally different range of evidence, such as artefacts, historical documents or old maps. Accurate dating is particularly important in establishing whether particular events – e.g. the Elm Decline in Neolithic times (Chapter 4) – were synchronous across a wide area or occurred at different times in different places. On the cultural side, firm dating evidence is also essential in order to establish that the so-called 'human responses' did actually occur after the environmental effects that are claimed to have precipitated them.

There is a vitally important point to note, however. Establishing that two sets of events occurred at the same time, or in quick succession, does not necessarily prove that there was a direct, straightforward causal relationship between them. This is an error of logic of which climatologists have sometimes been accused by historians (Parry 1978; Fagan 2000). It involves identifying and dating a phase of environmental change, then looking for contemporary evidence of any stresses or upsets in society – population crashes, migration or wars – and then claiming, without any further indications of a link, that the former directly caused the latter. This is a natural, but dangerous and misleading, fallacy which has given some scientists working at the environment–human interface a bad name and which has certainly produced some bad history.

Historians tend to be more cautious in their use of documentary evidence. A good example is the French historian Le Roy Ladurie's careful reconstruction of the history of climate in western Europe over the last 1,000 years and his even more measured interpretation of its effects (1971). Yet, even so, for their part, landscape historians have tended to regard the environment, unless altered by man, as being more or less constant. They often seem to consider that physical changes during the Holocene period have not been sufficient to have had much impact on the landscape unless in very marginal areas such as Iceland. Environmental changes are automatically assumed to have been due to human agency rather than to nature.

Even more dangerous, because it is less easy to detect, is oversimplification in interpreting human response to environmental change. For example, it is true, up to a point, that some unusually cold winters in London during the most severe phase of the Little Ice Age in the later seventeenth century encouraged the freezing of the River Thames, leading to the great frost fairs that have been captured in paintings and engravings. The Thames certainly froze over at London at least eleven times in the seventeenth century (Lamb 1982). But it is also likely that the design of the old London Bridge, with its many narrow arches, tended to pond fresh water back upstream, making this part of the river more susceptible to freezing than it is today (with its more free-flowing current and a dredged, scoured channel).

It will already be evident that the accurate dating of environmental changes is an essential prerequisite for drawing any serious conclusions about human responses. As we will see, fairly precise dating can often be obtained from a range of scientific techniques, but in many cases only relative dating – saying that a particular stratum in a sequence of deposits is older or younger than another one – may be possible.

Establishing a date for a specific stratum in a sedimentary sequence provides a marker which allows rates of change, such as erosion and deposition, to be calculated. In Iceland, for instance, a particular layer of volcanic ash, the Landnam tephra, was deposited at about the time of the earliest Norse settlement. When this survives in areas where later deposition of windblown material from eroded soils has occurred, it provides an ideal baseline from which subsequent rates of soil erosion elsewhere, caused largely by overgrazing, can be calculated (Chapter 6).

The Nature of Environmental Change

A long-established view of environmental change was that physical processes operated in a linear fashion, steadily and gradually over long periods under the impact, mainly, of climatic and tectonic forces. With change of this sort small forces produced correspondingly small effects. This view goes back to the early days of scientific geology. In 1785 James Hutton first produced his *Theory of the Earth*, in which he developed the idea of a continuous, slow cycle of change operating over what were then unimaginably long time-spans. He suggested that land was gradually uplifted from the oceans to form mountain ranges. Weathering and erosion then got to work on them and gradually reduced the land to an area of low relief, the sediments deposited in the sea eventually forming rocks which would in due course be uplifted in turn. He described this cycle of processes as having 'no vestige of a beginning, no prospect of an end' and was a firm believer in the ides of uniformitarianism: that the past can be fully understood in terms of the processes operating on Earth at the present. His view of gradual, slow change formed the basis of the more detailed cycle of erosion put forward by the American geomorphologist W. M. Davis in 1899, which continued to influence views of broad-scale landform development through the first half of the twentieth century and beyond (Chorley et al. 1964). The study of vegetation change over time followed a similar path, emphasising slow and progressive variations leading to a stable state or climax in which the vegetation reached its full potential for a given set of climatic and soil conditions.

Another early school of thought in geology was catastrophism: the belief that the major features of the Earth had been shaped by dramatic cataclysmic events, especially floods. Such ideas dropped out of fashion with many geologists and geomorphologists in the later nineteenth century. From the 1960s, however, more sophisticated dating techniques began to show that environmental change had indeed often happened much more quickly than had previously been suspected. At the same time the application of systems theory to environmental processes offered new, challenging perspectives (Thornes and Brunsden 1977). The Earth as a whole can be seen as a complex system subject to external forces – such as variations in the amount of solar radiation received – as well as internal forces – such as the growth of human population – both of which can cause change. The four major sub-systems of the Earth that have been identified – the lithosphere, the atmosphere, the hydrosphere and the biosphere – are closely interconnected and variations in any one may affect the others (Park 1997).

Scientists began to suggest that instead of change operating smoothly and progressively many processes actually proceeded via short periods of intensive change rather than in the gradual, linear fashion discussed above. Changes in any one element of a system could lead to complex adjustments elsewhere. Such mechanisms could incorporate feedback loops. Negative feedback tended to reduce the effects of change in a system due to outside influences, returning it to stability. Positive feedback, on the other hand, involved internal mechanisms that reinforced and accelerated change within an environment triggered by external influences, so that changes become more and more pronounced, destabilising the system. A good example of this is the ice–albedo feedback mechanism by which a build-up of snow and ice, beyond a certain key level or threshold, increases the albedo or reflectivity of the land surface so that more solar radiation is reflected away from the Earth. This causes temperatures to fall further, so expanding the area covered by snow and ice and so on until an ice age is initiated. We will see a possible instance of this nearly happening within historic times in Chapter 6. This downward spiral can be broken only by a change in external factors such as the amount of solar radiation, or variations in the planet's orbit.

Systems theory introduced the idea of change occurring rapidly and unexpectedly, triggered by small rather than major events. It began to be suggested that many environmental systems might remain stable despite a good deal of change having occurred, until some critical boundary was crossed. When this happened a further small-scale change might cause the system to suddenly flip over into a totally different mode. Sometimes an environmental system could be totally transformed, with a new one emerging from the change: for example, in a Mediterranean environment when fire totally destroys the vegetation cover and a new vegetation succession develops (Chapter 5). Similar responses can occur in environmental systems that are changed by human rather than natural forces. The significance of this kind of change is that, unless we understand properly how complex environmental systems work, we may be unable to spot the triggers which can set system change in motion. The crucial point at which an environmental system suddenly changes into a totally different mode of response to change is known as a threshold. Thresholds are often difficult to pinpoint, making it hard to predict how systems will behave as the result of changes. When a threshold is crossed the behaviour of a system can change unexpectedly in ways that are problematic to forecast. The more we learn about the nature of environmental changes the more complicated they appear.

Another related theme concerning environmental systems is the concept of the return periods of very occasional extreme events. In a river catchment in the British uplands, for example, relatively little sediment will be transported when streams are at a normal summer level. Every year, particularly in winter and spring, streamflow will be higher and erosion and transportation of sediment greater, as shown by the muddy colour of the water. The cumulative effect of such annual events, however, is still quite modest even in the long term. What can really transform an upland valley is the rare, extremely severe flash flood, often with a very localised distribution, which may have an average return period of only once in 200, 500 or even 1,000 years or more (Ballantyne and Whittington 1999; Curry 2000). Failure to plan for the possible occurrence of such an event can have catastrophic consequences; for example, in relation to dam construction (Chapter 8). Whether due to a severe thunderstorm, rapid snowmelt or other causes such a flood can generate more erosion, transport more material and cause more damage in a couple of hours than normal year-to-year processes acting over centuries. A more recent, well-publicised example of this was the flood at Boscastle in north Cornwall in England in August 2004.

Such events, however, are not specifically a feature of global warming, despite what was reported in the press. They are a normal, if occasional, part of fluvial processes in small, steep catchments. A historical example of the same phenomenon is the valley of the Mosedale Beck and the Vale of St John in Cumbria. In 1749 a severe thunderstorm over the fells north of Helvellyn caused a huge local flood which drowned livestock, swept away buildings and deposited spreads of large boulders which are still sitting today where they were dropped because there have not been any floods of a similar magnitude since then to move them (see Plate 6).

The impact of extreme events can be discerned even in the lower courses of major rivers. In the valley of the River Tyne, sections through the sediments deposited by the river contain an extensive layer of coarse sand up to 50cm thick. This is believed to be the result of a single severe flood in AD 1771, the most severe documented in England in historical times (Macklin et al. 1992). It is now thought probable that in many landscapes much of the erosion results from occasional extreme events and that the incidence of these can vary over time rather than being totally random. In Crete, for example, it is now considered that a concentrated period of flooding during the Little Ice Age, especially the 1590s and 1690s, has been of major importance in shaping many features of the modern landscape (Grove and Conterio 1995).

Reconstructing Past Environments and Dating the Changes: the Physical Evidence

If we are to measure and understand environmental changes and link human responses to them we need to find ways of dating both physical and human processes. First let's look at some of the ways in which scientists can date environmental changes. We will then consider the problems of dating events in human history and prehistory that may be linked to them.

Until the second half of the twentieth century relative dating was all that was available, apart from instances associated with particular environments where deposits were laid down in annual layers, like varved clays (see below). To geologists and archaeologists the law of superposition has long been established as a governing principle. This states that, in undisturbed stratified deposits, the oldest layers lie at the bottom of the sequence and the youngest at the top. The relative thickness of a deposit within such a sequence might provide some indication of how long it had taken to accumulate, but the process of dating was relative rather than absolute. The same sequence of rocks, identified in different areas, might cause geologists to conclude that the strata were of the same age but would tell them nothing about what that age actually was. The same principle was applied to the interpretation of archaeological deposits using human artefacts rather than fossils as indicators. Collections of artefacts – pottery, tools, weapons – were arranged by archaeologists in developmental sequences on the assumption that simpler, cruder forms were replaced by more complex ones but, of course, the rate of change could not be determined and the assumption that development was always a simple, one-way linear process might not always apply.

Trying to piece together and match up relative dating chronologies from different areas and, even more so, to convert them to absolute chronologies was an archaeological minefield. Before the 1960s, archaeologists had built up complex sequences of phases of human cultural development in areas around the Mediterranean by starting off with the longest 'absolute' historical chronology available – the dynasties of ancient Egypt, which went back to c.3000 BC. They dated artefacts imported into Egypt during particular reigns and then transferred the dates to the areas from which the goods had originated, and used them to date stratigraphical sequences there. Also, conversely, they used Egyptian exports in a similar fashion. This was difficult enough using pottery types, but it was even more problematic when applied to architectural styles. Using this approach, a date for the most spectacular phase of Stonehenge was worked out by relating the monument – with many intermediate stages – back to the Egyptian master chronology (Renfrew 1973). The problem with this approach was that mistakes and inaccuracies introduced at each stage tended to be magnified with increasing distance from Egypt, making the dates less and less reliable the farther away you got. The entire approach had the stability of a house of cards: remove any one suspect date and the whole structure came crashing down.

Such a system of transferring dates from one region to another was also based on the idea, widely held in archaeology at this time, that innovations – such as agriculture, monumental architecture or merely a different style of decorating pots – had a tendency to diffuse outwards from a single core area into more remote, less sophisticated peripheries as the result of population movement, the so-called 'invasion hypothesis'. Stonehenge was thus linked to the eastern Mediterranean as the end product of a developmental sequence via intermediate tombs in Malta and Iberia. When radiocarbon dates first became available it was with considerable dismay that archaeologists discovered that the absolute dates for Stonehenge showed it to be much earlier than the structures from which it had supposedly been derived!

Relative dating can also be applied to sets of landforms. It can be used to work out a sequences of features such as river terraces, lake shorelines or moraine limits. A classic example is Vita-Finzi's (1990) study of deposition in Mediterranean valleys. He identified two sets of deposits which he described as an older and younger fill that had been cut into by recent streams to form sets of terraces. The older fill went back to late Pleistocene times and was associated with the massive environmental changes that occurred at the end of the last glaciation. The younger fill was dated from artefactual evidence to the Roman period, suggesting that a major phase of soil erosion on the surrounding hillslopes, leading to deposition in the valleys, had occurred then

(Chapter 5). Sequences of moraines in front of Alpine and Scandinavian glaciers, relating to phases of retreat since their last most advanced position, provide another example of morphological dating.

Even when they do not form distinct landforms that can be mapped, stratigraphical successions can provide evidence of both relative dating and environmental change. This is particularly the case where deposits contain micro and macro remains of the flora and fauna that flourished when particular layers were laid down. Palynology – the study of vegetation change from pollen grains – was first developed in Sweden in the early part of the twentieth century. It has become the most important and widespread technique for the reconstruction of Holocene environments, for correlating sites and for identifying environmental changes.

The pollen grains of plants survive well in deposits such as lake sediments or peat bogs from which air is excluded so that decay is prevented. Laboratory processes remove other organic matter and leave only the pollen grains with their resistant, protective shells. Pollen grains can be identified under a microscope to the level of genus for trees and to family level for some grasses and herbs. In a sample of pollen, individual grains can be identified and the numbers or proportions of grains from different genera and families established to allow a reconstruction of the vegetation that produced the fossil pollen. Doing this at regular intervals throughout a core allows changes through time to be identified: inferences about the causes of these changes may then be made, by looking at a broad scale at features such as the changing balance between arboreal (tree) pollen and that of herbs and grasses, or at a finer scale by the presence of indicator species such as the pollen of domesticated cereals or weeds such as plantain (*Plantago lanceolata*) which are associated with cultivation. In western Europe the vegetation changes revealed in the pollen record are due to changing environmental factors during the earlier part of the post-glacial period, such as variations in climate and the development of soils, but from around 6,000 years ago they are increasingly the result of human activity. Where many cores containing pollen have been extracted from sites within a fairly limited area, such as the English Lake District, it is possible to contrast patterns of vegetation change between, say, valley bottoms, valley sides and upland ridges (Pearsall and Pennington 1973).

Extracting a core from the sediments in the bottom of a lake or a peat bog, preparing the samples for examination and identifying the pollen grains is one thing. Making inferences about what a pollen assemblage shows about the vegetation that produced it, and what factors influenced changes in that vegetation, is even more complicated. First, the pollen grains from different species may have different susceptibilities to decay in particular depositional circumstances. Also, different plants produce pollen in different quantities: alder, birch, hazel, pine and oak produce twice as much pollen as elm and eight times as much as lime and ash, which has caused the significance of the last three species as components of British woodlands in the past to be underestimated. Wind-pollinated plants, in general, produce more pollen than insect-pollinated ones, though heather (*Calluna vulgaris*), while insect-pollinated, produces pollen in huge quantities. Self-pollinated species such as cultivated cereals produce relatively little pollen.

Some pollen grains travel farther than others; Scots pine (*Pinus sylvestris*) pollen grains, with large air sacs, can be dispersed widely from their source, while the pollen of cultivated cereals, much heavier by comparison, has a very localised distribution. Most wind-borne pollen is deposited within a few kilometres of its origin but some travels farther. This probably explains the presence of some tree pollen, both in the past and today, at sites in treeless environments such as Shetland or Greenland. At any locality a proportion of the pollen will have been generated within the local catchment area of the lake or peat bog, whether transported to the place at which it was found by wind or water. At a very local scale the prominence of certain types of pollen grain in a sample will also be influenced by the character of the site and the direction of the prevailing wind: trees upwind of a coring location will be better represented than those downwind. Once allowance has been made for such influences the nature of changes in the pattern of pollen also need to be established with care (Roberts, N. 1989).

The principal factors affecting the vegetation patterns that are likely to be identified from the study of pollen are climatic and human influences – but the response of plants to climate is not just a straightforward reaction to temperature or precipitation, but to a whole complex of variables. With lake sediments the erosion of peat deposits elsewhere within the catchment area may result in older pollen grains being deposited on top of younger ones.

Starting with early-twentieth-century work in Scandinavia, the vegetation changes revealed by pollen analysis have been used to establish a chronology for post-glacial climatic change based on the idea of four broad zones: (1) Boreal (c.10,000–7500 BC), when a relatively dry, continental climatic regime characterised western Europe; (2) Atlantic (c.7500–5000 BC), during which average temperatures peaked but rainfall increased; (3) Sub-Boreal (c.5000–2500 BC), similar to the Boreal but less dry; and finally (4) Sub-Atlantic (c.2500 BC–present), which was colder and wetter with rapid growth of peat in many areas. It is now widely considered that the assumptions on which this reconstruction of climate is based may be flawed. It has long been recognised that there was a time lag between temperature rises in any area and that the spread of particular tree species depended on the existence of suitable soil conditions and the speed at which trees could migrate and colonise new habitats. More recently other interpretations, such as the expansion of alder being a reflection of increasing climatic wetness, have also been questioned (Edwards and Ralston 1997). It is now thought that this may have been related to purely local changes in hydrology. The initiation of peat growth may have been due to factors other than the onset of cooler and wetter climatic conditions, such as poor land management leading to the compaction of soils and poorer drainage. The trend of post-glacial climate is now being interpreted more as one involving rapid warming between 10,000 and 7,000 years ago with relatively minor fluctuations since then, though nevertheless punctuated by some sharper short-term variations (see Plates 4 and 5).

Sediments that produce pollen may also contain macro remains of plants – leaves, branches, even sometimes whole tree trunks relating to wetter climatic phases when peat bogs expanded and overwhelmed surrounding woodlands. In a similar way, lake and marine sediments contain micro and macro fauna. Diatoms are microscopic plants whose variations can identify habitat changes, such as lake and sea level fluctuations and the impact of human activities on aquatic ecosystems. Like pollen grains, diatoms have hard shells which resist decay and which can be differentiated to species level under the microscope. The assemblage of diatom species at a particular site is influenced by factors such as the acidity and temperature of the water and especially its salinity. They provide evidence of changing lake and sea levels and, in the case of enclosed lake basins in semi-arid areas, they generate information on climatic change.

Plant macrofossils have the advantage over pollen grains that they can often be identified to species level, though their occurrence is more variable. Animal remains are also preserved in sediments. Fossil insect remains can be a good guide to past temperature variations because insects, being mobile, can respond much more quickly than plants to warming or cooling conditions, and they often have very precise habitat requirements. As we will see in Chapter 6, insect remains from deposits inside the remains of a former house can indicate even the time of year at which the place was abandoned. Molluscs, ostracods, foraminifera and other creatures with shells can be extracted from aquatic sediments and variations in their habitats analysed.

Sediments may also contain distinctive layers relating to particular environmental events which have affected the surrounding area. Volcanic ash or tephra layers may provide evidence of past eruptions. The peat bog at Fen Bogs in the North York Moors has distinctive layers of light-coloured mineral material washed in from nearby slopes relating to phases of soil erosion due to woodland clearance by prehistoric communities (see Plate 3).

The kind of sedimentary sequences that we have been considering provide only relative rather than absolute indications of age. Incremental dating methods are based on the regular accumulation of biological or sedimentary material over time, preferably on an annual basis, and may give very specific and accurate dates indicating exactly when particular layers were laid down. Many sedimentary deposits are laid down with a seasonal rhythm, with bands of coarser and finer material accumulating according to the season. Where fine sediments are deposited in lakes at the snouts of glaciers they can accumulate as annual layers or *varves* in which the coarser sediments are laid down during the spring and summer melting period while during the winter fine material in suspension gradually settles out. The varying thicknesses of the individual layers provide clues to past annual weather conditions. Varves can be counted at individual sites, and sequences with different thicknesses matched from site to site, allowing patterns of deglaciation to be established, a process that has been used particularly widely in Scandinavia (Lowe and Walker 1984).

Dendrochronology is the most frequently used of these incremental dating techniques (Bradley 1985). It is based on the annual rings that are created as trees grow. The age of living trees can be worked out by using a coring implement and counting the number of rings outwards from the centre. Variations in the width of such rings from year to year also preserve a signal of past short-term environmental fluctuations. Groups of narrow rings indicate periods when growing conditions have been less favourable; depending on the environment this may indicate a phase of colder conditions – in the Alps or Scandinavia, for example – or drought, as in the south-western USA. The patterns created by such variations not only preserve a record of past climatic fluctuations: they also allow dead wood preserved in structures or in peat bogs to be dated by matching up the patterns where they overlap with those from dated living trees, using computer programs to detect the best fits. The technique was first applied to the very long-lived Bristlecone pine (*Pinus longaeva*) in the arid south west of the USA, but it has since been used for a range of tree species in many other environments.

Working backwards in time with various overlapping samples of wood this can, ultimately, allow chronologies covering several thousands of years to be constructed. One derived from oak trees growing in Irish peat bogs has been pushed back to 5479 BC and a chronology from southern Germany extends back beyond 10,000 BC. Ring patterns can also be compared between samples from different sites and regions, allowing the extent of environmental changes at a particular period to be established. Oak trees have been most commonly used for dendrochronology in Europe, being long-lived with some surviving English trees having ring patterns extending back to the early fifteenth century. In central and northern Europe chronologies based on conifers have also been developed. The ability to assign precise dates for certain kinds of environmental changes nevertheless needs careful interpretation (Baillie 1995).

There are problems with dendrochronology; samples with only limited numbers of rings may not have a unique match and may produce more than one possible date. The nature of the environmental change and a tree's response to it will vary with its local setting. A tree growing on the edge of a peat bog is likely to respond in a different way, or at least to a different degree, to a tree on a well-drained soil only a short distance away. Often the nature of the environmental change producing groups of wider or narrow tree rings is assumed rather than demonstrated. There are also problems in deciding on the scale of the factors affecting growth; whether they were purely local, such as changes in drainage, or more widespread.

Ice cores extracted from the centres of stable ice caps, such as Greenland or Antarctica, can also provide environmental information. Each year's accumulated snow forms a layer which traps within it a range of environmental information, including temperature – measured by the amount of the isotope oxygen 18, the amount of which varies directly with air temperature, or the presence of peaks of acidity caused by volcanic eruptions. Some ice core sequences extend back to the last interglacial period, but in practice the identification of individual layers of accumulation is not always precise and becomes more difficult with increasing depth, sometimes having to be estimated by the modelling of glacier flow rather than direct counting. Variations in oxygen isotope levels between ice layers can be used to date individual layers as well as providing a year-to-year plot of climatic variation throughout the post-glacial period and, indeed, far back into the Pleistocene. The technique was pioneered in Greenland, where the heavy annual snowfall allows the annual layers to be distinguished relatively easily, but it has since been extended to the Antarctic and to smaller ice caps and glaciers in areas like those in the Andes and New Zealand. One feature of these studies has been to show that the post-medieval cooler phase often called the Little Ice Age (Chapter 6) was not just a European phenomenon but occurred worldwide.

Lichens, organisms consisting of algae and fungi living together symbiotically, have been used since the 1970s to date surfaces such as boulders on moraines and river terraces. The rate of growth of lichens is slow, regular and measurable. The technique can indicate how long a rock surface has been exposed to the atmosphere, for example after the retreat of a glacier or following deposition in a major flood. The rate of growth of lichens in a particular area can be calibrated against dated surfaces such as tombstones. Lichenometry has been particularly useful for dating glacier fluctuations, especially during the Little Ice Age, in areas such as Scandinavia, the Rockies, Alaska and New Zealand where documentary evidence and maps are late and sparse.

Radiometric dating methods are based on measuring the rate of radioactive decay of material. Of these, radiocarbon dating is probably the best-known and most widely used technique, one which can be applied to a range of organic material including peat, wood, charcoal, shell and bone. Developed from the mid-1950s, it began to have a major effect on archaeology and palaeo-environmental studies from the 1960s. It is based on the principle of isotopic decay. Many elements, such as carbon, are mixtures of several isotopes with the same chemical properties and atomic numbers but different numbers of neutrons and different atomic masses. Carbon 14 is the least abundant variant of normal carbon 12. It is present in all living organisms but is unstable and decays after the death of the organism at a known rate with a half-life of 5,730 years. The level of carbon 14 in a sample, and hence the amount of time which has elapsed since its death, can be measured. Radiocarbon dates are statistical estimates rather than absolute dates and are given as years BP – before the present – which is conventionally set at AD 1950. Dates are given with margins of error which inevitably widen as you go back in time, so that dates for early prehistory have much greater margins of error than those for, say, medieval times. Radiocarbon dating cannot be used for very recent samples, say within the last 150 years or so. Since the onset of the Industrial Revolution the burning of fossil fuels on an increasingly large scale has released a lot of ancient carbon into the atmosphere, the absorption of which makes recent samples seem older than they actually are. Contamination with old carbon can also occur naturally in areas of limestone bedrock or coal measures. Comparisons of radiocarbon dates against ones established by dendrochronology show discrepancies, with the radiocarbon dates coming out too young. The variations are systematic worldwide, however, and they can be corrected or calibrated. One impact of radiocarbon dating has been to greatly lengthen the span of prehistory. In the 1950s, for example, the introduction of agriculture to Britain at the start of the Neolithic was placed at around 2000 BC. Now a date of c.4500 BC or even earlier seems more likely.

The decay of other radioactive isotopes with different half-lives can also be used – such as lead 210, with a half-life of a little more than twenty-two years, applicable to dating on timescales of up to 200 years. This can be used to date samples more recent in date than radiocarbon dating can handle – for example, lake sediments or the uppermost layers of peat bogs. Erupted volcanic ash (tephra) may spread over extensive areas and form a thin layer in peat bogs and aquatic sediments. The tephra from each volcano and, indeed, every individual eruption, has its own distinctive 'signal' when analysed in the laboratory and tephra layers can provide important data 'markers' throughout the world. Most tephra layers found in Europe are due to the activity of Icelandic volcanoes, sometimes on a massive scale (Chapter 4).

Historical Records and Environmental Change

There are problems in using many of the dating techniques that have been discussed when it comes to dating human events. While dendrochronology can sometimes give a surprisingly precise date to a year or even a season, most of the other techniques are less specific. Yet there is often pressure to use them to the limits of their precision and even beyond, creating a misleading impression of accuracy. The difficulties involved in trying to date the Bronze Age volcanic eruption on the island of Thera in the Aegean are discussed in Chapter 4.

The application of the range of dating techniques already discussed has also revolutionised interpretations of archaeological deposits. For varying periods, going back several thousands of years in the case of ancient Egypt but only a few decades in some less well-recorded parts of the world, human records are available to identify environmental changes and to show how societies have reacted to them. Historical sources comprise not just written documents but a range of evidence including monumental inscriptions, coins, paintings and photographs. The closer you get to modern times the greater the volume of material there tends to be and the better the amount of detail. This is not only because early literate societies produced less material than more recent ones, but also because the survival of historical evidence decreases steadily as you go back in time, and as you move from core to periphery within a state or an empire. Such sources may contain graphic first-hand accounts of environmental events, such as Pliny the Younger's description of the eruption of Pompeii in AD 79; more commonly they may shed light on such incidents accidentally and unintentionally. People in seventeenth-century French and Swiss peasant communities who recorded the dates at which the grape harvest began each year never dreamed that they were creating an archive of data for future climatic historians to study in order to establish year-to-year variations in the amount of summer warmth in central Europe (Ladurie 1971).

Data of this sort, available in a standardised format on an annual basis for consecutive runs of years, are often more frequent than might be supposed. Into this category, too, come early meteorological records, which began to be kept in Britain in the mid-seventeenth century. Professor Gordon Manley amalgamated short runs of temperature readings from different locations into a standardised time series for

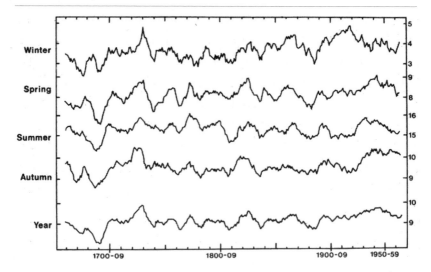

FIGURE 2.1 Central England temperature series 1659–1973
(after Manley 1974)

central England, making allowance for variations in the construction
and quality of the instruments during the earliest years and producing
the world's longest run of instrumental data (Manley 1974). Even longer
runs of environmental data survive, such as the measurements of the
flow of the River Nile on Roda Island from AD 715.

A wide range of evidence from different sources can sometimes
be pieced together to provide evidence of environmental change. For
example, paintings, engravings, photographs, old maps and documents
can be combined to show the positions of alpine glaciers at various
times from the sixteenth century onwards (Lamb 1982), and this information can in turn be correlated with the evidence of moraines and
other landforms on the ground.

The quality of the data available from historical sources can vary
considerably even within the same part of the world. For example, the
behaviour of Scandinavian glaciers is much less well recorded before
the later nineteenth century than many alpine ones because they
occurred in more remote, thinly inhabited areas (Grove, J. M. 1988).
Studies of glacier fluctuations in Scandinavia in recent centuries have,
as a result, had to depend much more on evidence from lichenometry

(Lowe and Walker 1984). Despite this, some relatively marginal societies have proved to be assiduous record keepers and chroniclers of environmental trends. Iceland, from medieval times onwards, was on the edge in terms of the vulnerability of its populations to environmental change, but fluctuations in glacier limits, eruptions and falls of tephra, and periods when sea ice beset the island's coast, are well chronicled (Byock 2002).

Establishing a date is one thing; interpreting its significance is quite another. Difficulties arise when dating information derived from different techniques and sources, with different degrees of reliability and precision, applicable at different geographical scales, is compared directly in order to determine relationships. An example of such a mismatch has been discussed in detail by Tipping (2005) in relation to interpreting the changing proportions of pollen from trees, grass, cereals and weeds at two sites in south-east Scotland. It is very easy to identify trends relating to the limited area around the site from which a pollen core was taken, and then to interpret them as being the result of regional or even national economic and political events, such as English invasions, or the introduction of new farming practices by medieval monastic estate managers. Political events in this region, such as the effects of an English invasion, are too short-term to show up in a pollen record, while other explanations such as monastic farming are far too generalised geographically. In terms of causation, then, it is deceptively easy but very misleading to make the kind of shifts of scale necessary to link national-level causes to possible effects on vegetation within an area of only a few hundred metres' radius.

Environmental Change and Marginality

Much work on the impact of environmental change focuses on human societies which have been in some way marginal – particularly in terms of their physical environment, but also their economic systems, social structures and their political position. Core areas of settlement tend to have more favourable environments, greater resources, and to be near centres of power and authority. They are likely to be less affected

FIGURE 2.2 Climatically marginal land in Britain (after Parry 1978)

by environmental changes, which may be felt as mere inconveniences or short-term problems rather than major disasters. Marginal areas, on the other hand, are often remote, poorer, with slender resources and thus less able to cope with environmental stresses (Pollard 1997). In such areas examples of land that was once used but has now been abandoned, or is at least used less intensively, are widespread whether abandoned lazy beds in the Scottish Highlands or terraces in the Mediterranean.

The belief that some environments are marginal while others are not has had a powerful influence on British archaeology, but the concept of marginality is not easy either to define or to apply objectively. In particular, the idea that certain environments may not be marginal under favourable conditions but may slide over a threshold into marginality as a result of long-term shifts such as climatic change or soil deterioration, has been widely used. Parry (1979), discussing settlement and cultivation in medieval and post-medieval upland Britain, has identified areas which were sub-marginal for cultivation, which could never have been seen as attractive or even feasible for agriculture at any time in the past. Such areas were surrounded by a marginal zone in which prospects for development were likely to vary over time. He suggested that in such an area a society, already operating at the limits of its viability, might be pushed over the edge by a gradual downturn in its resource base, perhaps reinforced by a particularly bad short-term crisis such as a run of harvest failures, leading to famine and the migration of population. Environmental marginality may be reinforced by economic conditions. What is a viable environment for one society with a particular economy may not be sustainable for another. The success of the Inuits in Greenland compared with the failure of the Norse settlers is a case in point (Chapter 6). Marginality may be reinforced by social characteristics, such as a distinctive religion, language or ethnicity, as well as by distance from centres of political power (Mills and Coles 1998).

The idea that certain landscapes are inherently marginal, however, may owe as much to perceptions as to reality. What may seem marginal now may not necessarily have been so in the past. The western islands of Scotland today seem a remote outpost of civilisation on the fringes of Europe. In prehistoric times, however, they formed part of an Atlantic route united by sea communication with active trade and interchange of ideas (Cunliffe 2001). This also comes out from topographic descriptions of areas of Britain between the sixteenth and the eighteenth centuries. Writers such as Daniel Defoe, brought up in towns and lowland areas, saw areas with extensive cultivation, industry and trade as wealthy and prosperous. Upland areas such as Wales, northern England and the Scottish Highlands were dismissed as backward and impoverished because of the limited extent of arable land and its poor quality. Writers who had been brought up in upland pastoral areas, however, emphasised the high quality of their grazings and the wealth of livestock and game (Smout 2000). It is difficult to look at an area like Dartmoor, covered today by acid peat bogs which provide only scanty grazing, and not believe that the people who colonised the area during the later Bronze Age did so reluctantly because of land hunger and a lack of any other real choice. But we know that environmental conditions were more favourable there 3,500 years ago than they are today (Fleming 1988). In addition, we cannot view Dartmoor through the eyes of a Bronze Age farmer. It is likely that the landscape and environmental contrast between upland and lowland areas in Britain was less sharp at that time than is the case today. It may even be that areas on the fringes of the upland areas were selected preferentially for their more free-draining soils and lighter woodland cover, compared with heavier more waterlogged lowland soils.

Where marginality is assumed rather than clearly defined and established, it is equally easy to postulate the existence of trends and relationships on the basis of limited evidence. The supposed widespread abandonment of the upland areas of western and northern Britain during the late Bronze Age hangs on a very flimsy framework of dating evidence (Chapter 4). For the same environment in medieval times Tipping has shown that the assumption that climatic deterioration drove cultivation limits a long way downhill and forced the abandonment of large numbers of farms is based on weak and imprecise historical chronologies, and is not supported by other forms of environmental evidence (Tipping 1998), or even historical data. A recent study of landscape change in the Ochil Hills of central Scotland has identified, and securely dated to the early eighteenth century, a phase of expansion of cultivation at high altitudes which occurred at a time when climatic conditions might seem to have encouraged cultivation limits to retreat downhill (Royal Commission 2001).

Assumptions about the effects of climate on cereal crops, such as those of Parry (1975), have been based on relatively recent, developed varieties of crops such as oats; yet the varieties actually in use in earlier times may have been hardier and more tolerant of severe conditions than has been allowed for. Structural changes within a marginal economy under environmental pressure – such as a shift away from arable towards livestock production – might well be interpreted in the archaeological record as abandonment and depopulation. There is also a tendency to select evidence when it fits the chosen argument and ignore it when it does not. The period which saw the construction of major prehistoric ceremonial monuments in an area like the western isles of Scotland, and which presumably required the diversion of a substantial labour force from farming activities, was also one of significant climatic deterioration.

Arguments about responses to environmental change have also had a strongly deterministic character. People in the past have often been seen as the mere playthings of the environment without recognising that much of their success, or lack of it, in coping with environmental change would have been due to their adaptability. This involved their capacity for making changes in both their economy and their society which would mitigate the worst effects of an environmental downturn, such as turning to the exploitation of a new resource, developing different subsistence strategies, or introducing technological innovations. Environmental factors might constrain but did not eliminate human choice. It should not be assumed that earlier farming systems, because they seem primitive by modern standards and had low outputs, were incapable of coping with short-term environmental variability (Dodgshon 1998). Indeed, many agrarian practices long established by custom seem to have been designed to protect societies in just this sort of way. The impact of environmental change on human societies is more marked during the earlier phases of prehistory than in later times, partly because identifying it becomes more difficult with more complex societies and also because archaeologists and historians have been less ready to look for it.

Human Responses to Environmental Change

How do individuals, societies and governments react and respond to the stresses and challenges posed by environmental change? A lot depends on individual and collective perceptions of environments and the opportunities and risks they offer. People are rarely unaware of hazards but their perceptions of the extent and frequency of the threat may differ widely from reality. Short-term gain may more than balance long-term risk, as when farmers cultivate rich soils on the slopes of still-active volcanoes such as Etna or Vesuvius (Burton et al. 1993). People may appreciate that a risk exists but may underestimate the frequency with which it occurs, as with farming in an area of drought hazard such as the American Great Plains (Chapter 7). The occurrence of the events may seem, effectively, random and unpredictable, such as the likelihood of a major earthquake occurring over large areas of the world. There may be no advance perception that a hazard even exists because the mechanisms causing it are not understood. When the glaciers above Chamonix were starting to advance in the sixteenth century the reaction of the local population was to call out their priests to pray for the ice to retreat (Ladurie 1971). Similar problems occur in areas like the Caribbean, which regularly experience tropical cyclones. The storms are known to occur each year but with varying levels of intensity and on different tracks.

The perception of risk and the responses of individuals and societies to short-term disasters such as floods, droughts, earthquakes and eruptions is comparatively straightforward to measure. More difficult to establish is their reaction to longer-term, more gradual shifts in average sets of environmental conditions. Folk memory in many societies was an effective repository of information on environmental changes. The received wisdom that ploughing and sowing a particular patch of land, above normal cultivation limits, was a high-risk strategy likely to lead to crop failure more often than not due to its exposure and marginality, may have been passed down from generation to generation within farming communities as a yardstick of what was, or was not, advisable.

Farmers may have coping strategies in place to survive a single bad year or even two successive poor ones. Traditional societies often have a range of famine foods which they would not normally touch but which they can eat if need be – such as 'bark bread' in Scandinavia or chestnut flour in parts of the Mediterranean. But longer-term runs of unusual conditions can cause greater problems. Under such circumstances people may hang on and accept, at least temporarily, lower standards of living, as in drought-affected areas of sub-Saharan Africa in modern times. Alternatively they may try to modify their enterprise and sources of income, or they may pull out and migrate to other areas. Abandoning the land in the face of environmental stress is an extreme response. Although more high-profile, it has probably been less common than other types of adjustments.

The capacity of societies to cope with environmental change has varied greatly between different locations at different times, as has the nature of the response to environmental threats. In the case of earthquakes the traditional approach in Japan was to build light, easily replaced houses, while in modern California the policy is to build strong to resist the shocks. Responses can vary between different groups within a society – witness the propensity of some Florida residents to sit out storm threats and even have 'hurricane parties', despite the efforts of state authorities to persuade them to evacuate.

CHAPTER 3

Hunters and Hunter-Gatherers

The Extinction of Big-game Species in North America

At the end of the last glaciation a huge wave of animal extinctions occurred, especially of *megafauna*, usually defined as large animals with weights of 450kg (990lbs) or more. The areas affected included Eurasia and especially North America, where many creatures which seem today quite fantastic died out. They included woolly mammoth (*Mammuthus primigenius*), which stood up to 3.6m. (11ft 9in.) high at the shoulder and weighed up to six tons. Their tusks were up to 2.5m. (8ft 2in.) in length and they would have cropped their way through some 182kg (400lbs) of vegetable matter a day. Even greater was the Columbian mammoth (*Mammuthus columbi*), over 4m. (13ft) tall and up to 5,600kg (9.5 tons) in weight, which ate grasses, plants and conifers at a rate of 250kg (550lbs) of vegetable matter a day. Slightly smaller was the mastodon (*Mammut americanum*), up to 3m. (almost 10ft) tall and weighing a mere 3,175–4,082kg (3.5–4.5 tons), which browsed trees, mainly conifers, and the woolly rhinoceros (*Coleodonta antiquitatus*). Among predators the giant short-faced bear (*Actodus simus*) was 30 per cent larger than a modern grizzly. Big cats included the American scimitar-toothed cat (*Homotherium serum*), which attacked young mammoths and mastodons. It was smaller than the sabre-toothed cat (*Smilodon fatalis*) of the Great Plains which, although not as large as a modern lion, carried twice the weight and had ferocious upper canines 23cm (9in.) long. Other large creatures included four species of ground sloth, armoured glyptodonts such as *Glyptotherium floridanum*, weighing nearly 1,000kg (almost a ton) and around 3m. (10ft) long, the giant deer (*Megaloceros giganteus*) and the native American horse (*Equus occidentalis*).

At the end of the Pleistocene some 200 genera of megafauna became extinct. In North America two-thirds of the large mammal species disappeared, including three genera of elephants, six of giant edentates (armadillos, ant-eaters and sloths), fifteen genera of ungulates and various giant rodents and carnivores. In all, some seventy individual species disappeared from North America, three-quarters of them large mammals (Fagan 1987). These extinctions appear to have occurred at different times spanning a period from about 14,000 to 10,000 years ago, but many seem to have been concentrated within a 500-year period. What caused this massive cull? One possible reason for these dramatic changes was the rapid warming of the climate that occurred at the end of the Ice Age and the equally marked changes in habitats which resulted from the temperature rise. The animals involved were mainly inhabitants of the tundra, an ecosystem that was gradually squeezed out northwards as the forests expanded. Another possible mechanism in some areas may have been drought, which led to crises in water supply for larger animal species (Gillespie et al. 1978). A similar sequence of climatic events, however, had occurred at the start of the previous interglacial period some 130,000 years ago (following even earlier glaciations), but the same mass extinction of species did not occur.

The idea that climatic warming at the end of the Pleistocene reduced the extent of habitats suitable for the big mammals until they became extinct does not find universal support. Professor Donald Grayson at the University of Washington has claimed that the range of species like the Columbia mammoth and Shasta ground sloth (*Northrotheriops shastensis*) had been shrinking steadily for thousands of years before they finally became extinct. Suggestions like this have encouraged the search for other causes. Human impact – the 'Pleistocene overkill hypothesis', as it has commonly been termed – is another favoured explanation. Since the middle of the nineteenth century, stone tools have been found in association with now-extinct big-game animals such as mammoths, indicating that our Stone Age ancestors hunted them. More recently, increasing appreciation of the sophistication of their hunting skills has led to growing interest in the possibility of human interference as a major, if not the prime, factor in the megafauna extinctions. The idea that people with such simple technology and low population levels could have caused such pronounced changes has proved to be a fascinating one.

According to this theory the date of the extinctions was closely related to the advent of the Clovis culture in North America around 10,800–11,300 years ago, marking what many archaeologists consider to have been the first appearance of humans in the Americas. The spread of the Clovis people, named from a site in New Mexico where their distinctive stone weapons were first identified, was followed by many species extinctions within 1,000 years or so. People of the Clovis culture are considered to have crossed the land bridge known as Beringia, where the Bering Strait between Alaska and Siberia is now located, at a time when sea levels were low due to vast quantities of water being locked up in ice sheets. They are then thought to have moved through an ice-free corridor between the huge Laurentide ice sheet over northern Canada and Labrador and the Cordilleran ice sheet over the Rockies into the heart of the continent and to have spread as far south as Tierra del Fuego within 1,000 years or so.

The original overkill hypothesis was put forward by Professor P. S. Martin in 1967 (Martin and Wright 1967; Martin and Klein 1984). He considered that when humans first crossed the Beringia land bridge they found themselves in a country full of animals which had no previous experience of humans and were easy prey for skilled hunters. This abundance of food in turn stimulated human population growth, which hastened the extinction of the megafauna. A human population growth rate of 2.4 per cent per annum on a front moving forward at 16km a year could have covered the distance from Canada to Mexico in 350 years.

The Clovis people were certainly effective big-game hunters. Their equipment is thought to have included a spear or dart thrower, which increased the accuracy and range of their weapons. Clovis points have been found in association with mammoth remains in over a dozen sites in the American Great Plains and south west. The idea that overhunting occurred as a wave of humans spread out across the continent, growing steadily in numbers in a favourable environment, is a fascinating one.

That hunting was a key factor in causing the extinctions is suggested by finds of kill sites where huge heaps of bones have been discovered at the base of cliffs, over which stampeded herds seem to have been driven. Another possible indirect influence which has been suggested is human modification of the original vegetation cover by the use of fire, with the major disturbance of existing ecosystems.

Yet, though superficially attractive, this is too simple a story to be totally convincing. Many of the animals that figure large in such kill sites did *not* become extinct – such as the North American bison (*Bison bison*), which continued to thrive until driven to the verge of extinction in the nineteenth century AD by hunters with repeating rifles rather than spears. The overkill theory would also suggest that the pattern of extinctions should have followed the spread of palaeoindians across North America from Alaska moving southwards and eastwards. Yet such evidence as we have does not conform to such a pattern (Beck 1996).

If simple explanations do not fit the evidence then more complex ones must be sought. Perhaps the addition of humans as competitors in rapidly changing environmental conditions affected the viability of some species in ways yet to be identified? It is significant that in Africa, where hominids had been part of the ecology of the savanna grasslands for millions of years, there were no major megafauna extinctions. But separating human and natural influences on environmental change is difficult even at the start of the Holocene (Roberts, N. 1989).

Another theory proposes that there was a period of prolonged drought around 11,000 years ago. This caused a shrinkage of the pastures that supported many species of megafauna, leading in turn to a concentration of the animals around watering holes which rendered them particularly vulnerable to human predation. Although the dry period was relatively brief – around 400 years – it may have been a significant factor in the extinction of megafauna by concentrating large animals near water sources and weakening them through starvation and dehydration (Haynes 1991). A combination of climate change and human disturbance may then explain at least some aspects of the megafauna extinction. In particular, Owen-Smith (1987) suggests that a substantial reduction in grazing levels by megaherbivores, due to human hunting, would have caused a major change in vegetation patterns which would have further reduced animal numbers, including even those of species not being hunted. On the basis of this theory it would have taken only the removal of a single key species to disrupt the ecology and change vegetation patterns. The behaviour of modern elephants in helping to create and maintain the African savanna may provide a model of the importance of such key species in habitat maintenance; remove the elephants (or the American Pleistocene megafauna) and vegetation patterns are totally altered.

Some support for this idea comes from Australia, where the earliest humans appear to have arrived around 55,000 years ago, during a period of environmental stability rather than change. Here a similar wave of megafauna extinctions, including 85 per cent of creatures over 100 pounds (45kg), seems to have occurred within about 5,000 years of their arrival. It has been proposed that large-scale burning of the vegetation by the Aborigines, possibly accidentally, possibly to try and control the vegetation, may have been the prime cause of these extinctions (Gillespie et al. 1978; Miller 1999).

The overkill hypothesis depends, of course, on accurate dating to show that the extinctions closely followed the advent of humans in the Americas. Certainly it is widely believed that humans first arrived in the Americas around 12,000 years ago at the time of the megafauna extinctions. Some of the extinctions seem, however, to have occurred before the arrival of the Clovis people. Of the thirty-five genera that became extinct, twenty may have been wiped out in *pre*-Clovis times

The overkill hypothesis rejects the possibility that the Clovis people were not the first humans in the New World. But there is also some evidence that human colonisation of the Americas could have occurred much earlier. A site at Monte Verde in southern Chile, discovered during the 1970s, has provided evidence of a settled community existing there over 12,800 years ago, before the advent of the Clovis people. One school of thought suggests that an ice-free passage down the Pacific coast of North America may have opened up by 14,500 years ago, i.e.

2,500 years before an ice-free corridor existed into the interior of the continent, giving migrants ample time to have reached the Monte Verde area by the earliest dates found there. A third possibility is that the first humans reached North America even earlier – perhaps 15,000 or even 20–40,000 years ago – but the dating evidence for this is still inconclusive. There are also indications that the dates of species extinction seem to be more spread out than was first supposed, from around 18,500 to 6,500 years ago. Only two of the species that became extinct can be shown to have been definitely hunted by humans. Mammoths and mastodons may have been hunted to extinction, but there is no clear evidence that this was the case with other species.

It has been suggested that climatic shifts at the end of the Pleistocene, and their impact on vegetation patterns, were the principal culprit with a dramatic shift in the interior of North America from relatively uniform conditions to climates like those of today, marked by cold winters and warm summers. MacPhee and Marx (1997), however, have put forward another theory: that human settlers from Asia brought with them a virus that killed off many mammal species. This theory speculates that new pathogens, to which the megafauna had no resistance, were carried by the dogs, rats, birds and parasites that accompanied the first human arrivals from Siberia. Canine distemper and rinderpest are known to have caused severe reductions in livestock populations, though not full-scale extinctions, in more modern animal populations. More likely candidates, however, are leptospitosis, a bacterium spread in rat urine, and the rabies virus: more detailed examination of mummified remains of Pleistocene animals might confirm this.

Mammoths appear to have become extinct between 13,000 and 11,500 years ago save for the survival of a population on Wrangel Island in the Canadian Arctic until around 4,500 years ago. It is not clear why they survived in this particular remote location, but they had become reduced in size, no more than 1.8m. tall compared with the 3–3.6m. of their predecessors. Their late survival may be linked to the continuation of a vegetation type richer in grasses and herbs than the boggy tundra which spread over most areas of the arctic as climate began to grow warmer and wetter from *c.*20,000 years ago. Farther south, this 'mammoth steppe' was lost to encroaching forests.

Of the fourteen sites from which Clovis points and megafauna remains have been found together twelve involved mammoths and two of them mastodons. Mammoths would have suffered in the droughts of the Younger Dryas period, 12,600–11,500 years ago – relatively weak animals gathered at water sources may have been easy prey to hunters. Mammoths were probably hunted for reasons other than their meat – their skins would have provided materials for tents and clothing, their bones for the tent supports. It has been *assumed* rather than proven, however, that the Clovis people were primarily big-game hunters. Some of their sites have produced evidence of the consumption of a range of smaller mammals as well. The efficiency of the Clovis hunters has also been questioned. Our impression of hunts on the Great Plains tends to be drawn from Indian buffalo hunts on horseback during the nineteenth century. We need to remember that the Clovis people hunted on foot with only stone-tipped spears.

In the early days of the hunters of the Great Plains, bison seem to have been the most attractive quarry but bones of the North American Plains camel (*Camelops*) have also been found. It was the camels that disappeared. Bison hunting involved, at one site in Colorado dating from 8200+/-500 BC, the stampeding of a herd over the edge of a narrow canyon where some 190 were killed. If this had happened only with mammoths, for example, it could have been argued that far more animals were killed than were actually needed for food, so hastening the decline of the animals. But bison – as we know – survived.

We know that the megafauna extinctions occurred, and we can date these events and the spread of the Clovis culture reasonably well, though not yet as accurately as we would like. Nevertheless, as we saw in Chapter 1 the occurrence of two events at the same time does not necessarily mean that one automatically caused the other. The jury is still out on the role of Stone Age hunters in wiping out the American megafauna, although the current consensus tends towards the view that climatic change was the main cause, with the activity of hunters possibly quickening the end of a few species that were already under pressure as a result of environmental change. The Pleistocene overkill hypothesis, however, lives on in the popular imagination and has been taken up by green propaganda writers as an indication of, in environmental terms, a kind of 'original sin' by early human societies. The strength with which this hypothesis has sometimes been put forward has not necessarily been matched by the quality of the evidence.

Mesolithic Hunter-Gatherers and Forests in Britain

In Europe, during the 2,000 years or so after the end of the last glaciation, the tundra that had supported the Pleistocene megafauna and their Palaeolithic hunters gradually gave way to deciduous forests. In these forests lived communities of hunter-gatherers using a technology of stone tools which has been classified by archaeologists as *Mesolithic* or Middle Stone Age. By 9500 BP temperatures had risen to levels comparable with those of today and at times average annual temperatures were up to 2°C warmer than today (Simmons, I. G. 2003). Almost the whole area was wooded by *c*.7000 BP except for some coastal and marshland districts and areas of heath and mountain grasslands on the highest summits. Although the forests were basically stable ecosystems at a broad scale, the idea that they developed into a uniform and unchanging 'climax' vegetation is misleading. Local-scale natural disturbances in the woodland caused change as did, at a larger scale, small variations in average temperatures and rainfall. Instead of a uniform mixture of tree species over extensive areas, the wildwood, as it has been termed, was probably a complex patchwork of different combinations of species, reflecting differences in soils, drainage, slope and altitude. Certain species were particularly common, however, over wide regions. Within Britain, in broad terms oak and lime were of major importance in the lowlands of England, with oak and hazel at higher altitudes. The tree line stood a good deal higher than today – at nearly 550m. on Dartmoor, where trees gradually thinned out into birch and hazel scrub at the highest levels. In the northern Pennines upland forest reached as high as 760m. – almost to the summit plateau of Cross Fell (ibid.). The animals that ranged through this forest included wild cattle (*Bos primigenius*), remnant populations of reindeer and moose, red deer (*Cervus elaphus*) and wild boar (*Sus scrofa*), wolf and bear.

This forest environment was exploited by the Mesolithic hunter-gatherers. Evidence about their lifestyle, how they affected the environment around them and how they were in turn influenced by environmental change is scanty compared with the evidence for later populations. They did not build substantial dwellings or monuments and the traces they have left behind them are often no more than a scatter of flint tools and charcoal fragments. Many of our ideas about how they lived have come from analogies with more recent hunter-gatherer societies. These, however, have tended to survive in harsh and marginal environments, lacking the variety of food sources that characterised the deciduous woodlands of Europe. The lifestyle of Mesolithic hunting groups has often in the past been interpreted as one of small, mobile social groups carefully exploiting seasonally fluctuating resources. Yet other models have been proposed with much more permanent occupation of particular sites as base camps, especially where the resources of coasts and freshwater areas were added to those of the woodlands. Analysis of human bones from a Mesolithic occupation site associated with huge shell middens on the island of Oronsay in the Inner Hebrides has indicated that marine resources supplied much of their protein, hinting at the possibility of year-round occupation (Richards and Mellars 1998). These bases were supplemented by temporary camps, associated with particular seasonal activities and tasks, in other parts of the territory occupied by each hunting group (Jones, C. W. 1994).

One can assume that these hunter-gatherers were good practical ecologists. Rather than hunting woodland animals indiscriminately the bone assemblages discovered at some of their campsites suggest that they may have preferentially culled older male animals, as these were least likely to have affected the future breeding success of the herds on which they depended (Edwards and Ralston 1997). As we will see in a moment, there are also indications that they practised quite sophisticated environmental management. The clearance of forests by fire or other means encouraged the spread of lower-level shrubs, which would have attracted the animals they hunted, or produced clearings which would be colonised by nut-bearing hazel trees.

Compared with the big-game hunters of the tundra, theirs seems a more attractive, less dangerous existence. But the woodland environments in which they lived were not immune to change. Today we may worry about the prospect of human-induced global warming occurring at a rate which, over the next century or so, is predicted to be greater than has been experienced during historic times. But it is easy to forget that the rate of warming at the start of the Holocene, during the early Mesolithic, was far greater than anything that has occurred so far in modern times – a rise of up to 2.8°C per century. Along with this, and resulting directly from the temperature changes, came major changes in vegetation patterns and rapid readjustments of sea level. Not only did forests push northwards and upwards at the expense of the tundra as conditions warmed, but even when deciduous forest had spread over much of Europe the botanical composition of the forest continued to change as forests adjusted to still-rising temperatures and developing soil conditions.

The hunter-gatherers for much of this period would have been aware, even within a single short lifespan, of significant changes in the environment around them and would doubtless have heard of more major transformations from folk memories handed down from one generation to another through each hunting band or group. To what extent such changes required them gradually to modify their lifestyles and subsistence strategies is still far from clear. The fauna of the deciduous woodlands were more widely dispersed and less easily located than the concentrated herds of big game that had roamed the tundra. Mixed deciduous woodland, however, offered a huge range of edible plants as well as nuts, berries, fruits and fungi; and foods that would find little favour today but were none the less nutritious such as the rhizomes of bracken or the roots of bulrushes, all of which could be collected with relatively little effort.

Sea levels rose and fell with the speed, in terms of geological time, of a yo-yo under the joint influences of isostatic recovery (the rebounding of the land surfaces that had been depressed by the weight of continental ice sheets) and eustatic rises (due to the return of water from the melting of these ice sheets at the end of the last glaciation). Sea levels at the height of the last glaciation had been as much as 130m. lower than in modern times. Down to around 8000 BP isostatic recovery occurred at a faster rate than eustatic rise, so that there was a fall of sea level relative to the land. Then came a phase of marine transgression when eustatic rises exceeded isostatic uplift, due to the rapid disintegration of the last continental ice sheets. The main post-glacial transgression destroyed many earlier Mesolithic coastal sites. Others became buried by the growth of peat as the climate became moister and more oceanic. In central Scotland the sea penetrated far up valleys such as the Tay and especially the Forth, so that the Highlands were almost cut off from the rest of Britain. At the same time Britain itself was separated from the Continent. Following this, eustatic changes levelled off but isostatic rebound continued, though at a lower rate. The result of this was a slow fall in sea level relative to the land until modern levels were reached. Now sea levels may be rising relative to the land once more as a result of thermal expansion of the oceans linked to global warming (Chapter 8). By later Mesolithic times, however, the scale of environmental change was reduced (Simmons and Tooley 1981; Tooley 1978).

Within the wildwood, human groups had to survive a lean season during the late winter and early spring: it may have been at this time that resources of freshwaters and coastal zones were particularly important. The vegetable element in Mesolithic diets has probably been substantially underestimated as such material is rarely preserved as well as animal bones or the remains of shellfish. Seasonal rhythms of plant growth and animal movements strongly influenced Mesolithic lifestyles. In the north east of England known Mesolithic sites tend to occur in two distinct altitudinal bands: close to sea level and on high ground from 250 to 500m. In the summer, small parties of hunters seem to have followed their quarry up to the edge of the forests, where the trees thinned out into a more open scrub of birch and hazel, providing cover for the hunters but at the same time giving clearer views of their quarry than under a continuous canopy of woodland. In winter, people may have congregated in larger groups at lowland camps, often adjoining coasts or wetland areas where shellfish, fish, wildfowl, seabirds such as gannets and guillemots with, sometimes, the bonus of a stranded whale, provided a more varied diet. On the small island of Oronsay, in the Inner Hebrides, analysis of preserved fish remains in a number of midden sites in different parts of the island has shown that some areas were occupied in summer, some in autumn and some in winter (Mellars and Wilkinson 1980).

One of the best-known occupation sites is at Starr Carr, an early Mesolithic site in the Vale of Pickering in eastern Yorkshire. It took the form of a campsite covering $c.250$sq. m. with a scatter of antler, bone and flint tools and bones of animals. A brushwood platform of axe-felled birch trees and branches lay between the settlement and the lake. It was located in birch woodland, with hazel and pine nearby, beside a lake, and its occupation has been dated to $c.10,500$ BP. Bones of red deer predominated, but wild cattle, moose, roe deer and wild pig were also found, some bird remains but no fish. Occupation in summer seems likely, and perhaps at other seasons, too. Pollen analysis suggests that even at this early date the opening out of the pine and birch woodland and burning of heath had commenced. The use of domesticated dogs to hunt game is suggested from remains at Starr Carr (Evans 1975).

Mesolithic hunter-gatherers were once considered to have had no more impact on their surroundings than the animals they hunted. Modern archaeologists have now revised this view, arguing that the modification and management of the woodland cover in western Europe began well before the introduction of farming at the start of the Neolithic period. Woodland clearance was the principal environmental impact of human activity in the Mesolithic and Neolithic but the opening out of the tree cover had a range of knock-on effects including reducing the amount of water lost from the vegetation and soil by evapotranspiration. This in turn increased runoff to streams by as much as 40 per cent, resulting in soil erosion, a higher incidence of flash floods, the deposition of colluvium (slope wash) at the base of valley sides and of alluvium lower down the valleys. The increasingly variable regime of streams caused them to cut into valley-floor deposits, producing series of terraces.

It must not be assumed, however, that evidence of woodland clearance automatically indicates human activity. Variations in the woodland cover could have occurred naturally as a result of disease, windthrow due to severe storms, and fires resulting from lightning strikes. More specific evidence is needed, such as finds of Mesolithic tools associated with charcoal layers or, after the advent of farming, evidence of cereal pollen or pollen of the weeds that characterise cultivated areas (Atherden 1992).

Later in Mesolithic times the evidence for the deliberate clearance of woodland becomes more abundant: pollen diagrams from peat cores show that the pollen of trees is replaced at some sites by that of plants on open ground in the period 8500–5500 BP. The clearance and then the gradual recovery of oak woodland allowed other tree species such as ash and hazel to spread. Much of the modification of vegetation occurred at the upper edges of the woodland, where fire was used to open out the tree cover and, in some cases, to drive the tree line downwards. In some cases such clearances were also associated with the formation of blanket peat, from 9000 BP onwards. The clearing of vegetation also had effects on upland soils. Fine charcoal produced by burning tends to block the pores of the soil and to increase the amount of surface water. The removal of trees, which can transpire large quantities of water, also encouraged soils to become wetter, generating more surface runoff. Depending on the detailed topography this could either encourage peat formation or cause more rapid soil erosion. The first extensive areas of heather moorland – as we have seen, as artificial a vegetation type as a field of wheat – date back to this period. Woodland regeneration following such burning was partial, if it occurred at all, and once heather moorland was established it tended to remain the dominant vegetation until modern times (Simmons, I. G. 2003).

Although, as we have seen, the opening out of areas of woodland could have occurred naturally, there are strong suspicions that human activity was also involved, though admittedly it can be difficult to separate human impact from natural causes. Mesolithic hunting bands did not have the efficient polished stone axes of their Neolithic successors, which archaeologists have shown by experiment to be quite effective in felling trees – so modification of the vegetation cover is thought by some archaeologists more likely to have been achieved by the use of fire. Much of this activity may have involved modifying the vegetation of the forest floor, which was readily accessible to browsing animals. Hunting groups may have tried to keep existing natural clearings free from encroachment by young trees, so as to maximise the amount of grass in order to attract deer and other game, or deliberately created clearings for the same purpose (Simmons, I. A. 2001). Fire may have been used to maintain areas of grassland and to prevent them from being taken over by bracken. Clearings would also have encouraged the spread of blackberries. At some Mesolithic sites layers of charcoal, suggesting fire, coincide with an expansion of hazel – a fire-resistant tree. This may have been done quite deliberately to increase the supply of hazel nuts, or to produce more browsable vegetation at a suitable height for deer. The deliberate coppicing of hazel trees to maximise nut supply is also a possibility. Hazel, however, is considered to have been favoured by post-glacial climatic warming, enabling it to colonise new areas faster than other warmth-loving tree species (Edwards and Ralston 1997), so natural process may still have been involved. It has even been suggested that some hunting groups may have partially domesticated deer herds, lopping off branches to provide leaf fodder for them. In Scotland, patterns of vegetation change in the Outer Hebrides and Shetland during the (later?) Mesolithic suggest grazing by deer in islands where the animals had not managed to penetrate after the last glaciation. A solution to this riddle has been proposed by the theory that Mesolithic groups deliberately introduced deer from the mainland to these islands in order to increase food supply there. At Flixton in the Vale of Pickering the charcoal layer was overlain by sand and clay, suggesting that burning was followed by soil erosion (Simmons and Tooley 1981).

Mesolithic society thus seems to have started the process of woodland clearance and environmental modification, which was continued, and greatly intensified, through the Neolithic period and into later prehistory. In upland areas in northern England sheltered sites not far from the crests of the ridges were favoured as occupation sites. These have scatters of tools and charcoal, presumably from hearths, sometimes with the remains of burnt hazel nut shells. The creation of clearings away from the edge of the forest was probably done by ring-barking rather than fire. Fire was used at the upper edges of the woodland and also lower down on the margins of lakes and rivers to maintain open grassy areas. Natural openings in the woodland canopy were also maintained by using fire to prevent regeneration. This small-scale modification of the landscape would, if carried out over long periods, have had a significant impact on the landscape.

Forest burning in the uplands may have encouraged the accumulation of peat between 9000 and 7000 BP as soils became more waterlogged. In areas like the North York Moors, parts of the Pennines and Dartmoor, the first signs of human interference with the vegetation cover coincide with the first development of blanket peat on watersheds, with Mesolithic flints being found at the junction between the original mineral soil and the lowest levels of peat (Evans 1975).

So even the earliest occupants of the post-glacial woodlands of western Europe seem to have been capable of modifying and manipulating their surroundings, rather than simply reacting passively to environmental change. Throughout the Mesolithic period their impact on the woodlands is likely to have remained localised. Although estimates of Mesolithic populations have been revised substantially upwards from the sixty to seventy for the whole of Scotland proposed in the 1960s (Piggott 1962), the environmental impact of these hunting bands across Britain as a whole cannot have been great. From around 5000 BP, however, the scale of environmental modification and the range of choices available to human societies were greatly extended by the introduction of agriculture, the most profound and far-reaching socio-economic change that occurred in prehistory, as we shall see in Chapter 4.

Early Agricultural Societies

The Origins and Spread of Agriculture in the Near East and Europe

The domestication of plants and animals has been the single most important change in human history in terms of providing a cushion against environmental fluctuations. In the process, however, it also had a major effect on the physical world. Globally there were several different source areas – or 'hearths' – in which domestication developed and from which farming spread out. The oldest of these was undoubtedly the 'Fertile Crescent' of the Near East, stretching from the River Jordan northwards through Syria into south-eastern Turkey and then swinging eastwards towards the headwaters of the Tigris and Euphrates in modern Iraq. Yet the reasons for the development of agriculture here remain a puzzle. After hundreds of thousands of years as hunters, why did people suddenly switch to farming? The change to agriculture did not simply involve an alteration in the ways in which food was obtained, but also the development of a different set of relationships between humans and nature, and different, more sophisticated and stratified social structures. This was recognised by early archaeologists, who identified a change to more efficient stone tools, which were more carefully finished than those of Mesolithic communities (hence the term *Neolithic* or new stone age, to describe the technology of the first farming communities), and the development of pottery for cooking and storage. While the environmental changes caused by hunter-gatherer societies were relatively modest in scale, the first farmers set in train a chain of events that began to transform the environment more and more profoundly, as well as leading to major changes in social organisation and the rise of the first cities.

Victorian interpretations of prehistoric hunter-gatherers pictured their lives as short, wretched and nasty, involving frequent and desperate struggles with fierce creatures. Yet studies of such communities in comparatively recent times have shown that it was often possible for such people to gain a comfortable sufficiency of food without undue effort, with a varied diet, and still have plenty of free leisure time. The switch from hunting and gathering to farming, especially the cultivation of cereals, involved more sustained hard work; and the more intensive agriculture became, the more labour was required in terms of the number of hours of effort in relation to the volume of food produced. It does not seem likely that people would have volunteered to adopt a life of harder physical labour whose reward was a poorer, less nutritious diet than they had enjoyed as hunters. So what changes or pressures occurred in the Fertile Crescent to lead people down the path towards agriculture?

Growing pressure of population is one obvious possibility, but the evidence in favour of this explanation is far from convincing. Population growth and agriculture were indeed related, but did population pressure encourage the development of agriculture or did agriculture simply allow larger populations to be supported (Boserup 1965)? The current consensus of opinion is that population growth was not a major force in precipitating the changes that led to agriculture. On balance, it seems that population expansion was an effect rather than a cause of the shift to farming.

Environmental stress is another possibility favoured by many archaeologists. In the 1920s and 1930s Professor Gordon Childe, believing that the ice ages in higher latitudes had been accompanied by wet phases or 'pluvial' periods nearer the Equator, suggested that conditions had gradually become drier in the Near East after the ice sheets retreated, causing game to become more scarce and forcing hunters to adopt other strategies in order to survive (Childe 1954). Although this simple chronology of ice age/wet – post-ice age/dry is no longer accepted, there can be little doubt that the rapid readjustment of climates at the end of the ice age must have caused considerable changes to Near Eastern vegetation zones, which in turn is likely to have put pressure on human populations.

The modern appearance of so much of the Middle East as barren

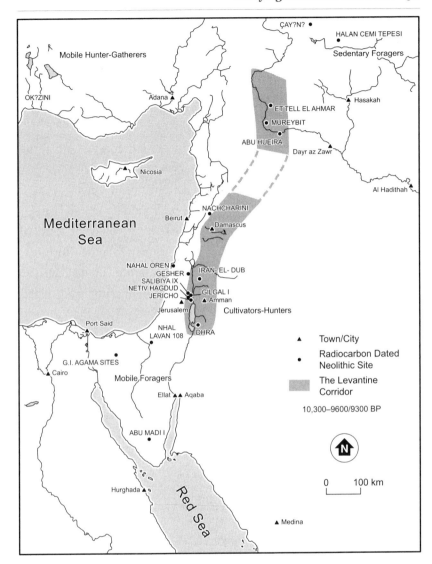

FIGURE 4.1 The Levantine corridor, with some of the earliest known agricultural communities

semi-desert is misleading. At the end of the ice age the landscape of this region was not as dry and poor as it appears today. In the Mediterranean Levant, a belt of country some 1,100km long and 300–500km wide, there was much more woodland than in recent times and also extensive areas of open parkland. Game animals included the mountain gazelle (*Gazella gazella*), wild cattle (*Bos promigenius*), wild goats (*Capra aegagrus*), fallow deer (*Dama mesopotmaica*), roe deer (*Capreolus capreolus*) and wild boar (*Sus scrofa*). The strongly territorial behaviour of the gazelles in particular may have encouraged the more intensive human exploitation of relatively small hunting areas. Because vegetable material survives much less well than animal bones, however, it is easy to forget that plant material was probably a major component in the Mesolithic diet in this region. The Mediterranean woodlands were rich in edible fruits, seeds, leaves and tubers. On the uphill fringes were extensive stands of wild grasses, the ancestors of modern cereal crops.

But exactly where within the Fertile Crescent, in what kind of environment and under what kinds of conditions did agriculture first develop? Various possibilities have been suggested by archaeologists. Professor Childe believed that the domestication of animals occurred under conditions of increasing aridity in oasis areas where humans and animals were forced into more intimate contact, but he was less clear about the origins of plant cultivation. On the other hand, Robert and Linda Braidwood, from the University of Chicago, favoured the idea that farming had arisen in the hilly flanks along the northern edge of the Fertile Crescent. Their early post-Second World War excavations at Jarmo in Iraq appeared to support their arguments (Braidwood and Howe 1961). In the 1960s Lewis Binford offered the suggestion that the domestication of plants had occurred in more marginal areas as the result of attempts by their inhabitants to obtain by artificial means what the people in more optimal areas were able to get naturally (Binford 1968). Modern research, however, suggests that the cultivation of crops and the domestication of animals developed in two different areas: the former among the woodland and parkland areas of the valley of the River Jordan in the southern part of the Fertile Crescent, the latter farther north and east on the fringes of the Zagros Mountains.

So within the Near East, cultivation appears to have emerged in areas of relatively abundant resources rather than in marginal environments. Farming seems to have developed as a supplement in areas where diet was already diverse and rich, rather than on the fringes of viable settlement as has sometimes been thought. The point has further been made that the inhabitants of marginal environments would have been less likely to experiment with new, potentially high-risk, subsistence strategies than their counterparts in better-endowed areas. This does not necessarily mean that climatic changes and other forms of environmental stress were not involved in the development of agriculture, though. Within these source areas, then, what climatic factors are likely to have encouraged people to turn to agriculture? Various possibilities have been suggested by archaeologists. At the peak of the last glaciation – between c.20,000 and 14,000 BP – the entire region was cold and dry, but from then onwards precipitation began to increase, reaching a maximum at around 11,500 BP, encouraging more stable human occupation of the drier areas. During the short-lived glacial readvance of the Younger Dryas period (11,000–10,000 BP), however, precipitation decreased once again. It is this period of renewed climatic stress that has been pinpointed by archaeologists as the key to the origins of farming.

On present evidence, it seems that the deliberate cultivation of cereals occurred before the domestication of animals. The first domesticated forms of barley and wheat that we know of are recorded from Jericho around 10,000 years ago, in the area of the Mediterranean Levant. Dogs had been domesticated long before – perhaps 100,000 years ago or even earlier – but sheep are thought to have been domesticated by about 9000 BC, goats by 7500 BC, pigs from 7000 BC and cattle from c.6000 BC. Early farming communities may also have herded gazelles in a semi-domesticated state. It is not entirely clear how the change was made from harvesting wild seeds to deliberately growing them, but archaeologists have proposed a gradual shift, from the opportunistic harvesting of wild grains to small-scale production of domesticated crop varieties with limited tillage of the soil and then eventually to larger-scale land clearance and more systematic preparation of the soil. Dependence on wild plants as sources of food was gradually reduced, as the cultivation of crops became more important, though hunting continued.

A major turning point in the history of the region came with the emergence of the Natufian culture in central Levant around 13,000–12,800 BP. The Natufians played a key role in the emergence of agriculture as a transitional stage between hunter-gatherers and farmers. Moister climatic conditions provided the Natufians with a wide range of food resources, but population increases may have made communities more vulnerable to short-term droughts. The sudden appearance of the Natufian hamlets may be a reaction to such abrupt climatic shifts, forcing people to adopt new patterns of resource exploitation and leading to a more intensive use of more clearly defined territories. Natufian base camps were located in the lowland oak woodland belt, with only limited occupation of the higher mountain areas of the Lebanon and the steppe areas of the Negev and Sinai. Natufian society adopted a more sedentary lifestyle in more permanently settled communities, much larger than those of previous societies in this area, with solidly built houses constructed with stone foundations and probably made of timber above. The greater permanence of occupation of these 'base camps' is shown by the occurrence at them of cemeteries. The Natufians still derived much of their food from hunting but may have deliberately cultivated unimproved wild grasses, rather than simply harvesting them wild.

Were the Natufians really the earliest farmers? The climatic downturn of the Younger Dryas may have reduced the area of wild cereals in the western part of the Fertile Crescent and may have led to the first experiments in the systematic cultivation of cereals. They certainly seem to have been the first to develop the intensive harvesting of wild cereals using sickles, a key technological development, but it seems more likely that the first real farmers, cultivating truly domesticated varieties of cereal, were their successors, people with a culture known as the Pre-Pottery Neolithic A, occupying sites such as Jericho, though these people had not yet domesticated animals.

The Pre-Pottery Neolithic A people, inhabiting villages that succeeded the hamlets of the Natufians, seem to have relied on the cultivation of domesticated varieties of wild two-row barley (*Hordeum*

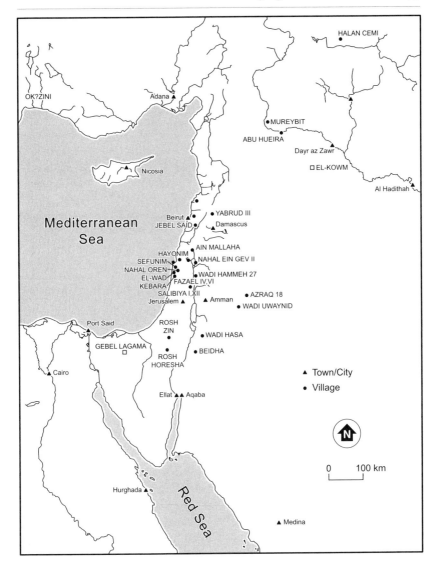

FIGURE 4.2 Natufian sites in the Middle East

spontaneum), wild einkorn wheat (*Triticum boeoticum*) and wild emmer wheat (*Triticum dicoccoides*), or at least the deliberate sowing of their immediate ancestors. These first farmers still hunted gazelle, wild cattle, deer and wild boar, as well as collecting wild fruits and seeds. Their settlements had houses with stone foundations and mud brick walls.

The best-known of these sites is Jericho, excavated by Kathleen Kenyon in the 1950s (Kenyon 1956). She interpreted it as a defended settlement with a protective wall and a tower, but more recent archaeologists have suggested that the wall may have been designed to protect the settlement against floods and mudflows rather than marauding enemies, and that the tower may have been a shrine rather than a defence.

There has been considerable debate regarding whether the shift from collecting wild seeds to the cultivation of domesticated crops was rapid or gradual. Indications are that, with certain forms of harvesting, particularly the use of sickles to cut the corn rather than wooden boards to beat the seeds out of the ears, the selection of grain varieties that retained the seeds in the ear for longer could have occurred within a few decades. It is also still far from clear whether during this phase a shift from the systematic gathering of wild seeds to deliberate cultivation occurred simultaneously in several places or spread out from a single centre of innovation. Was there, perhaps, a different place of origin for the cultivation of each cereal species? In either case the area around Jericho, in the valley of the River Jordan, seems the most likely location for the origins of true agriculture. Bar-Yosef suggests that cultivation began in the Levantine corridor, probably in its southern part between Damascus and Jericho in the late eleventh or early tenth millennium BC (Bar-Yosef and Meadow 1995). The domestication of animals in this area occurred in the succeeding Pre-Pottery Neolithic phase B around 9500–8500 BC.

Bar-Yosef has proposed that the onset of drier conditions in the Levant around 11,000 BP may have forced hunter-gatherers westwards into the woodlands and parkland environments nearer to the Mediterranean to compete with the existing inhabitants. Pressure of population may then have reduced people's mobility and helped to create the larger Natufian settlement sites, which later developed into the first farming villages. The onset of the drier conditions that characterised the Younger Dryas period may have forced the later Natufians to switch from harvesting wild cereals to the deliberate cultivation of crops.

Goats seem to have become domesticated in the foothills of the Zagros and Taurus mountains by the late tenth millennium BC, and sheep soon after that. The domestication of cattle and pigs came later, some 8-7,000 years ago, but the herding of animals, whose bones suggest smaller domestic beasts rather than larger wild animals, had spread to many parts of the Fertile Crescent by the later ninth millennium, probably by transmission among existing groups of hunter-gatherers rather than the migration of farming communities. The combination of the domestication of crops and animals into a single integrated farming system seems to have occurred by the ninth millennium BC.

The short cold period of the Younger Dryas was followed, from about 10,000 BP, by another increase in precipitation which encouraged cultivation to spread. Although, according to Bar-Yosef, agriculture developed under the pressure of drier conditions, the return of moister conditions after the Younger Dryas episode may have been a key factor in encouraging agriculture to expand within the Fertile Crescent. The moist early Holocene conditions lasted through the Pre-Pottery Neolithic Period B from around 7500/7300 to 6000 years BC. This in turn allowed the creation of early villages with populations of up to 300–500 people. There was a dramatic spread of agricultural communities from the areas occupied by the Natufians into neighbouring districts and, as food surpluses began to increase, other social changes such as the appearance of public shrines and temples began to occur.

What was the ecological impact of the change to agriculture? Human impacts on the vegetation cover of the Middle East before the Bronze Age are difficult to detect, but there are signs that despite the trend to wetter conditions, the spread of oak woodland seems to have been relatively slow. This has been interpreted as reflecting human agency, perhaps due to the regular burning of natural grasslands to improve grazings, to extend the area covered by wild cereals, or to encourage dryland cereal cultivation.

From this original heartland, farming began to spread out, notably into southern and eastern Europe. One major natural event which may have helped to propel agriculture into eastern Europe was the rapid flooding of the Black Sea basin around 5500 BC when the Mediterranean Sea broke through the narrow land bridge separating it from a great inland basin. The breakthrough created an inrush of water which has been estimated, at its peak, as equal to around 400 times the volume of Niagara Falls. The conversion of the original, much smaller lake into an arm of the ocean was slow enough for people to have moved out of the way of the rising waters, though it may have given rise to some interesting legends. Estimates of the amount of land that was flooded have been in the region of 20–60,000 square miles. Large numbers of farming communities must have been displaced and some of those who did not starve may have been pushed westwards, up the Danube valley. Even setting aside the possible effects of this spectacular natural change, the spread of farming across Europe between 8,000 and 5,000 years ago appears to have been partly the result of the physical migration of farming communities in search of new land, although it may also have involved the transfer of the idea of farming to indigenous hunter-gatherer societies.

The theory of a rolling frontier of colonisation is still widely held to explain the spread of agriculture over much of Europe and is supported by studies which have shown that the genetic make-up of the European population is characterised by a series of bands radiating northwards and westwards from south-east Europe. About 20 per cent of the modern gene pool in Europe seems to have been contributed by the population wave of farmers moving westwards from Turkey c.8,500 years ago (Cavali-Sforza et al. 1994). A far higher proportion, however, around 70 per cent, has come from groups migrating into Europe from the same direction in earlier times, between c.14,000 and 11,000 years ago. In many areas, such as south-eastern and central Europe, the advent of a new immigrant Neolithic population is suggested by the sudden appearance of pottery manufacture where it had not previously been recorded and a marked change in styles of houses, settlement patterns and burials. Other sites, such as ones in the Danube gorges between Serbia and Romania, suggest the transformation of a native Mesolithic population. In Britain, more weight has been given in recent years to the possible transmission of new skills and technologies to an indigenous Mesolithic population with only limited numbers of migrants. In southern Scandinavia, too, the adoption of agriculture by indigenous peoples is thought to have been more likely than large-scale immigration.

If we accept that migration was an important element in the spread of agriculture into Europe, we might expect it to have been a slow, cumulative process in which each new generation pushed the frontiers of settlement a few miles farther on. While change was slow overall, however, it was punctuated by phases of more rapid acceleration (especially around 5500 BC and 4000 BC), the nature of which are still not properly understood. Some Mediterranean islands, such as Crete and Cyprus, settled by Neolithic communities around 7000 BC, may not previously have been occupied at all by human populations. The relative uniformity of Neolithic material culture over extensive areas of central and eastern Europe also indicates a rapid spread of people; in the course of 500 years or so the frontier of agriculture seems to have shifted from the Ukraine to eastern France. The so-called LBK culture (from the German *Linienbandkeramik Kultur* relating to the style in which they decorated their pottery), which expanded from a core area in Hungary across Poland and Germany into the Netherlands, Belgium and France, was distinguished by substantial rectangular timber houses up to 45m. in length scattered along river valleys, possibly housing cattle as well as humans. They may have spread from what is now the Czech Republic to Belgium in as little as 200–300 years. But it is not clear what started this migration, or what sustained it. Traditionally archaeologists have associated these settlements with the cultivation of small plots of land for cereals. Despite the massive construction of these timber long-houses, however, they need not necessarily have been occupied permanently but may have been used on a seasonal basis, while there are indications that animal husbandry rather than cereal cultivation may have been the mainstay of their farming system. Certainly forest herding fits in better with the evidence for relatively limited clearance of woodland in the early phase of settlement.

The LBK culture had a remarkable homogeneity of material culture,

FIGURE 4.3 Location of the main LBK cultural area (after Whittle 2002)

FIGURE 4.4 Reconstruction of an LBK long-house (after Whittle 2002)

with no real variation in patterns of crops and livestock over a wide area. It was uniquely European, adapted to a very different climate than that of the Near East. The farming system involved the cultivation of emmer and einkorn wheat with legumes and some barley. Fields were probably quite small, with perhaps 10–30ha for a community with a population of between twenty and sixty. Livestock rearing focused on cattle, with sheep and goats in a secondary role. New strains of cereals were developed to cope with moister conditions. The speed of their movement may have been due, in part, to the preference of these early farmers for very specific habitats. They went in particular for light, well-drained, easily cultivated soils developed on deposits of windblown loess which had accumulated at the end of the ice age. Other areas of soil, even ones that would have proved fertile and easy to cultivate, were not colonised until much later. Within areas of loess they showed a preference for the smaller tributary valleys of major rivers.

As agriculture pushed further north and west it had to cope with increasingly different climatic and soil conditions than those areas of the Middle East in which agriculture had originated. The impact of the first farmers on the thickly wooded landscapes of north-western Europe has been vigorously debated by archaeologists, but it is clear that even in the early days of farming the scale of woodland clearance was much greater than in the Mesolithic. By around 4000 BC farming had reached

Britain. Many archaeologists currently believe that the concept of farming must have spread into Britain through the indigenous Mesolithic population as much the same areas that were occupied by hunter-gatherers witnessed the first signs of agriculture. Some colonisation from the Continent, however, may also have occurred. The transition from Mesolithic to Neolithic seems often to have been a swift one, with abandonment in some areas of coastal sites in favour of inland locations. The speed of the change again suggests the influence of immigrants and the import of domesticated livestock.

In Ireland in particular, which lacked large post-glacial mammals, even the red deer may have been a Neolithic introduction and the impact of the arrival of domestic cattle could have been considerable. Throughout the early Neolithic period, between 4000 and 3000 BC, the landscape remained predominantly a wooded one and clearings were still quite small. Settlement sites remain elusive for much of Britain and many are likely still to have been seasonal and temporary. Microscopic fragments of charcoal in pollen cores indicate the occurrence of fire, but whether due to natural or human agency is not clear. It is sometimes difficult to accept that fire could have seriously affected forests in western Europe because forest fires are such a rare occurrence in western Europe today. Oliver Rackham has suggested that such woodlands in the past might have burnt like wet asbestos, and Ian Simmons has claimed that they were as combustible as a pile of wet football socks (Rackham 1986; Simmons, I. A. 2001). But the susceptibility or otherwise of modern north European woodlands to fire may be a poor guide to how they may have been affected in the past. We tend to think of forest fires as having been very rare and very severe but natural fires, started by lightning strikes, or fire used deliberately by humans may have been more frequent, smaller-scale and less devastating than has been realised. It seems likely that the use of fire by early farmers was not random but was carefully controlled with quite deliberate aims.

Deliberate woodland clearance may have been accomplished by ring-barking the trees then leaving the stumps to rot. The rest of the vegetation may have been piled up and burned. The clearings, thus created, would have been kept in being by the grazing of saplings. Deliberate management of woodland using the technique of coppicing – cutting broad-leaved trees down at ground level and leaving the stumps to send up shoots which would eventually grow into a crop of straight poles – also developed in the Neolithic period.

So farming had spread, by around 4000 BC, to the western extremities of Ireland – a long way from the Jordan Valley and the Zagros Mountains and a very different environment. At the start of the Neolithic period, Irish woodlands were dominated by pine in many areas, with an understory of hazel, but elm, oak, birch and alder were also common species. The pollen record from all over the British Isles and elsewhere in western Europe is characterised by a particular marker level known as the Elm Decline: a date corresponding to the early Neolithic period, in which the pollen of elm trees falls off suddenly but the total amount of arboreal, or tree pollen, does not change too much immediately. What could have caused this selective attack on prehistoric elm trees? The Elm Decline has been variously attributed to woodland clearance by Neolithic farmers, the elms being preferentially cleared because they occupied richer soils, to the lopping of elm branches for animal fodder, to climatic change and to the attack of a prehistoric form of Dutch elm disease.

The Elm Decline in the limestone country of the Burren in County Clare is dated to *c*.5800 BP (see Plate 7). Finds of cereal pollen from before the Elm Decline indicate that it was not the earliest phase of agricultural activity in this area. Today disease is the explanation favoured by many archaeologists, disease perhaps brought into Britain accidentally by incoming farming communities. This would have created openings in the woodlands which may then have been exploited for cultivation and pasture. After the Elm Decline in Ireland there was a rapid rise in the pollen of tree species which exploited the more open woodland environment, especially yew. This was followed by a major expansion of the area cleared for farming, with a rise in the pollen of grasses, heather, bracken and plants of disturbed ground like ribwort plantain (*Plantago lanceolata*). The light loess soils of the Burren, with their thinner tree cover, may have been particularly attractive to farming communities. There is little evidence of the use of fire and the trees were probably cleared by felling or ring-barking. Once cleared of woodland many areas remained open for centuries – 300 or 500 years in some cases – before farming seems to have gone into a decline and regeneration of the woodland occurred. The farming system here seems to have involved only a limited amount of cereal cultivation and was mainly concerned with raising cattle, sheep, goats and pigs.

At Céide Fields on the coast of County Mayo an entire early Neolithic field system has been uncovered from under a peat bog with stone walls in long parallel strips and cross-boundaries defining large fields of up to 50ha in extent, which must have been used for livestock (probably cattle) rather than for cultivation. There is evidence of some small-scale disturbance of the woodlands from the centuries before the Elm Decline, some of which could have been due to natural changes but which in other cases might represent the first signs of farming. The discovery of bones of domesticated cattle in a Mesolithic context, from the Dingle Peninsula in south-west Ireland, points to pre-Elm Decline contacts with Neolithic incomers. Here the main phase of clearance followed immediately after the Elm Decline and lasted for around 500 years before agriculture was abandoned and regeneration of the woodlands began. With such a long-sustained period of use, and such a complex field system, permanent settlement rather than shifting, mobile occupation seems probable. The sequence of vegetation at a number of sites was woodland, changing to pasture then moorland and finally to peat bog. From around 4,500 years ago, at a number of sites, farming became more restricted or was abandoned altogether. At Céide Fields this may have been due, at least in part, to the encroachment of peat bogs although the expansion of peat had been continuing, on a more limited scale, from the time of the Elm Decline.

The early Neolithic period in Britain, then, seems to have been characterised by a mobile lifestyle with an absence of large, permanent settlements like those of farming communities in the Near East. The great timber long-houses of continental Europe are absent. Herding was much more significant than cultivation and the use of permanent, walled cultivation plots seems to have been rare. Although there was an increase in the amount of woodland clearance people still lived in a woodland environment. So far, no sites have been identified which demonstrate a transition from a Mesolithic to a Neolithic lifestyle and economy.

While the earliest agriculture in Britain must have involved small cultivated areas – garden plots rather than fields in scale, within still-extensive woodlands – within 1,500 years or so in areas like the chalk country around Stonehenge and Avebury the woodlands had been reduced to small patches in an open parkland landscape (Malone 1989). Much of this is likely to have been due to the impact of grazing animals preventing the tree cover from regenerating, rather than the direct clearance of land for crops. Older interpretations of the evolution of the English landscape saw the Saxons as the pioneers of woodland clearance over much of the country (Hoskins 1955). It is now clear that in areas like this the landscape was already an open, densely settled one, more than 2,500 years before the Saxon settlement.

The Neolithic period in Britain also saw the creation of the first landscapes associated with mining. As population increased and the demand grew for a wider range of tools, the mining of flint and other suitable kinds of rock became more specialised and larger in scale. The flint mines at Grimes Graves in Norfolk are well-known. Equally the working of particular strata of rock which, when chipped and polished, provided a durable cutting edge, started to alter areas such as the Langdale Pikes in the Lake District (see Plate 10), Teivebulliagh and Penmaenmawr (Claris and Quartermaine 1989).

By the end of the Neolithic the landscape in many parts of western Europe had been substantially opened out as a result of woodland clearance. Garden-plot cultivation with hand tools was starting to give way to larger fields cultivated with animal-drawn ploughs. The shallow groves scratched by these implements have been discovered on ancient land surfaces below Bronze Age barrows and other monuments. Towards the end of the Neolithic period population was rising rapidly and the landscape was becoming quite densely occupied. The scene was set for the spread of population, settlement and agriculture into the uplands that characterised the succeeding Bronze Age.

The Abandonment of the British Uplands during the Later Bronze Age

Throughout upland Britain, above levels subject to later agricultural improvement, landscapes from the later prehistoric period are well preserved. A wave of colonisation of these upland areas appears to have occurred between c.2300 and 1800 BC. On Dartmoor carefully planned and extensive field systems are still clearly visible (Fleming 1988). Dartmoor was occupied earlier in the Bronze Age, as cairns and stone rows from this period demonstrate, but after c.1300 BC, within a relatively short time period, the landscape was carefully carved up into a series of territories, each of which included valley land, higher slopes and open moorland. The unenclosed moor was divided off from the lower land by stone banks, locally called reaves, which may originally have been topped by hedges. Other reaves marked territory boundaries and subdivided the land within them into sets of long, narrow strips, some of which may have been worked by family-sized groups. Some of the parallel reave systems enclosed areas of over 1,000ha and reave boundaries could be more than 5km long (ibid.). The occurrence of *lynchets* (breaks of slopes caused by ploughing), and finds of cereal pollen from peat cores extracted from nearby bogs, indicate that at least some cultivation took place at these elevated locations. Settlements, marked by circular stone hut foundations, were scattered throughout the reave systems. All the available dating evidence for these boundary systems indicates a Bronze Age origin for them.

It has been suggested that this landscape was occupied only for some 300 years and that it had been abandoned by the early first millennium as a result of a climatic downturn, over-exploitation of the soil, or a combination of both, which led to the expansion of peat. A drop in average annual temperatures of around 2°C and a marked increase in precipitation have been claimed (Parker Pearson 1993). Similar settlements and field systems on a smaller scale are also known from Bodmin Moor. The Dartmoor reave systems run from the moors down into the lowlands, where they gradually fade out in areas which have been cultivated during medieval and later times, suggesting that they may originally have been a lowland type of land organisation extended into the uplands. Studies of modern field boundaries from areas like East Anglia have revealed traces of similar, regular field patterns over wide areas which appear to predate Roman roads (Fleming 1987). Systems of so-called 'Celtic fields', dated to the Iron Age but possibly representing a reworking of earlier field systems, once covered extensive areas of the chalk downlands of south-east England until post-Second World War deep ploughing obliterated much of them. So planned systems of prehistoric fields may once have been found throughout southern England. Within the uplands, boundary systems which appear to be comparable to the Dartmoor reaves in both function and date occur as far north as Yorkshire (Barnatt 1999).

Farther north the reave systems give way to a different type of landscape which appears to date from the same period. Cairnfields are a characteristic feature of many moorland areas and the lower slopes of upland areas like the Lake District (Leech 1983) (see Plate 8). Similar landscapes occur widely in upland areas ranging from Northumberland through Perthshire to the far north of the Scottish mainland in Sutherland (Johnston 2000; Horne and MacLeod 2001; Royal Commission 1993). Cairnfields comprise hundreds, sometimes thousands of small piles of stones, often interspersed with curving, irregular linear stone banks, the foundations of circular huts and the occasional larger burial cairn. The small cairns, which have no internal structure or evidence of burials, seem to be the result of simply removing stones from the land, either for cultivation or, probably more frequently, to improve the quality of the pasture. Studies of pollen from the soils buried under some of these cairns, and from nearby peat bogs, have shown that at the time the cairnfields were created the landscape around them, though bleak and open today, was often still partially wooded. The making of the cairns was associated with, or followed by, widespread soil erosion, evidence for which is sometimes clearly visible in soil sections downslope of the cairnfields as a thick layer of downwash.

It has been pointed out that in the original brown forest soils of the areas around the cairns there should not, initially at least, have been many stones near the surface, suggesting that the cairnfields were a response to a process of erosion that had already been initiated by woodland clearance (see Plate 9). The cairnfields often occur in clumps, separated by areas of empty hillside, suggesting either relatively fixed settlement occupation separated by uncleared boundary zones, or perhaps nomadic settlement where, after a few years, with soil exhaustion and erosion starting to set in, sites were abandoned and occupation was moved to new locations (Leech 1983). It takes some imagination to see these areas of bleak treeless moorland as a desirable proposition for settlement and improvement but their environment has changed significantly since the Bronze Age. In some areas, such as the Southern Uplands, settlements of circular huts standing on platforms cut out of the hillside are characteristic, often associated with areas of cairnfields (Wickham-Jones 2001). Whether they were occupied permanently, or were used only seasonally, like medieval shielings, is hard to tell.

The organisation of landholding and resource exploitation in such a careful manner has been interpreted as the result of population pressure which first promoted the colonisation of the uplands from Caithness to Cornwall and then, in some areas, led to the development of carefully planned boundary systems to maximise the efficiency of production. The earlier Bronze Age, during which this expansion into the uplands seems to have been initiated, had been a relatively favourable period as regards climate, warmer and drier than today. From around 1000 BC, however, climatic deterioration began to set in with increased rainfall and lower temperatures leading to waterlogging of soils and peat growth. This may have made cereal cultivation difficult in more marginal upland areas (Champion 1999).

It was once assumed that upland areas like Dartmoor were abandoned gradually in a piecemeal fashion as environmental conditions deteriorated. A slow climatic downturn caused by falling temperatures and increasing rainfall, leading to the acidification of soils, water-logging and the growth of blanket peat, perhaps exacerbated by soil erosion, were seen as likely causes (Burgess 1985; Turner 1981). More recently there have been claims that the abandonment of such landscapes was both sudden and widespread with a rapid retreat of settlement during the twelfth or eleventh centuries BC, and a minimum of occupation until the emergence of palisaded settlements from the sixth century BC onwards (Burgess 1985). Burgess (1989) subsequently widened the scope of his theory by identifying similar, apparently contemporary abandonment in France, Spain and parts of Italy. The suggestion was that conditions may already have been on a downward slide and that a short period of severe environmental stress may have triggered abandonment.

Certainly, looking at the ubiquitous remains of clusters of circular stone hut foundations in areas like the Strath of Kildonan in Sutherland, the idea of wholesale abandonment of settlement and rapid retreat from the uplands seems plausible (Fairhurst and Taylor 1974). The scale of abandonment and retreat has been visualised as having been more widespread and severe than the better-attested impact of the Little Ice Age (Chapter 6). Burgess (1989) has termed it 'one of the most fundamental breaks in the whole prehistory of these islands'. The occurrence in the Irish tree-ring chronology of a period of narrow tree rings lasting for about a decade, suggesting highly unfavourable conditions for tree growth, has been linked to an acid peak in the Greenland ice core sequence, suggesting the possibility that a major volcanic eruption may have caused a severe short-term subsistence crisis in northern and western Britain. A major eruption of Mount Hekla in Iceland, known as Hekla 3, has been considered to fit the evidence. It has been proposed that a short-term, severe drop in temperatures due to this eruption caused a 'nuclear winter'-type scenario. Solid and gaseous material from the eruption blotted out solar radiation for an extended period, with associated freak weather conditions, leading to serious crop failure and major livestock mortality, generating a precipitate flight from the uplands (Burgess 1989; Baillie 1989).

Finds of far-travelled microscopic volcanic tephra, however, while providing valuable marker horizons in sedimentary records, do not necessarily have much relevance to local environmental conditions (Buckland et al. 1997). The idea of a volcanic-induced weather disaster is, superficially, an attractive one for people who like catastrophe scenarios. Unfortunately, recent major volcanic outbursts appear to have had relatively minor effects on global climate. The eruption of Mount Agung in 1972 (which produced an output of sulphur believed to be similar to that of Hekla 3) caused a drop of average global surface temperature of only 0.2–0.5°C for little more than a year. The major eruption of Tambora in the Dutch East Indies in AD 1815 lowered average northern hemisphere temperatures by up to 0.7°C, enough to cause a poor summer with crop failures in Europe in 1816 (Post 1977) but hardly equivalent to a nuclear winter (Grattan 1998); although admittedly, conditions are likely to have been worse in more marginal areas like Sutherland than in lowlands farther south.

Other mechanisms for causing depopulation at this time have also been considered. For a while the idea of a major prehistoric plague was put forward as a mechanism. Even if upland populations were not decimated it was possible that a major cut in population due to disease could have led to a retreat from the uplands as people moved out to take up unoccupied better-quality land in the lowlands, as happened in England after the Black Death. Burgess (1985), entering the dubious field of estimating prehistoric populations, has suggested that the peak of Bronze Age population in England around 13,000 BC may have been as high as at the time of the Domesday survey in AD 1086 but had been halved by the end of the millennium. On this basis the expansion of settlement into upland areas could have been the result of population pressure and there may have been a cut of up to 50 per cent in population at the end of the second millennium BC (Baillie 1995).

Unfortunately for the volcanic disaster scenario, tephra from the appropriate period, accumulated as layers of microscopic silicic glass shards, has yet to be securely identified in Scotland (Buckland et al. 1997). Such a scenario also fails to explain why, if it was the upland areas that were especially hard-hit, a similar phase of abandonment appears to have affected the chalk downlands of southern England (Parker Pearson 1993).

Burgess has pointed out that since the population of Britain has been cut drastically twice during historic times – in the immediate post-Roman period and in the mid-fourteenth century with the Black Death – it is reasonable to assume that major population cuts may also have occurred in prehistoric times. Both these historic disasters involved major outbreaks of disease but, as Burgess has indicated, their impact was upon a population which, due to periods of favourable environmental (particularly climatic) conditions, had expanded to an extent that was already putting society under pressure. His suggestion that in many regions it is difficult to find any settlements from the post-Roman period at all, however, suggesting a major retreat from the upland landscapes, ignores important evidence for settlement continuity (Roberts, B. K. 1993).

Burgess's initial theory for a period of abandonment of the uplands lasting for several centuries was developed using evidence from the northern Pennines and the Cheviots, though similar arguments were also made for Wales and Dartmoor (Taylor 1980; Fleming 1988). A main element of the argument was the lack of evidence for Iron Age occupation in these areas. Much depends, however, on the interpretation of thin scatters of radiocarbon dates which do not allow the periods of occupation of sites to be determined with accuracy: so desertion on the scale suggested is still not clearly proven from the evidence of archaeological excavations. Nor can the surface features provide support, since features such as hut circles, cairnfields or systems of irregular linear banks are not sufficiently chronologically specific to date activity. Tipping's (2002) survey of data from pollen analyses for a range of upland and upland marginal sites in Scotland and northern England shows that at many sites, including ones with nearby cairnfields such as Stanshiel Rig in the Southern Uplands, there are no signs of cultivation, indicating that many field systems were designed for improving the quality of the pasture rather than for growing crops.

Equally at many sites there is no indication that grazing intensities dropped at the end of the Bronze Age. Indeed, at several sites in both the eastern and western Highlands, grazing was intensified between 1200 and 500 BC – the period of supposed abandonment.

One mechanism which could have operated at a more local scale than a blanket 'nuclear winter' is acid deposition, an idea for which there is some modern supporting evidence from the AD 1783 Laki eruption in Iceland. This not only caused huge livestock mortality locally but also killed fish in Scotland and damaged crops in England as the result of acidic fallout. In eruptions of this type acidic gases are absorbed by the surfaces of the tephra particles, which are then transferred to land and freshwater ecosystems as the tephra settles. If the area in which such deposition occurred is already an acidic one, the addition of more acid material could push ecosystems over a critical threshold, causing increased environmental stress for relatively brief periods, damaging vegetation and causing animal mortality (Grattan and Gilbertson 1994). The eruption known as Hekla 4, dating to around 3700 +/- 70 BC may have caused a sharp drop in the pollen of Scots pine in Scotland (Grattan 1998).

Livestock rearing may be less sensitive to climatic change than cereal cultivation. The continuation or even intensification of pastoral farming, however, does not disprove the abandonment model because, with systems of transhumance, upland areas need not have been settled permanently in order to be exploited. At only three sites, two in the Cheviots and one in the Grampians, does the evidence suggest the abandonment of cereal cultivation between about 1200 and 800 BC in accordance with the abandonment model, while sites from Galloway, the west Highlands and the Grampians provide evidence of an expansion of cultivation during this period. Because of its limited production and distribution, cereal pollen does not necessarily show up in pollen diagrams from sites quite close to areas of cultivation. Nevertheless, as far as the data currently go, neither the archaeological nor the pollen evidence demonstrates a pattern of widespread land abandonment during the later Bronze Age, no matter what the trend at individual sites may be.

We know relatively little about patterns of settlement and the economic structure of such areas. Cowley (1998) has examined the concept of marginality in relation to the Strath of Kildonan in Sutherland during the first and second millennia BC. He divides the clusters of hut circles in the area into three groups: the larger clusters within well-developed field systems defined by lynchets and banks; smaller clusters associated with clearance cairns and fragmentary clearance banks; and isolated hut circles with no signs of cultivation. These three groups form an altitudinal sequence, with the larger clusters on the best land, the smaller ones generally above and the single hut circles highest of all at altitudes comparable with later temporary shielings. Some excavated hut circles in this and adjoining areas have gone through more than one phase of occupation separated by phases of abandonment. It is not clear if this represented some kind of ebb and flow of settlement in response to environmental or population changes or a form of shifting occupation with the reuse of areas after periods of abandonment. Indications are, however, that the nature of settlement was more complex and structured than has sometimes been appreciated.

There is no doubt that many areas of upland settlement were abandoned during the later Bronze Age, but the case for this having occurred rapidly, over a wide area, as the result of a major environmental catastrophe, remains unproven. It seems more reasonable to assume that the timing, speed and nature of this retreat from the uplands varied from one area to another. It is also likely that more than one background influence was involved. The role of gradual climatic deterioration and the over-exploitation of marginal soils is still more convincing than the short, sharp shock of a disaster whose occurrence had yet to be convincingly demonstrated. We also need to bear in mind the possibility that social and political changes, possibly resulting from environmental changes but also possibly operating independently of them, may have been involved. Just because we cannot identify such changes from the nature of the surviving evidence does not mean that they may not have occurred.

The Eruption of Thera and Its Impact on Minoan Civilisation

If the abandonment of settlement in upland Britain really was a catastrophic event resulting from the eruption of Hekla 3, its existence has yet to be clearly proven. Another eruption that occurred during the Bronze Age, on the island of Thera in the Aegean, has also attracted the interest of archaeologists and environmental specialists. Thera, also known as Santorini, lies 100km from the north coast of Crete and rather farther from the Greek mainland. The present island is only a fragment of its former size, representing the rim of a volcanic caldera, the centre of which was blasted apart in a huge explosion forming an underwater crater covering 80 square kilometres. The explosion has been estimated at 7,500 megatons, making it one of the greatest natural disasters of the Holocene – not quite as severe as the eruption of Tambora in the Dutch East Indies in 1815, but more powerful than the eruption of Krakatoa in 1883. An estimated 30–40 cubic km of magma was erupted and the plume of debris may have extended 36km into the atmosphere. On those parts of the island that survived the eruption a layer of ash up to 50m. thick was deposited. Winds from the north west carried clouds of ash which drifted for as much as 700km and settled over eastern Crete in a thick layer, as well as over parts of western Turkey to a depth of 10cm. Severe tidal waves were also created which affected the north coast of Crete. The scale of the disaster has been considered by some to have been so great that they believe it may have given rise to the legend of Atlantis, the great civilisation supposedly destroyed in a major cataclysm.

A Minoan city at Akroteri on the southern part of Thera has been excavated to show that, unlike Pompeii, there were no bodies among the ash. The residents seem to have had sufficient warning of the erup-tion to evacuate the site. Archaeologists, however, have long speculated that it can hardly be a matter of coincidence that the Thera eruption appears to have been followed quite closely by the rapid collapse of the Minoan civilisation, centred on Crete. It seemed reasonable to suggest that the tidal waves and ash clouds must have had severe effects on coastal settlements and more generally on Cretan agriculture. But, as

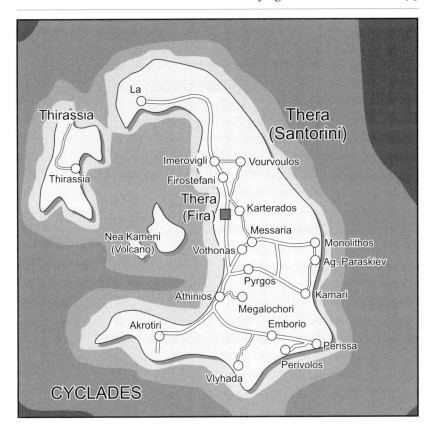

FIGURE 4.5 The island of Thera, formerly known as Santorini

we have already seen, close coincidence in time does not automatically prove a cause-and-effect link.

Part of the problem has been dating both the eruption and the Minoan collapse using different kinds of evidence for each event. One of the difficulties with arguments like this is the problem of pinning down environmental episodes such as eruptions to a human timescale. Spyridon Marinatos, the Greek archaeologist who first suggested the link between the Thera eruption and the downfall of the Minoan culture, suggested that the eruption occurred around 1450 BC, on the basis of correlating pottery from the immediately pre-eruption levels on Thera with that discovered at the palace at Knossos in Crete (Marinatos 1939; Doumas 1974). The evidence of ice cores in Greenland, however, indicated a date of 1645 +/- 20 BC for the acid layer believed to be the result of the Thera eruption while tree-ring data from different parts of northern Europe, including oaks from Irish peat bogs, point to a widespread cool phase of stunted tree growth lasting for several years around 1628 BC (Baillie and Munro 1988; Baillie 1995; Hammer et al. 1987). This is supported by the occurrence of a band of narrow rings from trees in the American south west, hinting at cold conditions which may have been the result of an eruption, again centred on 1628–26 BC. If this last adverse spell was caused by the Thera eruption then a gap of around 150 years might have intervened between the eruption and the Minoan collapse, so that the former could hardly have been a direct cause of the latter. There are problems with the radiocarbon calibration for the mid-second millennium BC, however, which generate two possible approximate dates for the Thera eruption: 1674–06 and 1554–34 BC with a 70 per cent likelihood of the date falling somewhere within the first band. There has also been a suggestion, not totally accepted, that the dating of the GISP2 Greenland ice core, which provided the date quoted above, has been miscalculated by forty years (Buckland et al. 1997). A layer of pumice in the Nile delta has provided a date for an eruption of around 1550 BC – which still leaves an awkward gap. More recently a date as early as 1650 BC has been suggested. So the eruption still cannot yet be pinned down within a span of 150 years. A recent survey by Manning (1999) favours the c.1628 BC date (but a review of this book argues for a 1645/1650 BC date).

To complicate matters even further, it is impossible to prove that the acid peak identified in the Greenland cores was actually the result of the Thera eruption. There may have been other major volcanic eruptions around the same time: a number of potential candidates has been identified: Avellimo (an earlier version of Vesuvius), Mount St Helens in the USA and Anakchak II in Alaska. Perhaps one or more of these erupted close to the time of Thera, but of course none of them is securely dated either.

If the timing of the Thera eruption poses problems, then so do calculations of its severity. The amount of sulphur released from the Thera eruption, worked out from geological evidence, has been set quite low in some estimates. On the other hand recent satellite measurements of major eruptions have suggested that such measurements may have greatly underestimated the amount of sulphur actually released by Thera (Baillie 1995: 112–14). Dating based on archaeological evidence, relating back to the Egyptian chronology, would put the eruption later rather than earlier, closer to the collapse of Minoan civilisation – but is this chronology accurate? There are serious doubts. It is deceptively easy to look at Egyptian inscriptions and other data for evidence of environmental stress which might have resulted from the Thera eruption. We have come across this fallacy before. One could postulate that atmospheric cooling due to a major eruption could have caused the failure of the monsoons at the headwaters of the Nile, leading to the failure of the annual Nile floods, and then to famine and political instability. But to identify famines or political upheavals from inscriptions and then use these as a means of dating the Thera eruption is a shaky circular argument with too many weak links. Perhaps the eruption did cause a dust veil over the Nile delta but this does not mean that any record of a major dust storm at about the right time can be interpreted as relating to Thera; dust storms occurred in Egypt under normal as well as abnormal conditions (ibid.: 154–5). Environmental scientists have emphasised the danger of allowing a single well-dated event to 'suck in' other dates for unrelated phenomena, the existence of which have been arrived at by different methods. On this basis a range of events around the eastern Mediterranean at about this period, such as the decline of particular cities or political shifts, can be claimed as evidence of the same environmental catastrophe. Establishing the precise dating of the eruption is thus important for a variety of reasons, not least of which is the claim that the exodus of the Israelites from Egypt, including the famous plagues and the parting of the Red Sea, represents some kind of folk memory of the effects of the Thera eruption. The sheer ingenuity involved in trying to link such a range of supposed disasters to this one source is impressive but ultimately it stretches the bounds of probability too far (Phillips 1998, 2002).

In the wake of scepticism about the large-scale climatic impacts of eruptions like that of Thera, more local, less severe impacts have been postulated, especially the occurrence of acid deposition which could have damaged vegetation and poisoned livestock. It was originally believed that much of the airborne debris from the Thera eruption was directed south eastwards but more recent work has indicated that a lot of the material went north eastwards towards Turkey and the Black Sea. A recent study of a site at Golhisa in south-west Turkey, some 400km from Thera, examined the effects of the eruption on the ecology of a lake catchment. The tephra indicated that the fallout of volcanic debris was a layer only 4cm thick. Studies of recent eruptions, such as Mount St Helens in 1980, have shown that a layer this thin settling on vegetation would soon wash out with only limited effects. In fact, the additional nutrients might even promote rather than hinder plant growth! Any adverse effects were too brief to be picked up by the lake sediments. At another site, Porsuk in south-central Turkey, a tree-ring sequence has a phase of wide rings caused by cooler summers and wetter conditions, which is thought to coincide with the Thera eruption. This suggests that on a regional scale the effects of the Thera disaster were not nearly as dire as has often been supposed (Eastwood et al. 2002).

Some archaeologists have claimed that a phase of severe economic dislocation in Crete was triggered first by a major earthquake and then by the Thera eruption. In such an earthquake-prone area, Minoan palaces had been destroyed on more than one occasion before the Thera eruption, but the earthquakes linked to this event seem to have been particularly severe and to have led to permanent rather than temporary abandonment. So some palace sites in Crete were undoubtedly abandoned after the eruption: society seems to have become more fragmented and localised as the traditional ruling elites lost prestige and control. Ultimately, as suggested by evidence of burning at many Cretan sites, society may well have collapsed into war and anarchy. The Mycenaeans from mainland Greece may have taken the opportunity to move in and take over, causing Minoan Crete to be absorbed into the Mycenaean, and eventually the Greek, world but the role of the Thera eruption in such events is still far from clear. The supposed cultural impacts of the eruption are not based on unambiguous, direct causal evidence or secure dates.

A recent study of environmental changes from the lowlands of north-west Crete shows that, while a thin pumice layer relating to the Thera eruption is present, there was no evidence at this site of tsunamis (tidal waves) caused by a violent eruption, or indeed of any significant long-term effect on the vegetation cover (Bottema and Sarpaki 2003). In dealing with a 'catastrophe' of this nature it is easy to underestimate the resilience of both environmental systems and human societies. The history of the Japanese and their ability to cope with the impact of volcanoes and earthquakes is a case in point. If we want to identify an eruption that may have threatened the human race worldwide we have to go back to the Toba event of c.740,000 BP. The Toba volcano, on the island of Sumatra in the East Indies, collapsed into its own magma chamber to leave a hole that subsequently flooded to create a lake 100km x 30km. The eruption was approximately forty times as severe as the one that affected Tambora in 1815, the most severe volcanic event in modern times. The Toba eruption is calculated to have ejected 2,800 cubic kilometres of material into the atmosphere. The ash fallout can be traced west to India where in some places it has accumulated to a depth of up to 6m. One school of thought, based on evidence from ice cores, claims that the eruption caused the equivalent of a 'nuclear winter' six years long, followed by a sudden shift into glacial conditions which lasted for around 1,000 years. Such severe impacts, it is thought, may have reduced the global population of *Homo sapiens* from c.100,000 to only 2,000, failing only narrowly to wipe out our species entirely. On the other hand, the alternative view is that the impacts of even this huge event were relatively localised and that they did not cause a worldwide catastrophe. On this scale, the Thera eruption, while locally impressive, seems likely to have been much less devastating than has sometimes been portrayed.

CHAPTER 5

Early Civilisations and Empires

The Effects of Agriculture in the Tigris-Euphrates Basin: the First Towns and Civilisations

Groups of early hunter-gatherers show no signs of having possessed surpluses of food which they stored from year to year rather than from season to season. The idea of a surplus at anything beyond the level of the individual family suggests the existence of some person or group in the community who wielded sufficient power and authority to allow the centralisation of food storage. Such accumulated surpluses could be used for more than just providing a reserve of food for the population during lean seasons: they could free individuals from agricultural labour to work as specialised craftsmen or feed a larger labour force which could be employed in major building projects such as constructing temples, palaces or defensive walls (to protect the food surplus as well as the community). Surpluses could also be traded in exchange for commodities that could not be obtained locally. More significantly, they might be used to further enhance agricultural production, for example by feeding the workforce needed to construct irrigation systems. The careful management of food surpluses thus encouraged a division of labour so that some people could be freed part- or full-time from agriculture to engage in other work.

We have seen that the earliest phases of agriculture encouraged the development of sedentary communities. Just as the domestication of crops and animals had proceeded gradually in a series of stages rather than occurring as a single dramatic revolutionary change, so did the size of farming communities gradually tend to become larger in the best-favoured areas. Larger communities could support more specialist non-agricultural workers and slowly, a very different type of community began to emerge, something archaeologists might label as a town or even a city. Because of problems regarding definition there is not complete agreement regarding which was the world's first true town. A case can be made for Jericho, as we saw in Chapter 4, and rather more convincingly for the settlement of Çatal Hüyük in Anatolia which, by about 6000 BC, may have housed around 5,000 inhabitants. The inhabitants not only grew cereals and peas but made pottery and smelted copper, trading these for a wide range of other commodities.

Archaeologists have doubted whether Jericho or Çatal Hüyük were real towns though, seeing them rather as just large nucleations of rural population without the full range of specialist functions and attributes which are normally seen as a prerequisite for the existence of urban life. Çatal Hüyük had many small shrines but no temples, many houses but no streets. But what is clear is that neither of these early settlements, even if they were true towns, led to a continuous urban tradition. When this happened it did not take place, as might have been expected, somewhere within the Fertile Crescent but in the much less promising environment of the lower Tigris and Euphrates river basins where, away from the main rivers, desert conditions were the norm. In this region an urban society rose which survived for some 3,000 years before becoming absorbed into the wider influence of the societies of classical Greece and Rome which were their inheritors.

During the seventh millennium BC farming had begun to move out of the Zagros Mountains in the eastern arm of the Fertile Crescent, down into the northern part of the Mesopotamian plain where, in the upper part of the Tigris valley, there was still enough rainfall to allow conventional agriculture. By around 6000–5500 BC, agricultural communities had begun to settle in the middle part of the Tigris valley, beyond the limits of rain-fed agriculture, so that crops could be raised only by using simple irrigation systems to draw water off from the rivers. The upper Euphrates, in contrast to the upper Tigris, had a very dry climate and here, too, agriculture was impossible without irrigation. Between 5500 and 4000 BC what has become known as the Ubaid culture became established not only throughout northern Mesopotamia but also in the even drier environment of southern Mesopotamia, where between the rivers (where irrigation could not reach) desert conditions occurred.

FIGURE 5.1 Location of ancient Mesopotamian cities
(after Whitehouse 1977)

Because so much effort has gone into identifying the earliest agricultural communities in the Near East we know relatively little about the
later agricultural societies which provided a springboard for the development of the first towns and cities. Certainly a number of later cities in
southern Mesopotamia appear to have had significant concentrations of
population during the Ubaid period. All older cities in this region that
have been excavated to their lowest levels seem to have originated at
this time. Typical were settlements such as Eridu, which covered an area
of 10ha and which may have had around 4,000 inhabitants. During the
succeeding Uruk period (c.4000–3200 BC) the first real cities emerged,

with monumental architecture, the use of writing, greatly expanded trading horizons and specialised industrial production.

In expanding out of its relatively moist areas of origin into the semi-arid landscapes of the Tigris and Euphrates valleys, agriculture had to adapt to very different environmental conditions. The returns of cultivated crops in the areas where they were first developed were relatively modest. It was only when agriculture shifted to the superficially unattractive environment of the lowlands of the Tigris-Euphrates basin that the full potential of agriculture was unlocked. Southern Mesopotamia lacked stone, timber, indeed any kind of mineral wealth, and was prone to sometimes disastrous floods. Agriculture was totally impossible if the only source of water was the limited rainfall.

Nevertheless the soils of its alluvial flood plains were potentially highly productive as long as sufficient water could be diverted from the rivers. It has been calculated that efficient irrigated farming systems in this area may have produced a return, in relation to the quantity of seed sown, of around fifty times. Irrigation was far from being a new phenomenon: on a smaller scale it had long been used in areas like the fringes of the Zagros Mountains of northern Mesopotamia, while the attractions of Jericho as a site for early agriculture were principally an abundant local water supply. But here the possibilities for irrigated farming were far greater. The adoption of irrigation systems allowed huge increases in output that freed a growing proportion of the population from direct labour on the land.

From about 4000 BC in southern Mesopotamia the first cities, including Eridu, seen by the later inhabitants of the region themselves as their oldest city, and Uruk began to appear with the rise of the Sumerian civilisation. From 3000 BC even more centres, including Ur, were established. Because the construction of buildings was based on the use of mud bricks (for want of anything else in this stone-free region) the sites of these cities were gradually built up in mounds, or *tells*, in which successive layers of structures were built up, protecting those below. The inhabitants of these early cities made high-quality pottery and, from around 3000 BC they were smelting metallic ores to make bronze.

The Sumerians developed the wheel, and from it the war chariot, simple pictographic writing systems, and sophisticated bureaucracies to organise the collection and redistribution of surpluses. The very poverty of resources in Sumer, apart from the fertility of the irrigated soils, meant that the cities were forced to engage in trade with surrounding mountain and plateau regions for a wide range of commodities that were not available locally. The ancient coastline of the Persian Gulf was much further inland than it is today so that cities like Ur and Eridu, the sites of which are now a long way inland, were close to the ocean and well-located for seaborne trade (Adams 1966).

Conditions for agriculture in Sumer were different from those in the other, more famous, Middle Eastern centre of irrigated agriculture, ancient Egypt. The rivers were fed by melting snow and a spring peak of rainfall in eastern Turkey, reaching a maximum flow in April and May. The annual floods of the Tigris, and especially those of the Euphrates, were less spectacular than those of the Nile because the rivers were much smaller in volume and did not spread annual layers of fertile silt so widely. Yet at the same time the spring floods could be dramatic in some years. One, which deposited a 1.5m.-deep layer of sediment at Ur, may have lived on in popular tradition to give rise to legends of the biblical Flood. The period of annual flooding, however, was out of phase with the times when water was most needed for agriculture, posing further difficulties for farming communities. The rivers flooded in spring but water supply was especially crucial in the autumn when the fields needed to receive water to prepare the soil for ploughing and sowing. As a result, water resources had to be carefully husbanded. Instead of simply letting the rivers burst their banks and then damming back the overflow, irrigation canals had to be laboriously constructed to bring water to the fields. Mesopotamian irrigation systems were built on a larger scale than those of the Nile valley. The natural levees on either side of the rivers, which kept the river channels slightly higher than the level of the surrounding fields, were carefully breached and water led away under gravity. At first this involved series of small-scale local canal systems. Irrigation systems at Choga Mami, dating from around 5000 BC, are among the oldest known. Later irrigation involved the construction of larger canals which ran parallel to the main rivers and spread water over a wider area. In their lower reaches the Tigris and Euphrates diverged into many channels, which helped to spread the availability of irrigation water over a more extensive area. Following the fuller development of city states in this area, however, even larger schemes developed, which involved the redirecting of river courses and supplied water for longer periods during the summer, allowing a wider range of crops including rice, sesame and cotton to be cultivated.

Water management required care, however, for once fields had been flooded the removal of excess water could be difficult. The canals required constant maintenance and dredging to prevent silting. As many of the cities of Sumer were so close to each other – the sites of several of their tells can be seen from the top of some of their ziggurats or temple mounds – close co-operation in water management between cities was an obvious advantage. A common language and culture encouraged the inhabitants of the various cities to see themselves as having a common identity, belonging to what they called 'The Land'.

The success of the Sumerian economy did not simply lie in its use of large-scale irrigation schemes but in the wider range of resources they exploited. The availability of archives of clay tablets detailing the collection and redistribution of produce has allowed the economy of these early cities to be reconstructed in some detail. In the fields barley seems always to have been more important than wheat because of its greater tolerance of salt. Two crops a year were possible on the irrigated land, but in practice the harvest was often restricted to only one crop to combat the problem of salinity. Peas, lentils and a range of fruits and vegetables were also grown. Date palms, very tolerant of salt, provided another nutritious source of food. Fish from the rivers, wildfowl from the marshes with deer and gazelle all helped to provide a more varied diet. Sheep and goats with some cattle and pigs were kept. The sheep provided wool which, made into cloth, was one of the region's major exports. Cattle provided dairy produce while oxen contributed the draught power for ploughing and hauling carts. Ploughs rather than hoes or digging sticks were used as far back as the Uruk period if not even earlier, making agriculture more efficient.

Sumerian agriculture and trade also depended upon harnessing wind power, via sailing vessels, and animal power via the plough and the wheel. These, with metallurgy, were discoveries which preceded the Early Dynastic phase of city development and can be seen as necessary precursors of civilisation. Early metal tools may have been only marginally more efficient that stone ones, but they lasted a lot longer without breaking or requiring sharpening.

The wide range of food sources may also have been important in encouraging an early trend towards specialisation as fishermen, herdsmen, fruit and vegetable growers, etc. The effect on population density was marked. Within the Fertile Crescent, hunter-gatherers may have lived at a density of around 0.1 people per square kilometre. Early farming may have allowed this to increase to between one and two people per square kilometre – an increase of up to twenty times – but irrigated farming could support around six people per square kilometre, a further threefold increase. It was this concentration of people in a relatively limited area that made the development of towns possible. Towns seem, then, to have been a result of local concentrations of population supported by intensive agriculture, but their development in turn precipitated further marked population increases. There was less of a contrast in population levels between the rural settlements of the pre-urban Ubaid culture and the first towns of the Uruk period than between these and the Early Dynastic cities.

The earliest phase of true urban development seems to have occurred in the Uruk phase, when the total population of Sumer was still relatively small. The growth of towns seems to have been due as much to the concentration of existing population in central places as to demographic growth. Although some kind of democratic 'citizens' assembly' has been suggested in these early stages of city development, by the time the archaeological evidence becomes more abundant the administration of these cities as well as much of their economic activity seems to have focused on their temples. Cities like Ur had at their centres ziggurats, huge stepped pyramids crowned by temples and shrines. Later on, however, secular warlords and kings seem to have taken over at least some of the power. Warfare between cities and their surrounding territories seems to have been not uncommon. Cities were fortified with walls and towers, while the use of chariots allowed more mobile warfare in the plains between them.

During the Early Dynastic period there were up to twenty cities at any time: independent, sometimes warring, with one generally being recognised as supreme, but with this primacy shifting from city to city over time. The cities had suburbs beyond their walls and satellite villages from which the more distant areas of land were cultivated. The largest city, Uruk, spread over some 450ha, and may have had a population of up to 50,000, though estimates of population based on the physical area covered by the cities are necessarily extremely imprecise. On this basis many of the other cities may have had populations in the region of 10–20,000. Uruk was defended with a circuit of walls nearly 10km in length with double ramparts strengthened at intervals with semicircular towers. Uruk started off as a small town serving a limited rural hinterland. From around 3000 BC, however, there was a rapid development with people from the surrounding countryside being packed tightly into the cities (Adams 1981). Inside the cities there was a maze of tightly packed buildings, sometimes with a regular grid of streets but more often unplanned. The streets were unpaved, but sewage systems were built. In addition to internal rivalries there were also periodic invasions from outside. The Early Dynastic period ends with the rise of the Semitic king Sargon of Akkad who united the Sumerian cities as well as conquering northern Mesopotamia and south-western Iran, parts of Syria and Turkey.

Early interpretations of the development of society in southern Mesopotamia claimed that, while towns could not exist without an efficient system of irrigated agriculture, the towns themselves were a mechanism for social control and needed to exist in order for the irrigation systems to be organised. Urban development then was a creation of the particular characteristics of the environment of this arid area. It is clear, however, that in many other societies complex irrigation systems have existed without the need for towns. Maisels (1990) has claimed that a dense rural population supported by irrigated agriculture came before the towns rather than vice versa. Within such communities central foci developed for religious, security or trading reasons and from these the first urban social elites developed to a point where the evolving cities became capable of transforming the structure of society as a whole. Irrigation helped the development of such elites but was not the only factor at work.

Within the cities high proportions of the population were still food producers – farmers, gardeners, herdsmen – but some of them were also part-time or even full-time tradesmen, while others had specialist roles as merchants, priests and scribes. The temples and palaces, in their own distinct quarters of the urban areas, were the foci of city life as well as the economic centres of the cities. During the Early Dynastic period some differences in social status are evident but without the sharper division into classes that had become evident by around 1800 BC. Priests, temple administrators and scribes had a relatively high status and were among the wealthier urban social groups. The palace retinues and the military also had high status. Slaves seem rarely to have been privately owned, but rather belonged to the temples.

Temples seem to have been key elements from the very start of urban life. At Eridu a series of eighteen superimposed religious buildings has been discovered, starting off with small shrines and ending with a massive ziggurat. A huge amount of labour was needed for the construction of these and other buildings within the temple precincts, as well as the palaces and the defensive walls. During the Early Dynastic period the work seems to have been done voluntarily by the inhabitants as part of their service to the god. Every citizen belonged to one of the temples and so did much of the land. One part of the land was worked communally, another was divided into individual allotments while a third portion was leased out to tenants. The temples thus controlled the organisation of both land and labour, as well as the distribution of food and other goods (Postgate 1992). Merchants traded goods as servants of the temple rather than on their own behalf. All this centralisation of economic activity required careful record keeping and led to the development of the first systems of writing. Over 90 per cent of the clay tablets recovered from these early cities are economic, legal and administrative documents. Although the temples wielded so much economic influence they were not sources of political power. Political power lay with the kings, although secular leaders do seem to have developed at a later stage than the temples. The palaces of Sumerian cities came to rival the temples in terms of wealth and land ownership but they never seem to have eclipsed them.

There was a down side to the increasingly complex irrigation schemes, though. The soils had to be treated carefully, with the amount of water supplied being strictly controlled and regular years of bare fallowing being used to prevent too much waterlogging and, even worse, the drawing up to the surface of salts dissolved in the river water. The result of excessive evaporation of moisture from the surface of the soil was the further upward movement of water by capillary action. Over time a salt crust might form which was highly detrimental to most plants. Incidentally, this was not a problem in ancient Egypt, where different conditions of flooding and drainage in the Nile valley helped to maintain soil fertility without increasing salinity.

It has been widely asserted that the cities of southern Mesopotamia and the farming systems that supported them contained the seeds of their own destruction. The urban elites may have thought that they were in control of nature but as population grew it became necessary to crop the irrigated lands more and more intensively. The net result was an increase in the rate at which salts accumulated in the upper layers of the soil. The cultivation of emmer wheat had to be phased out because of its lack of salt tolerance compared with barley. Around 3500 BC wheat and barley were being grown in roughly equal amounts, but by 2100 BC wheat had ceased to be grown almost entirely and crop yields generally were steadily falling (Jacobsen and Adams 1958). The decline in food supply ultimately led to the decay and then the collapse of many cities. Sumer was conquered by the more northerly Babylon around 1800 BC and many of the original cities of the south were abandoned leaving only tells to mark their sites. Extensive areas of the Tigris-Euphrates basin still remain virtually useless for agriculture due to the build-up of salt. On this argument the world's first intensive irrigated farming system had generated the first large-scale environmental disaster. Traces of old abandoned irrigation systems still criss-cross the area, mute testimony to the efforts of long-vanished farmers (Yoffee 1988).

The story, however, was undoubtedly much more complex than this simple deterministic argument might suggest. Not all archaeologists are convinced that the build-up of salt occurred on a scale sufficient to cause the major decline and depopulation of Sumerian cities. Mesopotamia, flanked by mountain peoples to the north and easily accessible from the Levant, was a much more open society than isolated Egypt, its city states always vulnerable to attack and invasion by outsiders. Periods of political disruption and instability were hardly conducive to the regular maintenance of complex irrigation systems. Equally, it is possible to suggest that, when society was under pressure, efforts may have been made to increase agricultural productivity in the short term by expedients such as reducing the period of fallow and so hastening the accumulation of salt.

It is now believed, moreover, that the argument for increasing salinity and declining yields is a fallacy based on the misinterpretation of a relatively limited and not necessarily representative body of written material. This view claims that it was relatively easy to prevent the undue build-up of salt in irrigated soils, first by the use of fallowing and second by flushing salts out from the soils through regular flooding: whatever the causes of the decline of the cities of Sumer, they lie in its social and political structures rather than its environment and how it was exploited.

The landscapes of southern Mesopotamia have become familiar as a result of the Coalition invasion of Iraq in 2003. The achievement of the first populations of this area in managing its water resources to allow irrigation and the development of a series of cities seems all the more striking in view of its unpromising appearance to modern Western eyes.

In a later section we look at how agriculture in an area which might seem equally unpromising, led to the rise of another great civilisation. In the case of the Maya, however, over-intensive exploitation of the landscape, plus unforeseeable environmental catastrophes, led not to slow decline but swift collapse.

The 'Ruined' Landscapes of the Mediterranean: Environmental Deterioration in Classical and Later Times

There is a widely accepted and persistent belief that the modern landscapes of the Mediterranean represent degraded, deforested, severely eroded versions of what was once a greener, more fertile, moister environment (Brandt and Thornes 1996). According to this 'ruined landscape' or 'lost Eden' argument Mediterranean forests in the past, unlike so many at the present, were composed of tall trees which, once cut down, exposed the topsoil to severe erosion causing land degradation and even a drying of the climate. In part this belief has been subconsciously influenced by the works of seventeenth-century French artists such as Claude Lorrain and Nicolas Poussin, who portrayed the landscapes of classical Greece as though they were as green and lush as those of their native country. The well-wooded character of the ancient Mediterranean also seems to be confirmed by evidence in the topographic accounts of some classical writers and it has been suggested that the landscapes of the Mediterranean world in classical times were very different from those of the present. There is a suspicion, however, that sources such as those mentioned above have been interpreted rather superficially or even totally misinterpreted. Yet surely the seemingly profligate use of timber in classical times and later must have devastated Mediterranean forests? One only has to think of the large numbers of triremes or war galleys in use when the Greeks beat the Persian fleet at Salamis in 480 BC, or for that matter at a later date when in AD 1571 the Turks were defeated at the battle of Lepanto. Events such as these certainly give the impression that large amounts of timber were consumed in shipbuilding, not to mention building construction or the production of charcoal for fuel.

Misunderstandings have also arisen over what constitutes 'forest' in the lands bordering the Mediterranean Sea. Many modern studies of Mediterranean vegetation have defined 'forest' in a narrow way and have not included types of vegetation such as maquis or savanna, whose character derives from grazing management. There has been a failure to appreciate that, when grazing pressure is reduced, rapid tree growth can occur in the Mediterranean, even today. Mediterranean vegetation needs to be understood on its own terms rather than seen as downgraded forms of a once universal forest cover (Grove and Rackham 2001).

The more recent experiences of other environments have seemed to echo that of the Mediterranean. Islands such as Madeira or St Helena, which were devastated by deforestation and over-cultivation from the late fifteenth century (Chapter 6), have often been considered as templates for what is thought to have happened in the Mediterranean at an earlier period. Once deforested, the lands around the Mediterranean, with their steep slopes, often made even more unstable by a complex geology and slope instability resulting from earthquakes, have been seen as especially vulnerable to erosion by flash floods. In this view of the evolution of the landscapes of the Mediterranean, erosion tends to be seen as less of a natural environmental process and more of an evil resulting largely from direct and indirect human activity. Erosion, moreover, is often assumed to involve mainly damage to the soil. In fact much of the material that has been eroded and deposited within Mediterranean river basins due to floods within historical times has been not topsoil but unconsolidated material which accumulated during or at the end of the ice ages. The modern landscapes of the Mediterranean, then, have been seen as the end product of massive ecological degradation which seems to have been especially prevalent in the classical, medieval and post-medieval periods. McNeill (1992), in his persuasive book, *The Mountains of the Mediterranean*, has claimed that extensive areas were depopulated as a result of deforestation and subsequent erosion, some of this occurring quite recently.

Bronze Age and classical times in the Mediterranean were certainly characterised by periodic high population densities and intensive human activity (Shipley and Salmon 1996). In Crete the rural population density during some parts of the Bronze Age was probably greater than it is today. But a closer look at some of the literature produced on the landscapes of the Mediterranean suggests that too often the evidence has been taken at face value, with too many processes being inferred rather than convincingly demonstrated. The amount of timber used for shipbuilding during classical times (and even later) can easily be exaggerated. For example, a Bronze Age Minoan 'ship' was roughly comparable in size to one of the ship's boats carried by HMS *Victory* at Trafalgar. Greek and Roman oared galleys were lightly built for speed rather than massively timbered for strength. They were designed mainly for inshore use during the summer and did not need to have the strength of construction to face winter storms. Shipbuilding has often been used as an indirect, proxy source of evidence for the existence of, the depletion of, and then the destruction of Mediterranean forests. It is often forgotten, however, that shipbuilding timber was frequently brought in from a considerable distance, sometimes from outside the region. It is also necessary to consider whether shipbuilding at any period was actually consuming timber faster than existing woods could replace it. Periods of political disruption, when fleets and armies were mobilised, were not necessarily detrimental to forests. As Rackham and Moody (1996) have observed, men who were rowing war galleys were not burning wood for charcoal or engaged in clearing trees for agriculture, while armies on the move tend to eat the goats that have been blamed for so much damage to woodlands in this region. Periods of war, then, might actually encourage the recovery of the woodlands rather than lead to their destruction.

In other cases the productivity of classical agriculture has been substantially overestimated in a viewpoint which sees this period as a kind of 'golden age'. North Africa, the so-called 'granary of Rome', has been assumed, on the basis of this title, to have possessed a moister climate in Roman times than now, plus a highly productive agricultural system.

In addition to shipbuilding the other favoured agent of destruction of woodlands in the Mediterranean from classical times onwards has been the production of charcoal, especially for use as a fuel in the smelting of iron and other metals. The myth that the charcoal iron industry stripped England of its ancient forests, however, has long been exploded (Chapter 7) and there are grounds for believing that the situation was similar in the Mediterranean. The production of charcoal did not necessarily – or even usually – involve the permanent clearance and destruction of woodlands. Methods of woodland management that treated trees as a long-term renewable resource through the processes of coppicing and pollarding were widely practised. Coppicing involved cutting deciduous trees down at ground level but leaving their stumps in place to send up clusters of shoots. These, after a dozen years or more, could be harvested to produce a crop of poles. The stump would then obligingly send up another set of shoots which could be harvested again.

Coppiced woodland produced a much greater volume of wood per unit area than clear-felled mature forest. All that was necessary was that the coppice shoots be protected from grazing animals. The technique of pollarding involved cutting tree trunks off some feet about the ground and allowing a set of shoots to grow out of reach of livestock without the need for fencing, so that forestry and pasture could be combined on the same plot of land. Some coppice stools and pollards surviving today in the Mediterranean are immensely old, going back over 2,000 years to Hellenistic times (Grove and Rackham 2001). The use of pollarding and coppicing not only protected woods from destruction: it actively encouraged them to expand in some cases where demand for charcoal was high. Coppicing is known to have been used in the Mediterranean since classical times at least, but many authors, McNeill (1992) included, while mentioning coppicing, assume that it was only of local or regional importance rather than something that occurred throughout the region. Circumstances where the expansion of iron production was limited by a shortage of charcoal may have been due to the growth of demand outstripping the existing fuel supply rather than a shortage of fuel caused by a reduction in the extent of woodlands.

Deforestation and subsequent erosion in the Mediterranean resulting from human agency has been assumed much more frequently than it has been convincingly demonstrated. Where deforestation is known to have occurred it needs to be shown that erosion actually followed soon after. Where erosion can be demonstrated it must be dated securely before links with human activity can be confidently asserted. All too often it has been suggested rather than proven that erosion was the result of vague unspecified human activities or a general 'expansion' of agriculture (Rackham and Moody 1996). This can lead to almost any activity being seen as a cause of soil erosion. The construction of agricultural terraces has often been claimed to lead to erosion but so, paradoxically, has the abandonment of terraces. In neither case has the detailed mechanism causing erosion been clearly stated.

The problem with erosion is that, by its nature, it involves the removal of evidence. It has usually been studied in mirror-image form by looking at the deposition of eroded material, whether at the foot of slopes, in valleys, in lakes or in the sea in the form of river deltas (Delano-Smith 1979). But establishing the period at which such deposits were laid down, identifying the sources of the material contained in them, and establishing precisely what forces set them in motion is a difficult task. Equally tricky is calculating rates of erosion and deposition over time, though this can sometimes be done where downwashed material has become banked up against a building of known date, such as a church.

In many Mediterranean valleys sequences of deposits have been identified which were originally divided by the geographer, Claudio Vita-Finzi (1969), into the Older and Younger Fills. The deposition of these was thought to span extensive periods of time. The former, which sometimes contained Palaeolithic implements, seemed to date from the late Pleistocene period and was much thicker than the overlying Younger Fill, which contained pottery and other artefacts suggesting dates of deposition between c.AD 500 and 1500. More recent research has indicated that the Younger Fill accumulated over a longer time-span than had originally been accepted by Vita-Finzi, stretching back in some cases to the Bronze Age, between 2700 and 1700 BC (Chester and James 1991).

Dating the Younger Fill is hard enough; linking it convincingly to erosion resulting from human activity is much more difficult. When evidence of phases of erosion in particular areas has been identified and dated reasonably closely, it does not necessarily coincide with periods when human activity is known to have been substantial – as during classical, Hellenistic and Roman times, for instance (Shaw 1981). When all the known dating evidence for the Younger Fill is assembled there seems in many areas to be a clear concentration of dates in medieval and post-medieval times rather than in prehistory. The erosion that produced the deposited sediments could still have been the result of deforestation and erosion due to human activities, but at a more detailed scale there is often no correlation between phases of deposition and known human events, such as periods of population growth which are likely to have had an impact upon the extent and nature of woodland cover and the rate of soil erosion. For recent centuries the date of the Younger Fill varies quite markedly from one location to another and matches more closely periods of abnormal weather conditions than any identifiable human agency (Grove and Rackham 2001).

Trees may have some effect on slowing down the rate at which moderate levels of rainfall percolate into streams and rivers, but against a really determined deluge their impact is minimal. In an environment like the Mediterranean, where flash floods are some of the most important natural hazards, much of the process of erosion and deposition is the result not of average winter storms occurring year after year but the level of flood that might occur once in a lifetime, or even the kind of storm whose return period is once every two hundred years or longer, the sort of deluge resulting from a cloudburst when a year's rainfall may occur within a few hours (ibid. 2001). An example are the floods that occurred in Provence on 8 and 9 September 2002 when over 650mm of rainfall – half the annual total – fell on the flanks of the Cevennes within twenty-four hours, producing floods in which twenty-one people were killed and a great amount of damage done to property.

During the Little Ice Age major floods, the prime cause of erosion and the deposition of alluvium in the Mediterranean, were more prevalent in some centuries than others. Such floods, however, were relatively localised in extent so that the Younger Fill is likely to have been laid down at different times in different areas depending on the local flood chronology. Other factors, including human activity, earthquakes (causing landslips) and unstable geology, may well have been contributory factors in producing Younger Fill deposits (Lewin et al. 1995). One of the most convincing arguments against agriculture or other forms of human agency having been a significant influence is that the accumulation of Younger Fill comes to a rapid halt towards the end of the nineteenth century at a time when population pressure in many regions was at a maximum. Population rose in the European Mediterranean from the late eighteenth century, typically at around 1 per cent per annum, after the ending of bubonic plague but not before the eradication of malaria. In many parts of Mediterranean France the peak of population was reached during the third quarter of the nineteenth century (Delano-Smith 1979).

McNeill (1992) attaches great importance to the intake of marginal land for agriculture in the nineteenth century as being permanently damaging to mountain environments. But Grove and Rackham (2001) do not necessarily see mountains as fragile environments. At a regional scale examples of environmental damage from the nineteenth century do occur. In the Sierra de Gádor in southern Spain, for example, between the 1830s and the 1860s the output of ore made this region the world's leading producer of lead. The demands of the mining industry and its workforce stimulated an expansion of cultivation and large-scale logging which did create a devastated landscape; but this was an extreme example (McNeill 1992). During the twentieth century, while activities such as agriculture, forestry and road construction have greatly increased, the opportunities for erosion, the rate of deposition has been markedly reduced. The incidence of major floods on a number of rivers has also decreased in the twentieth century due to the construction of dams which help to regulate river flow. The occurrence of serious floods during the Little Ice Age has thus been pinpointed as a major cause of erosion.

The deposition of eroded material occurred not only in the lower parts of river catchments, but also at their mouths in the form of deltas. In the near-tideless Mediterranean most of the sediment in these deltas comes from inland erosion via rivers rather than from coastal erosion. Historians have tended to assume that this deltaic material represents soil eroded from river catchments due to population pressure, deforestation and soil erosion. Post-glacial sea level rises created drowned coasts with numerous inlets and creeks, at the same time burying existing river deltas over 100m. below sea level. Since then sedimentation has gradually filled in the indentations of the coastline, a process that would have occurred naturally without any human intervention. When delta deposits had accumulated to a level where they were once more close to the surface then they were in a position for their visible part to grow rapidly. The Ebro delta in Spain hardly existed in Roman times but underwent rapid expansion during the sixteenth and seventeenth centuries at an annual rate of deposition over twice that of the early part of the Holocene. By the nineteenth century, however, the rate of growth was slackening rather than increasing. The Rhône delta has been built up in part by sediment derived from beyond the Mediterranean zone. In the fourteenth century the Alpine streams seem to have been generally well-behaved but after this time they became much more torrential, acquiring heavy loads of sediment and becoming braided. Like the Ebro much of the growth of the visible part of the Rhône delta seems to have come during early modern times when the limits of the delta were advancing by some fifty metres each year.

Deltas are difficult to study: it is rarely known from exactly where within a catchment area the source of their sediment at any period lies but, in broad terms, the evidence for their expansion seems to fit in with the deposition of Younger Fill deposits, being most dramatic during the worst part of the Little Ice Age, a period when Spain was in decline economically, and Italian river basins such as the Arno seem to have experienced no more intensive land use than had been occurring for centuries. So there is no consistent evidence that delta expansion was due principally to human-induced environmental activity. It has to be admitted that changing attitudes towards the practice of forestry with the spread of Enlightenment ideas in early modern times *were* potentially destructive of woodlands. Forestry and agriculture were increasingly seen as forms of land use that should be separated rather than integrated. But the damaging influence of these ideas in many areas did not have enough time to take full effect before depopulation started in the nineteenth century and vegetation began to recover (Grove and Rackham 2001).

One problem with most views of the Mediterranean and its landscapes is that climate is assumed to have been a constant factor with no significant variation throughout the Holocene. One aspect of the natural vegetation of the Mediterranean, which has been fully appreciated by ecologists only in recent years, is that it has had only a few thousand years of climatic stability to which, in some cases, it may not yet have fully adjusted. It was only as late as the Bronze Age that a true Mediterranean climate seems to have developed, with north European trees disappearing from areas such as Crete and southern Greece. Some of the changes in vegetation over the last few thousand years undoubtedly represent a delayed response to climatic changes rather than to human impacts. The present Mediterranean climate of dry hot summers and wet winters is quite a recent development, then (ibid.). During the earlier part of the Holocene, climate in the region was moister than today with less marked seasonal contrasts. The vegetation of the region may then have included fewer areas of evergreen forest and more deciduous woodland which was killed off by a change to a hotter, drier climate. The evidence from pollen analysis needs to be treated with care, however: many of the areas of deciduous woodland in the early Holocene are likely to have grown on the deeper soils which were later cleared for agriculture. Additionally, pollen deposits come from wetland sites that frequently have deeper soils nearby, so that the pollen from deciduous trees may be over-represented compared with that from evergreen trees, the commonest of which, the holm oak (*Quercus ilex*) and the kermes oak (*Quercus coccifera*) are tolerant of very poor soils. Even under these wetter conditions, however, the tree cover was far from continuous.

The two most important events in the environmental history of the Mediterranean during the Holocene period were first, the increasing aridity of the climate from the fifth millennium BC and, second, the spread of agriculture and pastoralism, not by Neolithic farmers, whose impact on the landscape seems to have been comparatively small-scale, but during the succeeding Bronze Age. By classical times the overall character of Mediterranean vegetation appears to have been very much like that of the present. In Sardinia, for instance, by late prehistoric times there was probably no more, perhaps rather less, woodland than there is today, and settlement had spread throughout the island (ibid.). Much of the making of the Mediterranean landscape, then, had already occurred before written records began. The changes which occurred from classical times onwards were less dramatic than those which had already occurred. The landscape of classical Greece was more like that of Greece in the nineteenth century than that of early prehistoric times. At a broad scale continuity rather than change has been the keynote during the last 2,000 years, with depletion and regrowth of woodland being much more characteristic than total destruction. Grazing in the Mediterranean, now and in the past, is not haphazard but carefully controlled, with animals being moved on regularly before they can do too much damage to the vegetation of a locality. The resilience of Mediterranean forests is demonstrated by the rapid rate at which abandoned cultivation terraces have been recolonised by trees since the start of depopulation during the twentieth century. Tourist developments, new roads and intensive agriculture have affected some areas, but many parts of the Mediterranean are more rather than less wooded than a century ago. As agriculture has contracted, and the numbers of sheep and goats declined, trees have spread rapidly. The example of the Mediterranean woods shows that we can manufacture human-induced environmental catastrophes where these may not actually have occurred. As we will see in the next chapter, however, there are plenty of examples of genuine disasters caused by environmental change, both natural and the result of human activity.

The Collapse of the Maya Civilisation

The Maya civilisation of Central America originated in the Yucatan peninsula around 2600–2500 BC. The Maya seem to have been related to the Olmec peoples of southern Guatemala and gradually spread to occupy an extensive area of Central America, including Guatemala, Yucatan, western Honduras, Belize and El Salvador, eventually occupying an area of 400–500,000sq. km in a region extending around 900km from north to south and 550km from east to west. They also developed contacts with the peoples of the highlands of Mexico to the north.

The Maya adopted many ideas from the Olmecs, such as writing, an accurate calendar and a complex religion, and improved on them. From around 2000 BC they developed agriculture, allowing a substantial increase in population. Towns began to appear from around 500 BC and from about 300 BC Maya society became increasingly complex with a hierarchical system of government based on the rule of kings and nobles. Maya cities appear to have developed first in the highlands, then in the lowlands, with elaborate ceremonial centres containing palaces and stone pyramid temples, squares, ball courts and inscribed stone commemorative pillars. Their culture reached its peak between about AD 600 and AD 800, with sophisticated astronomy and mathematics, hieroglyphic writing, and a monumental architecture which was all the more impressive for being constructed without metal tools. Their achievement was so impressive that some writers on the lunatic fringe of archaeology have attributed it to knowledge imparted by alien invaders from outer space! At its peak the Maya empire may have had as many as fifteen million inhabitants according to some estimates. When the Conquistadors arrived in the New World, however, there were only a few hundred thousand of their descendants left. What had happened to them?

Between c.AD 800 and AD 900, Maya civilisation appears to have declined rapidly and dramatically. The building of monumental architecture and the cutting of inscriptions came to an abrupt end in most cities, suggesting that a collapse of the ruling dynasties had occurred. There are signs of a massive cut in both urban and rural populations. Rather than just involving a collapse of power structures and elite groups the Maya disaster seems to have affected the entire population very severely. Many cities were abandoned, to be lost for centuries in the encroaching jungle. Some were reoccupied, but the evidence suggests that it was by squatters camping out in the ruins of the great ceremonial squares. Estimates of the scale of population decline, though necessarily highly imprecise, have varied from 66 to over 90 per cent. There has been a lively debate about the reasons behind this collapse and theories have been legion. Disease, overpopulation, warfare between city states, invasions from outside, deforestation and environmental degradation have all been suggested as possible causes.

Many books on the Maya have tended to ignore the environmental context within which their civilisation developed, but more recent studies have redressed this imbalance. Early explanations tended to emphasise single factors in explaining the collapse. More recently more complex and subtle theories have suggested that a range of influences worked in concert to undermine Maya society and bring about a system collapse. J. W. G. Lowe (1985) has proposed that a combination of growing population pressure and a top-heavy administration started the crisis. The current evidence suggests that environmental factors, long suspected but now clearly demonstrable, may also have been a major contributor to the catastrophe. In particular the onset of a period of severe drought is currently favoured as the prime suspect, although its effects may well have been worsened by an over-intensive cultivation system which may already have been on the point of collapse, causing malnutrition, disease and rising infant mortality.

The environment of the Maya heartland included volcanic mountains along the Pacific coast, but mostly it was a lowland region, moist and heavily forested in the south, while the drier northern lowlands had a more scrubby forest cover. Much of the lowlands were underlain by limestone, with a consequent lack of surface water. The rainy season extended for six months of the year from May to November with as much as 4,000mm of rainfall in an average year in the south but falling steadily to as low as 1,000mm in the north.

Much of the recent evidence for environmental disaster comes from lake sediments. Sediment cores from lakes in Yucatan have been analysed to show variations in the ratios of oxygen isotopes extracted from the shells of ostracods, microscopic lake crustaceans. Variations in the isotope ratios were caused largely by changes in the balance between precipitation and evaporation in the lake, providing a measure of rainfall. From this evidence a number of periods of drought have been identified, around AD 585, 862, 986, 1051 and 1391. The second of these values coincides well with the period of Maya collapse. The sediments used in this study, however, had also been affected by local deforestation and soil erosion, so that the climatic signal has been considered by some specialists to be a blurred one.

A sediment core from Lake Chichancanab in Mexico's Yucatan province has revealed variations in gypsum levels which reflect the amount of evaporation and thus, indirectly, variations in rainfall. Between AD 800 and 1000 the level of the lake was low, indicating an exceptionally dry period, perhaps the worst in 7,000 years. A longer-term cyclical pattern extending over some 2,600 years was also visible, with serious droughts occurring at intervals of around 208 years, a pattern that links closely to peaks of solar flare activity. In the Cariaco basin, northern Venezuela, on the Caribbean coast, changes in titanium levels from the sediments provided another indication of variations in rainfall. A drier phase appears to have set in from around AD 750. This was punctuated by three periods of severe drought starting around AD 810, 860 and 910. Each of these lasted for several years (Hodell et al. 1995, 2001).

These three data sources point independently to a serious drought having occurred at the peak of Maya civilisation. But once again it is important to stress that demonstrating a coincidence in time does not prove causation. Nor does it explain the broader climatic context within which drought occurred. As we have seen, solar flare activity has been linked to the 208-year cycle, but the occurrence of drought has also been tied in with variations in atmospheric pressure patterns over the North Atlantic and to volcanic eruptions. Studies of recent climatic variability have linked drought-related famines in the Yucatan between AD 1440 and 1840 to volcanic activity, with famine following within two years of eruptions. Some of the recorded droughts within historic times have led to mortality levels of up to 50 per cent, even with the improved transport introduced by the Spaniards, strengthening the argument for the impact of droughts in the more distant past (Culbert 1973).

During the early part of the first millennium the city of Tectihuacan in the Mexican highlands developed as the premier city of Central America, the only pre-Columban superpower, with a population estimated as high as 200,000. The Maya lowlands were one of the areas that fell under its influence. Its power declined rapidly, however, between c.AD 530 and AD 590, the period of the so-called Maya Hiatus, and it is possible that upland Mexico was hit by a major drought as well as the lowland zone. The Hiatus has often been attributed by archaeologists to the effects of the collapse of Tectihuacan, but it is possible to reinterpret the evidence to suggest that both events were in fact the result of common environmental problems.

It would seem reasonable to suppose that a severe drought accompanied by a major famine would have caused at least some movement of population towards the least affected areas. It may be within this context that we can interpret the temporary flourishing of some of the northern Maya cities, which experienced a short-lived building boom at the same time as other cities further south declined.

The ninth-century Maya collapse has often been viewed as a major but isolated event. Certainly the scale of the apparent population cut can make it seem a disaster almost without parallel in global terms. Maya archaeology, however, is revealing other periods of political instability, economic dislocation and population decline which occurred in conjunction with evidence of severe droughts, suggesting a more regular pattern in which the ninth-century disaster, though undoubtedly severe, was not unique.

There is evidence of a phase of depopulation in pre-classic Maya times. Around AD 150 the city of El Mirador was abandoned and a contemporary phase of drought affected much of the Maya heartland for as long as fifty years. During the war and social disruption of the Maya Hiatus a number of cities, including Rio Azul, were abandoned totally while in others construction projects came to an abrupt halt and population seems to have dropped substantially. A post-classic phase of abandonment between AD 1110 and 1160, affecting cities on the Yucatan coast, has also been identified. So the collapse at the end of the classic Maya period, between c.AD 790 and AD 950, was far from being an isolated occurrence. The identification of four periods of difficulty, each associated with evidence of contemporary drought, is much more suggestive of an environmental problem than any single event. There may well have been other periods of droughts, less severe or less widespread, which have left less substantial traces in the archaeological record.

But was drought the sole cause of the collapse? Gill (2001) has reminded us that according to Occam's Razor, the simplest theory which fits all the evidence is to be preferred to more complex, convoluted explanations. This is fine in some respects but, as studies of recent global warming demonstrate, environmental trends can have complex causes. So can human responses. In order to understand why drought appears to have hit the Maya so hard we need to understand more about their rise and the subsistence base which supported their civilisation. There is evidence of a remarkable growth in population from pre-classic times to the peak of the classic Mayan era. How did agriculture support such an increase?

The Maya lowlands were occupied by scattered village communities as early as 2000 BC. Gradually these became more numerous and larger until by late pre-classic times the area had developed most of the attributes of a complex society. There was a major division between the northern and southern lowlands, with different styles of architecture and artefacts, forming a distinct cultural boundary for much of the Maya period. From around AD 100 to AD 250 villages began to grow rapidly in population size and cities began to develop.

Traditional pre-classical Mayan agriculture appears to have been of the slash-and-burn or swidden type, with areas of forest being cleared and cropped for between two and five years before being left for several years to recover. Maize was the staple crop, with squash and beans. This system was a relatively ecologically-friendly one. With the rapid expansion of population, however, agriculture had to intensify. Shortening the fallow cycle may have been sustainable for a while, but the dangers of soil exhaustion, plant diseases, insect pests and weed infestation would have increased markedly. More intensive systems of agriculture, including double cropping in moist areas, terracing and the construction of raised fields in low swampy areas, were developed. The cultivation of extensive wetland areas was a key element in the expansion and intensification of farming.

Nevertheless, despite this remarkable achievement there were serious weaknesses in the Maya economic system. The thinness of the tropical soils was one. Another was the difficulty of supplying the cities with food surpluses. In a society lacking the wheel and draught animals, the cities depended on food being carried to market on human backs. This in turn limited the distance over which cities could be supplied, while increasing their vulnerability if the supply system should break down. It is not likely that much food could have been brought in from distances of over thirty miles and this may have helped to ensure that for much of the time Maya cities remained numerous but relatively small. Large cities such as Tikal were often located on hills with rainwater being channelled into reservoirs from which it was fed, under gravity, to surrounding fields so that the city was surrounded by a dense ring of intensive garden agriculture.

How much control did the city rulers have over the populations of their rural hinterlands, and the kind of farming systems they practised? There must have been a tension between the need for labour in the fields and for monumental construction projects. There were also problems regarding the supply of water for drinking and agriculture, especially in the extensive limestone lowlands. In the limestone Yucatan there was little subsurface water and the population depended on surface supplies in rivers, lakes and storage reservoirs for both drinking and agriculture. The reservoirs at Tikal could hold a maximum of around eighteen months' supply, enough to survive one dry year but not a succession of them.

Calculations from the sizes of the cities and the numbers of house platforms suggest that while swidden agriculture may have supported up to sixty persons per square kilometre, rural population densities at the height of Maya culture may have reached close to 200 people per square kilometre, a very high level for a population with a Neolithic technology and one not often equalled today in agrarian societies. There are signs that Maya society may have reached an unsustainable level before the mid-tenth-century drought set in. Maya agriculture was then a system already under intense pressure without the added problems of droughts. Vast areas were cleared of forest, and agriculture was extending into more marginal areas. Environmental degradation due to deforestation, erosion and soil exhaustion may well have been a widespread problem.

Limitations of water storage must have seriously reduced the ability of the Maya to respond to an environmental crisis, but its social and political structures may not have helped either. Indeed, one school of archaeological thought blames the collapse entirely on internal, structural causes (Lowe, J. W. G. 1985). Kingship seems to have developed soon after the appearance of the first cities. A network of small independent city states arose, competing for resources and often in conflict. During the classic period many small cities became dominated by a few major power blocs. Inscriptions record some bitter wars during this era. There is a tendency, however, for archaeologists to focus on the better-recorded ruling elites and to lose sight of the bulk of the population. Mayan armies, like those of most ancient states, are likely to have been quite small. It has been suggested that the great city of Tikal may only have been able to field an army of just over 1,000 warriors (Harrison et al. 2000). The ability of a group of this size to cause major economic dislocation should not be overestimated.

The disintegration of society could also have occurred from the bottom upwards. It has also been speculated that the downtrodden rural population may have risen up against their masters in the cities, who had tried to squeeze too much labour and tribute from them. It may well have been that in the face of environmental stress the secular and religious leaders of Mayan society, until then successful, forfeited the trust of the bulk of the population, who had formerly maintained them through labour and tribute, as a result of their inability to cope with the crisis.

Maya civilisation at its peak may have been dominated by two powerful city states – Tikal and Calakmul – engaged in protracted conflict (ibid.). Inscriptions in the smaller city of Dos Pilas, 70km south west of Tikal, confirm the frequency of these wars. Dos Pilas was first established around AD 629 as a military stronghold of Tikal, which strengthened their power at the edge of the Maya lowlands and acted as a gateway for trade. The city was later conquered by Calakmul. We can perhaps think of better-recorded parallels in the rise of city states in ancient Greece and their eventual coalescence into two warring blocs headed by Athens and Sparta. Many archaeologists believe that warfare was a significant factor behind the Maya collapse, with Tikal and Calakmul fighting each other to a standstill and Maya society then distintegrating into regional kingdoms engaged in intensive petty warfare. At Dos Pilas and La Toyanca crudely built defensive walls were hurriedly thrown up at the end of the classic period.

The idea of a collapse of Maya society, in terms of a short-lived but widespread catastrophe, has probably been overstated and some archaeologists have claimed that reality was less dramatic with longer-term decline having occurred rather than short-term collapse. There were certainly problems evident before the collapse. From around AD 750 there is increasing evidence of malnutrition in the skeletons of non-elite groups, with a decrease in stature and signs of scurvy, which may indicate a lack of animal protein in their diet. Changes were also sequential geographically with the wetter southern highlands of Guatemala being affected before the more arid northern Yucatan lowlands. This is shown by the last dates carved in monumental inscriptions, which range from AD 810 to AD 910.

Nevertheless, the cumulative impact of drought, possibly exacerbated by structural factors within Mayan society, had profound effects. For a century or so a few survivors seem to have continued living in some of the almost empty cities, leaving their domestic rubbish in what had been palaces and squares. Then they, too, departed, leaving the forests to encroach on the abandoned cities. In Tikal the population seems to have been reduced from its estimated peak of 100,000 or even 200,000 to around a third of this and within a few generations the site was entirely deserted. A few cities lived on; significantly those that continued to survive were ones with an assured water supply, close to lakes and rivers. Tulum, on the Caribbean coast of Mexico, reached the peak of its development as late as AD 1200 and was still flourishing when the Spanish conquistadors arrived. In northern Yucatan, along the Caribbean coast and around inland lakes, Maya populations survived, but one estimate suggests that the overall population may have been cut by around 85 per cent.

If a prolonged major drought was indeed the key factor behind the collapse of the Maya, it is likely that food shortages would have produced not only malnutrition, starvation and disease but also internal unrest within individual city states and wars between them. Political disintegration would hardly have encouraged the most efficient use of labour or resources to combat the effects of the drought. Dependent on outside supplies of food, the cities would have been especially vulnerable. As cultivation was abandoned, the land would rapidly have become overgrown with dense thorny scrub, which would have discouraged clearance. The irrigation ditches would have silted up and become choked; terraces would have collapsed.

The response of the Maya to the problem of drought may have been limited in part by the inflexibility of their environment, and particularly the widespread problem of water storage. But it was also worsened by the high population densities which required an intensive system of agriculture that even in wetter years may have been pushing the boundaries of what was sustainable in the short term, never mind the long term.

So the evidence available at present suggests that the collapse of the Maya was due to a particularly severe and prolonged drought in an area prone to cyclical dry phases. This drought had an especially severe impact because it occurred at a time when population densities and levels of agricultural exploitation had reached unsustainable levels. There are few more striking images of the danger of taking the environment for granted as an inexhaustible resource than photographs of the great Maya cities overgrown by forest (see Plate 11).

The nature of the archaeological evidence is such that it tends to encourage catastrophe scenarios and there is a school of thought that suggests that population losses may have been less severe and more protracted, that the collapse was essentially that of the ruling elites and the cities they had dominated, while the ordinary urban populations merely abandoned the cities when the food supply system broke down and melted into the surrounding jungle.

CHAPTER 6

Medieval and Early Modern Societies

Viking-age Greenland and Iceland: Medieval Societies at the Margins

The story of the Norse settlement of Iceland and Greenland in medieval times provides a fascinating study, and perhaps a cautionary tale, of a European society right on the margins of viability. The settlers encountered an environment that, when they arrived, was difficult enough but which subsequently deteriorated, partly as a result of their own activities but also due to climatic shifts over which they had no control. In the case of Iceland the colony struggled on and survived though beset by volcanic eruptions, plagues and famines as well as environmental degradation. The Norse colony in Greenland, though, was just too small and too isolated to cope with the stresses. Tragically, around the time that Columbus was (re)discovering North America, the last of the Norse Greenlanders, whose ancestors had explored the coasts of Newfoundland, named the area 'Vinland' and established at least one temporary settlement there, were dying out (Jones, G. 1986).

A major wave of expansion in the ninth and tenth centuries AD carried a homogeneous Norse culture, technology and economy to a wide range of environments around the North Atlantic including Ireland, the Outer Hebrides, Orkney, Shetland, Faeroe, Iceland and eventually Greenland (ibid.). They brought with them a farming system based on livestock rearing with some cereal cultivation and an opportunistic willingness to exploit whatever resources of land and sea they discovered, including seabirds, seals, walrus and fish. After the period of initial settlement and exploitation the economies of various Norse-settled areas began to diverge, partly as a result of adaptations to local conditions and resources but also due to variations in the distance from, and levels of integration with, their homelands in Scandinavia (Amorosi et al. 1997).

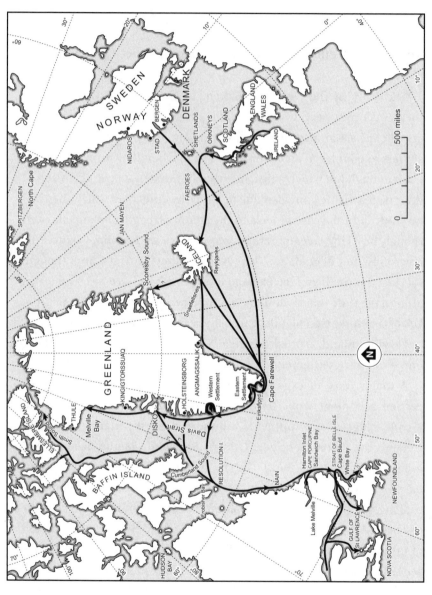

FIGURE 6.1 Viking sailing routes in the North Atlantic (after Jones 1986)

The Norse were great seafarers but their exploration of the North Atlantic was aided by a relatively favourable phase of climate, characterised by calm, anticyclonic conditions, with warm dry summers and cold but dry winters. In addition, the distribution of land around the rim of the North Atlantic in a series of stepping stones ensured that, with favourable weather, a vessel need not be out of sight of land for more than brief periods. From the Scottish mainland to Muckle Flugga at the north tip of Shetland you are never out of sight of land in clear conditions. From Shetland to Faeroe the passage is under 200 miles (320km), from Faeroe to Iceland only a little farther: around 240 miles (384km). Indeed the Norse were not even the first to discover Iceland. They had been preceded in the late eighth century by Irish monks in their leather curraghs, seeking remote places in which to worship God and also, no doubt, to escape from Viking raiders at home. The Irish monk Dicuil, writing in 825, discusses the Irish settlements in Iceland, but he did not make it clear how many monks were living there or how permanent was their occupation (Jones 1986).

The monks must have been disconcerted when the Norsemen arrived, the first occasional explorers around 860, with full-scale settlement beginning some fourteen years later. By about 930 all the habitable land in Iceland – more extensive than in modern times – had been taken into possession. The population of Iceland had risen to around 80,000 by 1100. Traditionally the motive for migration to Iceland was to escape the tyranny of Harald Fairhair, who was mopping up various earldoms and petty kingdoms to make himself sole ruler of most of Norway, but population growth and land hunger at home may well have been another factor behind migration (ibid.).

The Norse seem to have discovered Iceland by accident; the island had first been sighted by the crews of ships that had been blown off course. Climatic conditions early in the settlement period in the ninth to twelfth centuries were relatively calm and there was little sea ice off the coast. Floki Vilgerdarson's description of extensive sea ice in the 870s, which gave the island its rather forbidding name, is almost the last for 300 years.

The discovery of Greenland followed the same pattern. Some time between about 900 and 930 Gunnbjorn Ulf-Krakuson was driven west of Iceland and sighted islands, backed by a larger landmass, to the west. The first proper explorer of Greenland was Eirik the Red. Banished from Iceland for three years in 982 for some killings, he spent his period of exile exploring the fjords of Greenland, finding the east coast inhospitable but the western fjords distinctly promising. He returned to Iceland in the summer of 986 with favourable descriptions of Greenland and fitted out a colonising expedition. Some 400 people reached Greenland and settled in the inner reaches of the 120 miles (190km) of fjord country north from Herjolfsnes to Isafjord. This became known as the Eastern Settlement, comprising eventually some 190 farms, a cathedral at Gardar, and a dozen parish churches. At a later stage the smaller Western Settlement was established 300 miles (480km) to the north in what is now the Godthaab area, with ninety farms and four churches (ibid.).

At first the Greenland colony thrived: at its peak population may have been around the 4–5,000 mark. There was regular contact with Iceland and around AD 1000 the coasts of Baffin Island, Labrador and Newfoundland were discovered. At L'Anse aux Meadows in Newfoundland a Scandinavian settlement, now a World Heritage Site, was excavated in the 1960s by Helge Ingstad (Ingstad 1969). It probably served as a base from which the area farther south into the Gulf of St Lawrence and beyond was explored. The Norse Greenland economy, however, was based, potentially precariously, on livestock rearing. The settlers were mostly neither hunters nor explorers but solid, conservative farmers, though they did kill seals and caribou for meat. Fishing seems to have made only a minor contribution to their diet. Settlement and activity focused on the best areas of grazing land, which were located at the heads of the fjords, below the huge outlet glaciers pushing down from the ice cap. The gathering of a good crop of hay as animal fodder for the long winter during which the cattle were housed indoors was a prime necessity. The discovery of extensive irrigation systems at Brattahlid, the site of Eirik the Red's original home (though probably dating from

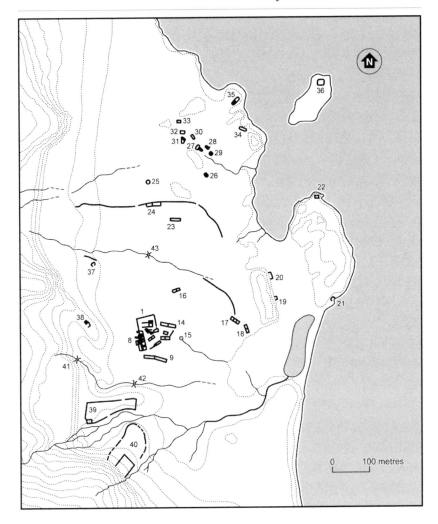

FIGURE 6.2 Norse settlement site with cathedral and associated
buildings, Gardar, Greenland (after Jones 1986)

a somewhat later period in the fourteenth century), to bring lake water
to pastures that would have tended to dry up in summer, argues for
an element of ingenuity: other smaller areas of irrigation have been
reported from the Western Settlement (Jones 1986). A little corn may
also have been grown but recent opinion argues against this (Barlow et
al. 1997). The Norsemen also exploited the resources of the high Arctic
in summer expeditions to what they termed Nordseta – the Disko Bay

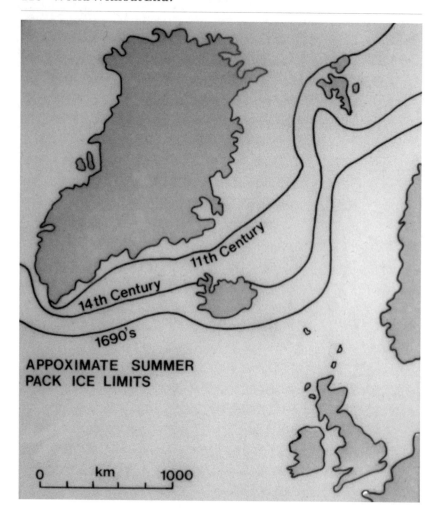

FIGURE 6.3 Summer sea ice limits around Iceland

area – to obtain live polar bears, a prestige symbol at European courts, and walrus ivory. In 1824 a small inscribed stone was discovered in one of three cairns just short of seventy-three degrees north. The inscription dated from around 1333 and commemorated the passage of three Norsemen on a hunting trip. There is also documentary evidence of a late-thirteenth-century expedition which got almost as far north as the seventy-sixth parallel (Jones 1986).

The Greenland colony was fortunate during its early years that the climate was more favourable than it has been at any time since. As we have seen, between the ninth and twelfth centuries air and sea temperatures in the North Atlantic area were relatively warm. Average annual air and sea temperatures in southern Greenland may have been as much as 3–4°C higher than in later times. Drift ice must have been rare south of seventy degrees.

The economy of the Norse Greenlanders was viable – just – as long as climatic conditions remained favourable, but from around 1300 they began to deteriorate. Average annual temperatures may have fallen by around 1.5°C or perhaps even more, according to some scientists. One immediate effect of colder conditions was to bring summer sea ice limits much farther south. There was an immense increase in drift ice down the east coast of Greenland and around Cape Farewell, threatening the direct shipping route from Iceland to the Greenland colony and blocking the fjords so that a round voyage from Iceland to Greenland and back within a single summer became more and more difficult. At the same time cooler conditions, and particularly wetter summers, began to affect the pastures, reducing the value of the summer grazings and cutting the amount of hay that could be mown for winter fodder. Colder conditions also brought the native Inuit inhabitants of Greenland farther south. Although there is some historical evidence, not necessarily accurate, of warlike relations between the Inuit and the Norsemen, the archaeological evidence does not bear this out. But undoubtedly the Inuit, with their skin boats, fur clothing and fishing and hunting lifestyles, were far better able to cope with cooler conditions than the farmers who clung tenaciously to a failing economy, to timber boat construction, and to European diets and styles of woollen clothing. The comparative paucity of fish remains in their domestic middens, or rubbish heaps, compared with other areas of Norse settlement, suggests that their diet was based on meat and animal products. The unwillingness of Norsemen to learn from the Inuit by adopting their seal-hunting techniques, skin kayaks, and fur clothing argues for a lack of flexibility, as does their persistence in maintaining the time-consuming summer hunting trips to Nordseta in the high Arctic, which continued well into the fourteenth century (McGovern 1983; Arneborg 1990).

Other forces not connected with the climate were also working against the Norse Greenlanders. They accepted Norwegian sovereignty in 1261, a year before Iceland. Making the Greenland trade a royal monopoly caused a substantial reduction in the frequency of voyages to a colony that was totally dependent on the outside world for many basic commodities such as timber and iron (Jones 1986). Other aspects of Greenland society may also have affected their ability to cope with harsher climatic conditions. The Church had come to own some two-thirds of the best grazing land, and maintaining the fabric and the priesthood of so many churches, in addition to a nunnery, a monastery and the cathedral, must have placed a severe strain on a population already in difficulty. McGovern (1981) has suggested that the colony may have turned inwards, focusing upon religious observances rather than thinking laterally and developing strategies such as increased fishing and hunting, which would have given them a better chance of survival.

The fate of the colony can be reconstructed in a fragmentary way from sporadic historical references and the archaeological record. The Western Settlement, the smaller and more vulnerable of the two, seems to have been abandoned around 1350 (Jones 1986). Detailed excavation of two farmhouses at Nipaatsoq and Sandnes, in which the occupation layer of the last inhabitants was well preserved, paints a grim picture of what happened. The inhabitants seem to have run out of food during the critical late winter/early spring period. They subsisted on arctic hare and ptarmigan and then, presumably in desperation, killed and butchered their hunting dogs (Barlow et al. 1997). But no human remains were found. Perhaps access to the early summer sealing grounds on the coast was blocked by ice or by Inuits. Perhaps they decamped to the Eastern Settlement. The failure of the inhabitants to adopt Inuit harpoon technology meant that they were unable to hunt seals throughout the year (Buckland et al. 1996). Records from the GISP2 ice core show that there were some periods of particularly severe conditions

PLATE 1 Glacier, Austrian Tyrol: the uplands of Britain would have looked like this some 12,000 years ago.

PLATE 2 Hummocky moraine, Great Langdale, England, marking the extent of the last phase of the Ice Age, just over 10,000 years ago.

PLATE 3 A peat core from Fen Bogs in the North York Moors of England. The light-coloured part of the core on the left represents mineral material washed in from soil erosion on the surrounding slopes caused by vegetation clearance.

PLATE 4 Examining a peat core from Devoke Water in the south-west Lake District of England.

PLATE 5 Preparing a peat core for pollen extraction in a laboratory.

PLATE 6 Boulder bar, Mosedale Beck, Cumbria, England, caused by
a major flash flood in 1749.

PLATE 7 Neolithic chamber tomb, the Burren, County Clare, Ireland.

PLATE 8 Bronze Age cairnfield, Barnscar, Lake District.

PLATE 9 Downwash of eroded soil material on top of old land surface below cairnfield, Devoke Water.

PLATE 10 Neolithic stone axe factory site, Langdale Pikes, England.

PLATE 11 There a few more striking images of the danger of taking the environment for granted than photographs of great Maya cities overgrown by forest. View of the Temple of the Warriors (or 1,000 Columns) post-150 AD (photograph by Mexican School © Chichen Itza, Yucatan State, Mexico).

PLATE 12 A degraded landscape: view from Thingvellir, Iceland.

PLATE 13 A landscape under heavy pressure from tourism: Alpine scenery, Seefeld, Austria.

PLATE 14 Plaque at the site of Boscobel Oak.

PLATE 15 The Gosforth Cross, Cumbria. Its shaft is carved to represent the world-ash, Yggdrasil.

PLATE 16 Ancient woodlands, Borrowdale, with just a hint of original wildwood.

during the fourteenth century, especially between 1343 and 1362. The Western Settlement, farther north than the Eastern one, had longer, harder winters and needed more hay per animal for the livestock to survive, as is shown by the larger size of barns in relation to cowsheds. The Eastern Settlement struggled on: from the mid-fourteenth century a ship came from Norway once every few years but after around 1367 or 1369 these voyages tailed off. In 1406 a party of Icelanders, driven off course, ended up in Greenland and were stuck there for four years – presumably being trapped by drift ice. Damage to pastures due to soil erosion may have reduced hay yields even further. The Greenlanders were caught not just by environmental changes but by their own poor land management and an inflexible culture that rejected the technology and lifestyle developed by the Inuit.

In 1921 excavations of a cemetery at Herjolfsnes in the southern part of the Eastern Settlement discovered bodies buried in clothes the styles of which were current in mainland Europe in the early fifteenth century, and even contained a few from later in the century, indicating some continuing contact with the outside world, but not necessarily on a regular basis. There were no signs of assimilation to an Inuit way of life in any of the graves. It is likely that the Eastern Settlement was finally extinguished by the end of the fifteenth century or, at the very latest, soon after 1500 (Jones 1986). The wonder is not that they disappeared but that they survived so long.

Attacks by Inuits, and the depredations of English pirates, have been blamed as possible contributory factors in the ultimate demise of the colony. A combination of climatic deterioration plus environmental degradation, however, and an inability to be flexible and adaptable in the face of environmental stress seems the most likely set of circumstances which finally pushed the colony over the edge. The Norse Greenlanders had tried to transplant a way of life, and particularly an economy, that had worked in Scandinavia but was less well suited to the much more marginal environments of Iceland and Greenland. In Orkney, Shetland and to a lesser extent Faeroe their subsistence strategies proved to be more sustainable than in Iceland and Greenland, partly because environmental conditions were less marginal and also due to the fact that these areas maintained stronger trading links with core areas of mainland Europe. At first the Norse pastoral system was maintained quite well in Greenland. Neither Iceland nor Greenland, however, had any native herbivores, so their livestock had an even more drastic effect on vegetation and soils than might otherwise have been the case (Thorarinsson 1961). The animals of the settlers denuded extensive areas of Iceland as well as Greenland within a few generations. Soils formed at a very slow rate in such marginal environments and damage due to over-exploitation was difficult or impossible to repair.

It is dangerous, however, to assume that the Icelandic landscape was a stable one before the Norse arrived; rates of sedimentation before the Norse settlement were high, indicating a very dynamic environment (Dugmore et al. 2000). Occasional massive flash floods due to the occurrence of volcanic eruptions in glaciated areas, falls of volcanic tephra and glacier retreat in the centuries before the Viking settlement all affected the landscape.

Recent research on the timing and scale of Holocene land degradation in north-east Iceland has emphasised the natural physical vulnerability of Iceland to erosion in a situation where soils are mainly of volcanic origin, the low-density tephra being easily disturbed and removed by rain or wind. In particular, the identification of two major phases of land degradation, between 5500 and 4500 BP and from c.3000 BP, both linked to the occurrence of more severe climatic phases, suggest that the episode of climatic deterioration from the fourteenth century might well have caused substantial environmental damage on its own without the effects of human interference (Olafsdottir and Gudmundsson 2002).

In Iceland rapid erosion occurred in many areas following the initial settlement because of removal of the turf for construction, tree felling and overgrazing. The woodland cover was mostly cleared within a couple of generations of the first settlement period: there is evidence that some of this was done by burning. The birch woodlands also provided suitable wood from which to make charcoal for iron smelting. By 950 some 80 per cent of the original woodland cover had been cleared. But by the eleventh or early twelfth century, much of the original woodland that the first settlers had found had been used up. Pigs, woodland grazers, drop out of the archaeological record at this time, as do goats. Numbers of cattle also declined in favour of hardier sheep. (In Scandinavia the far more extensive pastures and woods could sustain large concentrations of cattle and pigs.) The best wood for shipbuilding and house construction was soon exhausted and Icelanders became major importers of timber (Byock 2002). Once disturbed, the volcanic soils were extremely vulnerable to erosion: rain, wind, snowmelt, frost action and trampling by animals affected any areas denuded of vegetation, with gullying and windblow of soil particles resulting (Dugmore et al. 2000). The situation stabilised for a while in the fourteenth century, but between 1450 and 1750 more phases of erosion occurred. There were, however, significant variations through both space and time in rates of erosion.

Many farms in Iceland, still occupied today, were established during the Viking era and have been occupied continuously ever since. Yet this stability is misleading. Erosion due to overgrazing had, by the nineteenth century, drastically diminished the island's biomass. This, together with climatic deterioration after the thirteenth century, meant that Iceland's population came under increasing pressure from resource depletion. The first generations of Icelandic settlers, like those of Greenland, were using up their 'environmental capital', making it unavailable for their successors. For example, early Norse settlements in the Reykjavik area have produced the bones of young walrus, indicating the existence of local breeding colonies, yet walrus had been hunted to extinction by the later Middle Ages.

Byock (2002) has suggested that in Iceland the upland grazings in particular were damaged by sending the animals to the summer pastures too early in the year, i.e. before the grass had recovered from the long winter, so that the thin upland soils became rapidly exposed and eroded by overgrazing. Initially deposition of the eroded material in the surrounding lowlands deepened the soils there, but as pressure on the vegetation spread these soils, too, became vulnerable to erosion. While settlement and agriculture was expanding over most of mainland Europe during the thirteenth century that in Iceland was starting to contract as higher-lying, more marginal settlements were abandoned first (ibid.; Dugmore and Buckland 1991). In some parts of the interior whole valleys dotted with abandoned settlement sites can be found (Sveinbjarnardottir 1991). In lowland areas some settlement abandonment was undoubtedly due to coastal erosion and the expansion of sandur – areas of blown sand on the margins of the Icelandic glaciers. By the fourteenth century the climate had started to become cooler than during the first settlement phase, a deterioration that continued, with cooler, wetter summers in particular reducing fodder yields and forcing the abandonment of cereal cultivation (Byock 2002). To compensate, the Icelanders turned increasingly to the sea. In Greenland, seals and seabirds rather than fish had been the main marine food sources. In Iceland, however, large-scale fishing developed from the fourteenth century (Hastrup 1985). By the thirteenth century, fishing was already becoming the most significant element in the economy as livestock husbandry declined. Large-scale export of dried cod began from about 1320 (Byock 2002).

It is going too far to suggest that without the cod fishery Iceland may have gone the same way as the Norse Greenland colony, but it undoubtedly provided a major lifeline. To make matters worse, volcanic eruptions with outpourings of lava added to the pressures on the population, forcing the abandonment of some farms. A major eruption of Hekla in 1104 caused much destruction. Volcanic activity had occurred during the settlement period, layers of volcanic tephra providing valuable datum levels for calibrating settlement and human-induced environmental change (Dugmore et al. 2000), but the frequency and intensity of major eruptions seems to have increased after around AD 1500, reaching a climax with the great famine of 1783–84 due to the Laki eruption, following which the island's population was reduced by about a fifth to 38,000, little more than at the end of the original period of settlement in 930 (Thorarinsson 1961). An epidemic disease, possibly bubonic plague but also thought by some to have been influenza, which reached Iceland in 1402, may have killed at least a third of the population (Byock 2002), as did a smallpox outbreak in 1707.

TABLE 6.1 Changing land use in Iceland (%)

	At the time of settlement	Today
Water	6	6
Glaciers	11	11
Grassland	40	22
Scrub and forest	25	1
Waste land	18	58

The net effect of these pressures on land use in Iceland is shown in Table 6.1. The area of grassland and woodland has declined drastically while the proportion of sterile wasteland has expanded. It has been suggested that human-induced soil erosion has removed about half of Iceland's soils (Dugmore and Buckland 1991). Rates of soil thickening due to the accumulation of windblown deposits from erosion elsewhere increased by around four to five times after about AD 1100. Climatic deterioration and volcanic activity may have contributed to increased soil erosion, but the main cause has generally been considered to be overgrazing (Gerrard 1991). The rate of erosion has varied from one district to another and also over time, but the overall trend is clear. Erosion continued into recent times, though increasingly balanced by reclamation and reseeding. In the Rangarvellir district forty farms were abandoned during the nineteenth century due to continuing soil erosion. Grazing pressure continues: numbers of sheep have risen from 152,947 in 1802 to 750,000 in 1981–82 (ibid.) (see Plate 12).

One result of this is a marked shrinkage of the area fit for livestock farming. In Iceland early farms are found farther inland and higher than later ones. An example is Sveigakot, near Lake Myvatn at the edge of what is today, because of erosion, a desert of sand and rock. It has been dated to the tenth century. Bones of cattle, goats and sheep and also pigs have been found, the last of these becoming rare after about

AD 1000. In the fourteenth and fifteenth centuries there was large-scale abandonment of settlement (Byock 2002). By AD 1100 farms had, in some places, pushed up on to the inland plateaus, as high as 400m., but this expansion was not sustainable for long. The first population census of Iceland in 1703 recorded 4,059 inhabited farms but also around 3,000 abandoned sites (Thorarinsson 1961).

The experience of Iceland, and particularly Greenland, shows that an economy that works adequately in a reasonably well-resourced area like the Viking homelands in Scandinavia and areas of colonisation such as north and west Scotland, can come badly unstuck in the face of more marginal conditions if people are not prepared to be flexible and adaptable. A similar story may lie behind the late Bronze Age abandonment of areas of upland Britain (Chapter 4). The climatic deterioration that affected the Norse inhabitants of Iceland and Greenland, however, worked its way eastwards and southwards to cause problems in many parts of Europe, as the next section demonstrates.

The Little Ice Age and Its Impact in Europe

The Little Ice Age is a term in widespread, though not universal, use to describe a phase of cooler and wetter climate which followed the relatively warm and dry medieval optimum. In global terms average annual temperatures may have been around 1°C lower than in medieval times, but in some more marginal areas the difference may have been 2°C or more. Because it occurred relatively recently, at a period of increasing documentation, a wide range of historical sources, ranging from late-medieval manorial accounts to nineteenth-century photographs of Alpine glaciers, have been used to try and measure the scale and impact of the Little Ice Age. This, however, has tended to focus attention on the relatively literate societies of western and northern Europe. As a result, it was initially thought that the Little Ice Age was essentially a European phenomenon, but an important feature of recent research in areas such as Alaska, east Canada, the Rockies, the Andes, Patagonia, Ethiopia and New Zealand has been the identification of a similar cold phase with only minor variations in chronology (Grove, J. M. 1990). The Little Ice Age was evidently a global phenomenon. Even so, this statement must be qualified by stressing the uncertainty surrounding the timing of the period.

There is closer agreement about when the Little Ice Age ended than when it began, with a rapid rise of average annual temperatures occurring in the later nineteenth century. The start of the Little Ice Age is much more difficult to pin down. Various dates between the early fourteenth and the late sixteenth centuries have been suggested. In addition, it is clear from a range of evidence that, whatever its terminal dates, the Little Ice Age was by no means a period of uniform severity. Relatively good runs of years and even decades were interspersed with cooler, wetter phases, the worst of which, in Britain, probably occurred at the end of the seventeenth century (Lamb 1982). This helps to explain why some environmental historians prefer to avoid using the term 'Little Ice Age' altogether or even question its very existence. It also shows why its impacts on human society are far from easy to establish.

Before the Little Ice Age is dismissed as being of no consequence, however, it is instructive to consider the plateau country of Baffin Island in northern Canada. Aerial photographs showed a marked colour contrast on the land surface with a sharp boundary which, when traced on the ground, turned out to be caused by a contrast in the size of lichens on boulders and rock outcrops. Lichenometry made it possible to show that the lichens within the boundary had been growing only from the eighteenth century, while those outside were older. The boundary marked the limit of the permanent snowfields which accumulated during the most severe phase of the Little Ice Age. It has been suggested that, in this area at least, permanent snow was close to building up to a point where positive feedback might have set in, with the extent of the snowfields reducing summer temperatures sufficiently to encourage the survival of more and more extensive areas of snow (Williams, L. D. 1978). On this interpretation the Little Ice Age can be seen as an abortive glaciation which only just failed to tip environmental systems over a threshold from interglacial to glacial conditions, due not so much to lack of severity but insufficient time.

Whatever the causes of the Little Ice Age, it is certain that such a widespread climatic phenomenon was not the result of any human activity, providing a salutary warning about the range of natural variation that can occur within the climate system. In the context of current concerns about human-induced global warming it is also salutary to reflect that we have not yet returned to the peak of warmth reached during the medieval optimum. Whether or not recent climatic warming has been due to the enhancement of the greenhouse effect by human agency, we are still within the natural range of climate during recent centuries.

This section focuses on Europe and, in addition to the various kinds of evidence discussed in Chapter 2, a range of documentary sources is available to study the severity, and the potential impact, of the Little Ice Age. First, from the mid-seventeenth century onwards, we have instrumental records of air temperature. Professor Gordon Manley created a continuous set of readings for 'central England' by amalgamating short runs of data from various sites and making allowance for variations in the nature of the instruments used (Manley 1974). By the later eighteenth century enough scientists were making daily weather observations of temperature, precipitation, atmospheric pressure, wind speed and direction, and cloud cover to allow the reconstruction of daily weather maps for much of Europe, though coverage was still patchy for eastern and southern areas of the continent (Lamb 1982). For earlier periods, such as the fifteenth, sixteenth and early seventeenth centuries, proxy measures of changes in temperature and precipitation can be used, such as the dates of the grape harvest, and historical records of other climatically related phenomena such as glacier advances, sea ice limits around Iceland, the presence or absence of sea ice in other locations at particular seasons extracted from ships' logbooks, and the freezing of rivers and lakes. Many of these measures need to be used with caution, though, as we saw in Chapter 2.

The human impact of the Little Ice Age in Europe was quite dramatic in some ways. We have already seen how the limits of summer sea ice spread southwards after the fourteenth century, cutting the established shipping route between Iceland and Greenland and freezing in the north coast of Iceland in some years. At its worst, during the later 1690s, summer sea ice limits lay even farther south, between Iceland and Faeroe. It is at this time that some Scottish writers report instances of 'fin men' being sighted around the coasts of Orkney and Shetland: skin-clad men in single-seat skin boats, apparently Inuit in kayaks who had become separated from the edge of the pack ice when it lay between Iceland and Faeroe and had ended up in British waters (ibid.). The name 'fin-men' is supposedly derived from the belief that Finland and Greenland were joined across the high Arctic. Some doubt has been cast on these claims, particularly concerning one of the kayaks preserved in a museum in Aberdeen, but a number of independent contemporary accounts tally and this seems to be the most reasonable explanation for these unusual visitors to Scottish waters.

We have also seen how cold conditions, especially in summer, reduced hay crops in Greenland and helped cause the demise of the Norse Greenlanders, some of whom were buried in ground that was then unfrozen but is now still affected by permafrost. Greenland, however, represented the extreme fringe of European viability. What effects did the Little Ice Age have on farming and settlement elsewhere in Europe? In the 1970s and 1980s it was widely believed that the Little Ice Age had caused major difficulties for agriculture, leading to a lowering of the altitudinal limits of cultivation throughout western and northern Europe and a retreat of settlement from higher, more marginal locations. The occurrence of colder periods is shown (albeit with a time lag) by evidence of the damage caused by advancing glaciers in Alpine areas and in Scandinavia. In the Alps in the 1590s and the earliest years of the seventeenth century glaciers around Chamonix, Grindlewald and Zermatt were advancing, obliterating fields and farms and sometimes blocking side valleys, leading to periodic serious floods (Ladurie 1971). At the end of the seventeenth century, and the start of the eighteenth around the fringes of the Jostedalsbreen ice cap in Norway, farmers were petitioning for tax reductions due to avalanches, floods and other damage caused by the expansion of the outlet glaciers (Grove, J. M.

1990). A frequently cited British example was the abandonment of the hamlet of Hound Tor, located at around 350m. on Dartmoor. Excavations suggested that the community, with its surrounding fields, was first established in the thirteenth century at the height of settlement expansion and was deserted around 1350 (Beresford 1981). Given the high-lying nature of the site, it seemed reasonable that climatic deterioration with the onset of cooler and wetter conditions had at least played a part in the decision to abandon Hound Tor. Yet the link between climatic change and settlement abandonment has often been assumed rather than proven. This can be shown by the shrinkage of many more marginal settlements following the Black Death of 1348–49 compared with villages in more favoured areas. It was not a run of poor weather conditions that caused the survivors of the plague to pull out of less well-endowed areas but the fact that there was now ample land available in areas with better soils (Hey 2000).

Other sites in different kinds of environment have been suggested as potential candidates for Little Ice Age-induced abandonment. The deserted village of Goltho in Lincolnshire, sited on low-lying clays whose cultivation might have been feasible for the first time during the medieval climatic optimum, contained peasant houses which in the thirteenth century required no special measures for drainage, but whose replacements in the fourteenth century did, suggesting a shift to wetter conditions and more extended periods of soil waterlogging, leading in turn to the desertion of the site in the second half of the fourteenth century (Beresford 1981). But once again the link between abandonment and climatic deterioration was made on the basis of evidence which, while suggestive, is not unequivocal. The discovery of thousands more deserted village sites in England abandoned at various times between the fourteenth and the seventeenth centuries, and occurring over most parts of England, suggests a range of causes for desertion (Muir 1982). These included fifteenth- and sixteenth-century enclosure with the conversion of arable land to sheep pasture requiring less labour and also, as a background feature, the adjustment of settlement and farming to the drastic cuts in population caused by the

Black Death of 1348–49 and subsequent outbreaks of bubonic plague. So a wide range of factors was at work causing settlement change and desertion. Distinguishing and isolating the effects of climatic change is far from easy. The problem is compounded by difficulties of scale: the environmental histories of deserted late medieval settlements were clearly highly individual, making generalisations from a handful of case studies problematic.

The first attempt to apply a broader-scale theoretical approach to the links between climatic change, farming and settlement was by Martin Parry in the mid-1970s. His work was based on a study of the Lammermuir Hills south east of Edinburgh, separating the lowlands of the Lothians from those of the Tweed basin. Rising to 1,730 feet (527m.), the Lammermuirs are gently rolling plateau country broken by shallow, gently sloping valleys. A shift of cultivation limits of, say, 200 feet (61m.) in altitude would be reflected in this area by a broad band of country, while in areas of higher, steeper hills this would be only a narrow strip along the hillside. Using aerial photographs and fieldwork Parry identified the sites of a number of abandoned settlements and associated field systems at altitudes well above those of any present-day or recent cultivation. He then used cartographic and documentary evidence to date, as far as possible, the period at which they were abandoned. He then calculated the minimum conditions of warmth under which oats, the hardiest cereal crop grown in the area now and in the past, would ripen under modern conditions. Minimum thresholds for the commercial cultivation of oats in modern times were then identified. These two limits, when mapped, defined a belt of country which was climatically marginal for the cropping of oats under modern climatic conditions. The altitude and location of this marginal band was then calculated back to the seventeenth century using meteorological records and to medieval times using less specific climatic information.

Parry suggested that a subsistence-orientated peasant farmer, interested more in a guaranteed minimum return for his crops rather than a maximum yield under the best conditions, would have pushed cultivation to approximately the height where there was a probability

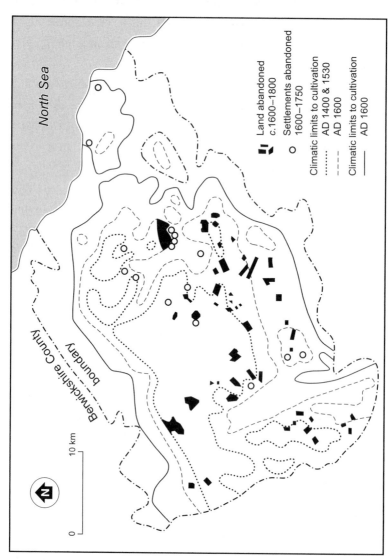

FIGURE 6.4 Settlements and areas of cultivation abandoned in the Lammermuir Hills, south-east Scotland, between 1600 and 1800 because of deteriorating climate (after Parry 1975)

that two successive crop failures might occur in a generation. The basis of this argument was the assumption that peasant farmers could survive a single bad year by tightening their belts but that two successive years of bad harvests would wipe them out. When this level was transformed into altitudinal limits on the map for the period of the medieval climatic optimum, it was clear that in the Lammermuirs at around AD 1250 all but the highest plateau areas would have been viable for subsistence cereal cultivation which, on the basis of Parry's calculations, stood as high as 450m. From the fourteenth to the eighteenth century, however, cultivation limits were driven downhill and outwards from the centre of the Lammermuirs, so that by 1600 cultivation limits stood at 260–75m.: almost all the uplands were now sub-marginal for the cultivation of oats. Parry showed that the dates at which particular settlements and their surrounding areas of cultivation had been abandoned had followed a similar chronological trend, with the highest-lying ones being abandoned first and lower ones at a later period (Parry 1975).

Parry was careful not to suggest that climatic change was the only, or even the most important, influence behind settlement abandonment. He cited economic, social and political factors as immediate short-term influences, such as changes in land ownership and the effects of English invasions. But he did claim that, as a background to this, perceptions of environmental deterioration could also have been influential. He believed that his approach had wider relevance than simply as a single regional case study and that his model was applicable not only to other upland areas in Britain but more widely throughout Europe.

More recent work, however, has challenged many of Parry's conclusions. First his focus on cereal cultivation has been called into question. While it is clear that farms in areas like the Southern Uplands continued to have a substantial arable element into the eighteenth century, it is also evident that livestock rearing was their main activity. Moreover, rather than being based on small-scale peasant subsistence farming, livestock rearing in this area had been operating on at least a partially commercial scale since medieval times. Much of the Lammermuirs themselves had been converted into large sheep farms run by Cistercian monks (Dodgshon 1981). It has also been pointed out that, by using the crop tolerances of oats as recorded by nineteenth-century agricultural writers, Parry may have underestimated the hardiness of the crop varieties in use in earlier times. A lot depends on the accuracy of his assumptions regarding the conditions under which arable land would remain in cultivation or be abandoned. Additionally, his dating of the abandonment of settlements, compiled as it was from scattered documentary sources and limited cartographic coverage, was necessarily imprecise.

The existence of deserted settlements in a country like Scotland, however, where settlement patterns could be quite fluid, need not necessarily be evidence of abandonment. Because the lifespan of individual farmhouses and outbuildings tended to be short, the locations of entire settlements could gradually drift over long periods, a process which has also been identified in England. Additionally, the process of splitting townships that became too large into two or more new settlements could sometimes lead to the abandonment of the original settlement (ibid.).

A different perspective is obtained from examining the impact of weather conditions on farmers in an adjoining area during the better-documented 1690s, the nadir of the Little Ice Age in terms of temperatures in Britain. Data are available from the chamberlains' annual reports on the estates of the Dukes of Buccleuch, covering valleys such as Eskdale, Ettrick, Teviotdale and Yarrow. The Duke of Buccleuch petitioned the Scottish Privy Council in 1675 referring to a 'great and extraordinary storm' the previous year 'whereby the greatest part of the cattle belonging to their tenants were destroyed'. Worse was to come. There are indications that the decade from 1684 to 1694 was unusually wet throughout the Scottish Borders. In 1684 and 1685 rent arrears were running at high levels in Ettrick Forest and Teviotdale with some tenants owing two entire years' rent. Farms such as Altrieve near St Mary's Loch were untenanted due to flood damage. The years 1686 and 1687 seem to have been less eventful, but in 1688 the harvest was late and much of the crop was lost by shaking and rotting due to heavy rain. The winter of

1688–89 was hard with heavy losses of sheep. Whether this was due to a lack of fodder after the previous poor summer or the result of a delayed start to spring growth – or both – is not clear. The harvest of 1689 was again bad and conditions for cereal cultivation in the lower parts of the Border dales had become so precarious that much land in Teviotdale went out of cultivation. Heavy rain caused flood damage to hayfields in Ettrick Forest, Eskdale, Liddesdale and Teviotdale. The unfortunate occupant of the now retenanted Altrieve had about ten acres of cereals and two days' mowing of hay destroyed.

Loss of winter fodder by the effects of rain on the hay crop may have contributed to the continuing heavy livestock mortality but in 1690, another bad year for storm and rain, flooding and crop damage, tenants were also complaining of heavy losses due to 'traik' – sheep maggot fly, a pest that lays eggs in the fleeces of sheep, especially when they are kept constantly moist through prolonged contact with rain or wet vegetation. The summer of 1691 brought a drought which stopped watermills from operating but the respite from wet conditions was brief. Between 1692 and 1693 several tenants petitioned for abatements of rent due to high mortality of sheep through rot, or sheep liver fluke, another parasite particularly favoured by wet summer conditions.

Continuous heavy rain reduced the time sheep spent grazing and if this was prolonged their food intake and weight were reduced, weakening their resistance to disease and severe weather conditions. Wet summer conditions not only favoured sheep diseases such as liver fluke and sheep maggot 'flu but also sheep ticks and foot rot. Wet autumns made haymaking more difficult and reduced the food value of the hay through loss of digestible carbohydrates due to increasing respiration, by the leaching of soluble constituents, and by moulding. Flooding due to heavy rain caused damage to valley-bottom hayfields. The resulting lack of winter fodder was critical when cold wet springs delayed the onset of fresh growth of grass in spring. Reduced cereal crops meant that farmers had to buy in grain for bread they would normally have produced themselves, thus eating into their cash reserves.

Another possible effect of poor weather was an adverse long-term change in the ecology of upland pastures. In the late 1680s many tenants in Teviotdale were complaining about a lack of heather. The tenant of Dowislees claimed in a petition that his ground was bare of heather, which had formerly provided food and shelter for his flocks, and that as a result the carrying capacity of his farm had been reduced by a third. The onset of wetter conditions might, at a local scale in less well-drained areas, have resulted in the replacement of heather by acid grasses and cotton sedge, which were less nutritious for sheep. More generally the wetter conditions may have disrupted the burning of heather, making it more woody and less fit for grazing.

The picture then is of a run-up of at least a decade of difficulty to the 'ill years' of the later 1690s. The winters of 1694–95 and 1695–96 were severe. Shortage of fodder and heavy snow in the spring of 1696 led to further heavy animal mortality. The annual meeting of Buccleuch tenants at Hawick in April to renew leases was abandoned as many of the farmers' horses were too weak to allow them to make the journey. Early frosts in September 1696 led to the almost total destruction of the grain harvest, while late frosts in spring 1697 dangerously delayed sowing. Summer floods in 1697 washed away crops on many farms or buried them under sediments, while early frosts again blackened any grain that had survived. The continuation of cold wet conditions in 1698 and 1699 resulted in the abandonment of cultivation on many farms.

There was undoubtedly great hardship among the tenant farmers in this region, though the lack of surviving well-kept parish registers means that levels of mortality are unknown. Recovery from such a run of harsh years would have taken longer for upland livestock farmers, as building up new flocks and herds took time as well as money. The picture, then, for the Borders is one of difficult conditions extending over at least fifteen years, more severe and more prolonged than those in lowland arable areas.

But the important point to note is that this long period of harsh conditions did not cause wholesale abandonment of farms and depopulation at a regional scale. A series of maps of the Buccleuch estates in 1718 and a recent archaeological survey of east Dumfries-shire allows a number of farms that seem to have been abandoned after these difficult years to be identified, mostly in the higher, more remote valleys (Royal Commission 1997). Yet the striking feature is that overall, despite livestock losses and temporary abandonment, most farms continued to be occupied, being marked on the 1718 survey, though a detailed study of tenancy changes would be interesting to determine the rate of turnover of occupancy. It appears that the farming system was quite resilient in the face of a period of hardship and misfortune extending over two decades or so. It is possible that the Buccleuch tenants may have reduced stocking densities of cattle and sheep and that tenant numbers in turn may have fallen. Some of the deserted sites may have been the result of the amalgamation of holdings rather than straightforward abandonment of the land, a process which may be associated with growing commercialisation as much as a response to deteriorating conditions. The lack of a phase of farm abandonment and settlement desertion at this time in the Pennine areas of northern England or in the Lake District is also notable.

The resilience of Scottish upland farming systems is also demonstrated from a recent landscape survey of Menstrie Glen in the Ochil Hills east of Stirling. Here detailed estate documents demonstrate that there was a substantial expansion of cultivation to altitudes of up to 350m. in the early decades of the eighteenth century, a period when one might have expected, on theoretical grounds, that cultivation would have been abandoned rather than extended (Royal Commission 2001). It is sometimes easy to forget that seemingly 'primitive' peasant farming systems often have built-in 'shock absorbers' which help to buffer them against poor years (Dodgshon 2004). South of the border, but in a similar kind of environment, the pastoral community of Tebay in Westmorland was expanding rather than contracting during the seventeenth century, with areas of land being enclosed for cattle rearing from the open rough pasture of the commons and new farmsteads being created on the improved land. Desertion of some of these sites came only with farm amalgamation during the twentieth century, particularly after the Second World War (Lambert, J. 1996).

Another line of evidence that challenges Parry's assumptions comes from palynological work in the Cheviot Hills on the Anglo-Scottish border, an upland area which is higher than the Lammermuirs but which, like them, is rolling rather than rugged. Pollen analysis backed by radiocarbon dates has shown that at sites in the valley of the Bowmont Water at altitudes of 365m., cultivation in the surrounding catchment was continuous throughout the period from the thirteenth to the eighteenth centuries. The pollen evidence was not sufficiently sensitive to rule out the possibility of short periods of abandonment – say up to a decade long – but it is clear that there was no long-term retreat of cultivation in this area (Tipping 1998).

In a rather similar situation, in the valleys at the head of the River Clyde, there is evidence of a phase of prosperity rather than poverty among livestock farmers some decades earlier. The excavation of a hamlet cluster or *ferm toun* at Glenochar shows that at the very end of the sixteenth century or the early years of the seventeenth a solid stone bastle house, a two-storey defended farmhouse, was constructed among the peasant long-houses with walls of dry stone and turf. Estate records show that the bastle was occupied by a well-to-do tenant farmer rather than a small landowner. A cluster of ruined bastle houses has been identified in this area. The fact that they had been built well away from the Anglo-Scottish border at a period when cross-border livestock raiding had greatly diminished suggests that these bastles were built for display rather than defence.

Evidence of this kind highlights first the difficulty of generalising in terms of settlement and agricultural change in the face of climatic fluctuation and also the need for care in developing behavioural models based on limited evidence. It is worth remembering that, apart from some very high mountain environments, very little land in western Europe has been totally abandoned in recent centuries, although the nature and the intensity of land use may well have varied.

The Little Ice Age, as well as being cooler and wetter at times, was also a stormier period than the preceding medieval climatic optimum. This fact is of considerable significance in coastal areas where, with cliffs cut in relatively easily eroded glacial till, as in Holderness and parts of East Anglia, many medieval villages have disappeared into the sea (Muir 1982). Another coastal hazard was the encroachment of blowing sand, a feature of parts of the Welsh coast in the fourteenth and fifteenth centuries and particularly notable on the north-east coast of Scotland and parts of the Hebrides in the seventeenth century. The disappearance under sand of the entire barony of Culbin in Moray, including the church and manor house, as the result of a storm in 1694, is well recorded, prompting the Scottish Parliament to pass in 1695 an Act forbidding the pulling of grass on sand dunes, an enlightened piece of conservation legislation for its day. Estate records from the western Highlands and Islands also identify settlements lost to sand blow in this way.

There is, however, a danger of attributing a wide range of social, economic and political changes in early modern Europe to the Little Ice Age. Behringer (1999), for example, relates peaks of witch hunting to the mid-sixteenth-century Little Ice Age cold phase, claiming that witches were considered to have been responsible for 'making weather'. Such simple cause-and-effect links lack conviction. Undoubtedly the impacts of climatic fluctuations such as crop failures and livestock mortality did have effects, but they were mediated in complex ways through social, economic and political systems. To try and rewrite the history of post-medieval Europe in terms of the impact of weather conditions on the quality of the harvest is a temptation that should be resisted. The impact of the Little Ice Age was felt mainly in more marginal environments where conditions were already precarious. What is more impressive is the sheer resilience of peasants and their farming systems; their ability to survive in the face of severe pressures and bounce back from disasters. By the seventeenth century many commercialised farming systems were widely established in the core areas of Europe, including the Low Countries, and south-east England. But European expansion overseas had already started to introduce highly commercialised agriculture to new environments and it is to a consideration of the impact of European settlement on these new environments that we now turn.

The Colonisation of the Atlantic and Caribbean Islands

Between the fifteenth and the twentieth centuries, European peoples had a huge impact on a range of environments in all other parts of the world through the processes of exploration, settlement and colonisation. The settlement of the Atlantic islands provides the first example of the effects of a relatively technologically advanced society on environments that were either previously unsettled by humans, such as St Helena or Madeira, or that had only been lightly touched by them, as with the Canary Islands. The rapid changes in vegetation patterns, soil quality and even climate that affected them following European settlement have provided a paradigm and a cautionary tale for later generations. The nature of the human impact on these fragile environments was frequently similar to that experienced in mainland areas, but the intensity of the effects was often far greater because of the small size of the islands involved. In particular, it was the rapid introduction of intensive plantation agriculture that changed the character of the islands' natural ecosystems. The Atlantic islands were Europe's first tropical laboratories, where European crops and farming systems could be tried out and modified in a different environment and new techniques experimented with. The experience of colonising them showed that Europeans could do well in such environments, in sharp contrast to the Norse settlers in Greenland.

In this section we look at human impact on a number of islands ranging from the Canaries and Madeira to the Caribbean.

The year 1492 is one of the dates most people remember – the year in which Christopher Columbus first discovered the New World. As we have already seen, the Norse Greenlanders got there centuries before him, but their impact was both small-scale and short-term. Columbus's first voyage led directly to large-scale exploration, conquest and settlement, but it was not planned in isolation. The year 1492 was also, not coincidentally, that in which the last Moorish kingdom of Granada finally fell to Christian Spain. This was the last phase of a long process, known as the Reconquista, in which Christian forces in Iberia had gradually pushed southwards against the Muslims. It was one of the frontiers of expansion of medieval Christian Europe, fuelled by population growth and land hunger as well as political imperatives and religious fervour. The switch from internal conquest within Iberia to overseas expansion was merely a diversion of effort and energy into a different channel, aided by improved shipbuilding and navigation technology. This outward movement had been spearheaded by the great Portuguese navigators who, in the fifteenth century, had pioneered the route down the west coast of Africa and, eventually, around the Cape of Good Hope. It was this process that led to the discovery of the first of the Atlantic islands.

The Canary Islands were known to the Romans (who may also have discovered Madeira and the Azores). The island of Lanzarote was discovered in 1336 by Lanzarote Malocello. The Canaries were unusual among the easterly Atlantic islands in that they already had an indigenous human population, known to the Spaniards as Guanches, who appeared to have originated from Berber stock in North Africa. Though only hunter-gatherers, they existed in sufficient numbers to constitute real opposition to the first European settlers. Between 1402 and 1496 a series of campaigns was waged by the Spanish against them and, island by island, they gradually succumbed to a combination of European weapons and European diseases. Any survivors were enslaved, some of them being sent to the plantations in Madeira. The Guanches thus had the misfortune to be the first non-European victims of European imperialism. The introduction of sugar cane from the Mediterranean transformed the prospects and appearance of the Canary Islands (Fernandez-Arnesto 1982; Braudel 1972). The first sugar mill was established in 1484. In a pattern that was to be repeated on both sides of the Atlantic, deforestation to make way for sugar plantations led to a rapid decrease in moisture (Crosby 1986). By the early sixteenth century wood was becoming scarce and regulations to protect the remaining forests were being introduced (Parsons 1981).

The Cape Verde Islands, 500km from the west coast of Africa, were uninhabited, though known to Senegalese fishermen. Europeans first landed in 1456 and the islands were claimed by Portugal in 1460. Once covered by dry forest and scrub, their volcanic soils were quite fertile but large parts of the islands were too dry for agriculture. Slaves were imported to work on sugar plantations; overgrazing and cultivation of the steep slopes led to soil erosion and desertification, made worse by the climate, which was characterised by marked wet and dry seasons with periodic droughts and water shortages.

The island of Porto Santo to the east of Madeira was discovered in 1418 by Golçalvez Zarco and Tristaö vaz Texeira while on a voyage to Guinea. A few colonists were left behind while the expedition returned to report their discovery. On their return in 1419 the people that they had left reported seeing distant high land: the island which came to be called Madeira, a word meaning 'the wooded isle' in Portuguese. This state of affairs did not last long. Zarco landed on the south-east side at what is now the town of Machico and explored some of the countryside. Before leaving, according to tradition, he set fire to the forests and the fires are claimed to have burned for seven years; the scale of the burning seems to have got out of hand. The first act of European explorers in Madeira, then, was woodland clearance on a catastrophic scale.

Two years later Zarco and Texeira returned to initiate full-scale colonisation of Madeira. The climate and fertile soil proved to be ideally suited to the growth of sugar cane. From 1452 onwards, when the first sugar mill was authorised by the Portuguese government, sugar production expanded rapidly and within a few decades the island was the world's foremost producer. The plantations were increasingly worked using slave labour brought from west Africa and the Canaries. Settlement was so rapid that by 1508 Funchal, the capital, had been elevated to the status of a city. By 1514 the population of Madeira had reached c.5,000 and by 1580 c.21,800. After Columbus's voyages the island became an important stopping place for vessels sailing to the Americas and, as a result, a focus for pirate attacks (Bryans 1959). Madeira, like the Canary Islands, was covered by a subtropical humid mountain forest of a kind which had once been widespread in southern Europe and north-west Africa. The widespread removal of this – the forests cover only about 16 per cent of the island today – had the effect of reducing soil moisture (and precipitation). The impact of this was that most perennial streams dried up. As early as the fifteenth century irrigation canals, or levadas, were being dug to distribute water from the moister areas in the north of the island to the drier, more sunny areas of the south, the first in a network that eventually extended to over 2,150km. One of the problems of colonisation, then, from an early date, was the provision of sufficient water for agriculture. Madeira was, then, already a major sugar producer by Columbus's day and the great explorer was well aware of the history of deforestation and desiccation that had characterised the settlement of the islands when he set sail on his famous voyage in 1492.

The Canary Islands and Madeira had a basically Mediterranean climate, but the Azores, discovered *c*.1432, though farther out in the Atlantic, lay more to the north and the cooler winds there did not suit the cultivation of sugar cane. A mixed farming system rather than plantation agriculture developed there following settlement in the 1440s.

More remote still was St Helena, 1,200 miles (1,920km) from Africa and 1,800 (2,880km) from Brazil. Volcanic in origin, it was colonised only by winged immigrants – birds and insects – or by plants whose seeds had been blown there or washed ashore. As a result the island developed a distinctive flora and fauna which existed in complete isolation. Many of St Helena's plants had as their closest relatives plants in Africa which had long been extinct. On St Helena distinctive woodlands developed dominated at different altitudes by characteristic species – scrubwood (*Commdendrum rugosum*) at lower levels, gumwood (*Commdendrum rubustum*) at 4–600m. and *Trochetiopsis erythdoxylon* up to 650m. It was the tragedy of this, and other, Atlantic islands that their unique ecosystems were so vulnerable to human interference.

St Helena was discovered in 1502 by the Portuguese. It came to act as an important staging post and watering point on the route to the Cape of Good Hope. The interior of the unpopulated island was largely covered by forest. It did not experience the development of plantation agriculture as early, or on such a large scale, as some of the islands we have been considering, although some orange groves were planted.

Although its resources were described very optimistically by early visitors, the first Portuguese settlers in the mid-sixteenth century introduced goats, which proved to be highly effective agents of deforestation. They were not solely to blame, though. During the middle and later seventeenth century, Anglo-Dutch rivalry led to the crews of visiting ships from each country cutting down the groves of fruit trees to deny their enemies the benefit of them. Development by the English East India Company in the later seventeenth century rapidly led to land degradation. When the Dutch annexed the Cape of Good Hope the English established a permanent colony on the island in 1659, leading to the rapid development of plantation agriculture. The effect of this on a mountainous island with variable rainfall was devastating. Erosion was being reported as early as 1670. Today over 60 per cent of the island is barren, known appropriately as the Crown Wastes. The colony's early administration seemed unaware of contemporary developments in the West Indies, where the undesirable impact of deforestation and the establishment of plantations was rapidly becoming evident (Grove, R. 1995). The danger of adopting stocking densities and land use methods which had been derived from England, under different conditions of climate and terrain, was not appreciated.

By the time that St Helena was starting to experience environmental problems these had already become manifest on some of the Caribbean islands. From Cuba to Trinidad the islands of the Caribbean are spread over an arc more than 4,000km long with great variety in terms of geology, topography, climate and vegetation. Many of the islands are tectonically unstable: witness the recent eruptions on Montserrat. The aboriginal population of the islands had lived in fairly close harmony with their environment, hunting, fishing and practising shifting agriculture with a wide range of crops including beans, cassava, maize, peanuts, peppers and sweet potatoes. Early Spanish settlement was on quite a small scale – there were still under 10,000 colonists in the whole region by the end of the sixteenth century – and by the 1520s most of the native population had been wiped out by European diseases against which they had no immunity, allowing the islands' forests to encroach on the former cultivated areas (Watts 1995). As in the Atlantic islands the introduction of European domesticated animals such as pigs and sheep to islands lacking in natural predators caused an explosion of their population and the start of major human-induced impacts on the environment. Much worse was to come, though, in the seventeenth century with the spread of plantation agriculture, especially on British-controlled islands. Tobacco was the first popular plantation crop but it was soon realised that it rapidly exhausted the soils, a more critical problem on relatively small islands where the area of cultivable land was limited relative to the American mainland. It was soon realised that sugar cane was a less exhausting and equally profitable crop.

There were other motives behind deforestation in the British Caribbean, though. In Britain there was a long-established association between woodland clearance and improvement. In the eighteenth century, changes in landscape taste also favoured more open parkland landscapes with trees in scattered clumps and more open vistas. It was also commonly believed that tropical forests gave rise to harmful vapours, which caused illness. Removing the forests would, it was thought, cause the sun to disperse the harmful miasmas (Grove, R. 1995). Unfortunately, despite the Spanish and Portuguese experience on the other side of the Atlantic, British planters in the Caribbean failed to realise that the lush tropical landscapes of the islands were terribly vulnerable to change. Most of the nutrients were locked up in the vegetation rather than in the soils. Once deforestation occurred the soil rapidly lost its fertility. The resources of the tropical world were far from being limitless.

The sugar industry was first established on Barbados when, in the late 1640s, immigrant Portuguese Jews from Brazil introduced the skills for producing high-quality sugar, causing a revolution in agriculture and a transformation of the landscape of the island. The scale of ecological change on Barbados was unprecedented: within twenty years the island was so short of timber that it was being imported from New England. Trees were killed by ring-barking them and then burning them at the end of the dry season (Watts 1987). Within a few years

Barbados became a gem among Britain's overseas possessions in the same way that Madeira had once been for Portugal (McFarlane 1992). Sugar cane grew well in the Caribbean but it needed light, quite a lot of water and careful weeding. On Barbados sugar cane had virtually replaced forest by 1665, covering 80 per cent of the island. The same pattern was repeated on St Kitts, Nevis and Montserrat in the later seventeenth century and on Antigua, Guadeloupe and Martinique during the first half of the eighteenth (Watts 1995).

What had happened on Barbados was repeated in the eastern Caribbean on various islands, including Dominica, Grenada, St Vincent and Tobago, which were acquired by Britain under the Peace of Paris in 1763 at the end of the Seven Years War. Official policy regarding these islands favoured the rapid development of sugar production. With the experience of Barbados clearly in mind, though, scientific opinion was starting to move towards a more conservation-orientated approach. The establishment of forest reserves on Tobago and St Vincent in 1764 was influenced by concerns that wholesale deforestation on these islands might lead to a drier climate and shortage of moisture for crops. Attitudes were influenced by the Royal Society for Arts, Manufactures and Commerce which, from 1758, had offered prizes for tree planting in England and which took a particular interest in the West Indies. By 1790 signs of sheet erosion and gullying were plain on St Vincent and were causing serious concern.

On St Helena the response to deforestation was more measured and interventionist. Evidence of erosion was first noticed soon after the island was acquired from the Dutch in 1659. The problem grew as the expansion of the East India Company's trade increased the island's strategic significance as a staging point on the route to the Cape. Felling of trees by the crews of passing ships and especially the damage caused by a population explosion of feral goats caused severe erosion, as did the introduction of sugar cane plantations by the East India Company. By the early eighteenth century reduced streamflow was leading to concern about drought and governors of the island were starting to develop schemes for replanting.

Out of this ecological damage, however, developed some important modern conservation ideas. There has been a widespread belief that modern approaches to conservation developed in the USA under the influence of writers such as George Perkins Marsh, Henry David Thoreau and John Muir. In fact, as R. Grove (1995) has shown, they emerged in the context of the deforestation and degradation of small tropical islands like those of the Caribbean and Atlantic. We also tend to think that worries about human-induced climatic change are modern – a product of recent global warming – but, as early as the eighteenth century, scientists were making a direct link between deforestation and climatic desiccation in the context of small islands.

One place where such ideas crystallised was the island of St Vincent where, in the 1790s, there were serious worries about the sugar crop during a period of severe drought which climatologists now realise was a distant spin-off from a major El Niño event over the Pacific. These concerns led to the passing of the King's Hill Forest Act, which aimed to encourage reafforestation due to worries that the wholesale removal of the island's tree cover, to make way for sugar plantations, was causing a reduction in the rainfall and a drying up of streams and rivers. This has been seen as the first pioneer legislation to encourage reafforestation, though the thinking behind it also drew inspiration from the experience of the British occupation of St Helena and Jamaica from the late seventeenth century, representing a more sustainable approach to land management, a different form of concern from that in contemporary Britain, where tree planting in the eighteenth century was in part a response to the concern to maintain timber supplies for the navy (Grove, R. 1997).

Similar enlightened ideas had been responsible for the creation of a botanical garden on St Vincent in 1763, the first of its kind in the Americas. Another one followed on St Helena in 1788, partly under the influence of Sir Joseph Banks, the botanist who had sailed on Cook's first voyage. By the early years of the nineteenth century a tree-planting programme was under way on St Helena. This impressed Joseph Hooker, the eminent botanist, who had visited St Helena and Ascension

Island. In 1843 he acted as an adviser to Lord Dalhousie, the Governor General of India from 1847, on the value of tree planting in combating desiccation. In reality, if the precipitation situation had improved in the Caribbean and the Atlantic islands it is probably because El Niño events at the end of the eighteenth century and the early years of the nineteenth had become less severe with a reduction in the occurrence of drought conditions – but the idea had nevertheless struck chords in the right places. In 1854 Lord Dalhousie founded the Indian Forest Service and a generation of retired Indian foresters taught at British universities (Barton 2002). Their impact had a significant influence on forestry in Britain and ultimately on the development of the Forestry Commission from 1919.

CHAPTER 7

Modern Developed Societies

Tourism in the Alps

In assessing the scale of environmental change that has occurred in the modern world the tendency is to focus on the growth of manufacturing industry and of major urban centres as the most dramatic and widespread environmental transformation. Another spin-off from the growth of population, however, from the increased wealth and greater leisure time in the developed countries during the twentieth century, has been the dramatic expansion of tourism which now, in the early twenty-first century, is starting to affect even the most remote areas of the planet, including Antarctica and the Galapagos.

Within Europe, mass tourism is perhaps most closely associated with the shores of the Mediterranean, especially the Spanish costas and the Balearic Islands, but it has also had a profound influence on other kinds of environments, notably mountain areas. In some ways the most extreme example of this is the world's highest peak, Mount Everest, which now, only fifty years after its first ascent, has a base camp buried in rubbish and a summit littered with corpses. Not only have its lower slopes become a standard trekking venue, but various expedition companies will take to the summit clients who, although fit, need not be experienced climbers – by routes which were once attempted only by the world's top mountaineers. The paradox of tourism – that tourists destroy what they come in search of – is particularly evident in the Himalayas. In this section, however, we look at some of the environmental problems arising out of the growth of tourism in another mountain environment: the European Alps.

The Alps have for centuries had an ambivalent attitude to the outside world. In medieval and Renaissance times they were isolated and remote, an abode of danger and horror, yet at the same time, crossed by numerous passes carrying high volumes of traffic between the cities of Italy and those of the Low Countries and Germany. Remoteness brought the benefits of clean water and comparative protection from epidemics such as bubonic plague, but the down side was that marginal conditions could make agriculture precarious (before the spread of the potato). Incomes from upland agriculture were bolstered in many areas by regular seasonal migration to lowland areas and cities (Netting 1981; Viazzo 1989). Although the mountains provided a harsh environment, seeming to offer only a poor living, the availability of gold, silver, lead, copper and salt in many areas provided riches for some. From the later eighteenth century the growing interest in sublime mountain landscapes attracted aristocratic visitors on the Grand Tour and Alpine tourism was born (Schama 1995).

Nevertheless, the development of Alpine tourism on a significant scale had to wait until the railway network began to penetrate the high valleys in the later nineteenth century. Some centres, such as Bad Gastein and Bad Ischl in Austria, developed as spas, attracting wealthy invalids. Others, notably Chamonix and Zermatt, became famous as mountaineering centres, benefiting especially from British patronage (Ring 2000). Downhill skiing was introduced to the Alps at the end of the nineteenth century. After the Second World War the activity developed rapidly from a minority sport for the wealthy elite to a mass pastime with the development of package holidays and charter flights. The technical expertise of engineers in constructing roads, mountain railways and cable cars opened the valleys and the mountains to summer as well as winter visitors, leading to the mushroom development of many Alpine resorts and their associated infrastructure of access roads, hotels, ski lifts and ski runs.

Within the Alps, however, there have been marked regional contrasts in the way in which tourist development has been handled. In the French Alps planning policies have favoured the construction of modern purpose-built ski resorts which have little contact with, and bring little income to, the population of the surrounding area. By contrast, in Switzerland and the Tyrol tourist development has tended to focus on existing settlements, with a greater number of businesses being run by local families. As a result the French Alps have continued to suffer from substantial depopulation while parts of the central and eastern Alps have maintained population levels and even experienced growth. Population in the Vorarlberg, Tyrol and Salzburg Alps increased between 10 and 20 per cent between 1961 and 1971, largely due to tourism (Kariel and Kariel 1982).

All this development has come at an environmental cost, though. Woodland clearance to create ski runs and the provision of high-level access roads to ski facilities has scarred the landscape and increased run-off and erosion. This in turn has increased the risk of flooding and avalanche damage. The growing popularity of particular resorts has caused growing traffic congestion and pollution, a demand for water and the need for waste disposal. The proliferation of ski runs, roads, tracks and paths has damaged Alpine meadows and threatened many plant species. The expansion of winter-sports facilities, and the need to keep them in operation throughout the year in order to make them pay, has led to the expansion of summer activities such as walking, mountain biking, riding and white-water rafting, which have spread the impact of tourism on the landscape even further.

A particularly serious problem has been an increase in the threat from floods, landslides and avalanches due to deforestation and soil modification in critical areas. An example of the increased flood danger was the flash flood that devastated the community of Le Bez near the French resort of Serre Chevalier in July 1995 when cars and even buildings were swept away, trees uprooted and mud deposited on surviving buildings almost to ceiling level.

The Alpine tourist industry and the environment it exploits are already under heavy pressure from present levels of activity (see Plate 13). Potential future environmental changes may make matters even worse. With global warming winter-sports resorts are increasingly at risk from shorter winter seasons and less reliable snow cover, particularly at lower altitudes. There has been a significant reduction in winter snow cover throughout the Alps in recent years. Predictions for the future are that a 3°C rise in average temperatures will push the snowline as much as 300m. higher in the central Alps. The first winter snowfall will be increasingly late and below about 1,200m. there will be no continuous winter snow cover at all, threatening some major resorts, such as Kitzbuhel, at lower levels. Within fifteen years many of the low-level resorts may have no snow; temperatures have already risen by around a degree Centigrade within the last ten years, pushing the snowline higher by as much as 150m. As the winter season has shortened there has already been an increasing recourse to the generation of artificial snow; its use doubled in Switzerland between 1992 and 1995. Making artificial snow, however, is expensive and consumes a lot of energy as well as water (Elsasser and Messerli 2001).

Continuing tourist expansion is undesirable, but in some places it is scarcely possible. Zermatt admirably illustrates some of the constraints on Alpine tourism. With 13,200 tourist beds and the industry employing – directly and indirectly – virtually the entire population, the village is heavily dependent on tourism. The attractive, traffic-free atmosphere of the settlement, however, can be maintained only by ensuring that no further growth occurs. Zermatt's tourist industry has already reached its limits.

Worldwide, mountain regions are the second most popular category of holiday destination after coastal areas. Mountains form a high-energy environment in which changes in the frequency and magnitude of extreme events can have major implications for the safety and enjoyment of visitors as well as residents. The growth of tourist demand is threatening to destroy the very foundations of Alpine tourism: its attractive landscapes and wealth of habitats. The popularity of the Alps as a tourist destination is still thought by some to be rising at around 4 per cent per year. The Alps receive around 120 million tourists a year with a resident population of only around thirteen million – which still makes it the most densely populated mountain area in the world. The area attracts some 10 per cent of total world tourism.

It has been calculated that as many as 700,000 skiers use the Swiss mountains on a peak day during the winter season. Some 60 per cent of all traffic in the Alps is tourist-related. Tourists use fifty million vehicles in the region each year and three million mountain bikes. Tourist development in the Alps has arguably reached its ecological and economic limits: the Alps may be one of the world's most saturated tourist areas. Traffic crossing the St Gotthard Pass in Switzerland each weekend deposits thirty tonnes of nitrogen oxides, twenty-five tonnes of hydrocarbons and 75kg of lead into the surrounding air and on to the vegetation. For a long time tourism was seen as a more benign source of income for mountain communities than, say, mining, but it is not necessarily viewed so positively today. There has been a rapid shift of employment in Alpine communities from farming to tourism and in the process the traditional social structure of whole communities has been altered.

Some of the most striking areas of Alpine landscape receive protection through designations as national and regional parks. In the last decade the German, Austrian, French and Italian governments have created eleven new national parks in Alpine areas plus thirty-five regional parks. But even so only around 10 per cent of the Alps are protected by such designation and the creation of national parks often leads to conflict, as in the recent examples of Lechtal in Austria and the Engadine in Switzerland.

Global warming has already had some marked effects on the physical environments of Alpine areas and these are likely to intensify in the future. Since about 1850 Alpine glaciers have lost between 30 and 40 per cent of their area and around half their volume. The hot summer of 2003 saw unprecedented melting not just of glaciers, but of mountain permafrost, leading to a dramatic increase in landslides and rockfalls: deaths from rockfalls were double those of previous years. All but the largest Alpine glaciers may have vanished by the end of the present century.

The avalanche hazard is nothing new in the Alps. Residents and travellers have been exposed to this risk for centuries or even millennia; Hannibal is said to have lost a significant proportion of his army from avalanches when crossing the mountains. Nor is the recent spate of avalanche fatalities something new – the frequency of major avalanches has fluctuated throughout history and may have reached peaks during the first half of the seventeenth century and around 1830 (Jomelli and Pech 2004). Many modern fatalities have been due to a failure to appreciate the extent and nature of the hazard by visitors, with skiers ignoring warning signs and going off-piste into areas of known danger. In around 95 per cent of avalanche incidents the victims themselves trigger the disaster. There have also been a number of recent examples, however, where avalanches have destroyed property and killed people in the ski resorts themselves rather than high on the slopes. One of the most widely reported disasters occurred in the village of La Tour near Chamonix in the French Alps in February 1999, when twelve people were killed by an avalanche that swept away seventeen chalets. Worse still was Galtur, in the Austrian Tyrol, where in March 1999 some thirty people were killed when two avalanches converged in a massive slide that demolished dozens of homes. These and other avalanches were caused by some of the heaviest snowfalls in half a century, bringing the winter's death toll from avalanches to more than seventy. While winters may have been getting shorter and less cold this has, paradoxically, encouraged heavier than usual spring snowfalls, dramatically increasing the risk of major avalanches. Predicted changes with global warming include more variability in precipitation and more rapid spring thawing, which might cause an increase in the frequency and intensity of large-scale avalanches.

Avalanches are most likely to occur on slopes of between thirty and forty-five degrees. Documentary evidence and field data allow avalanche-prone areas to be identified fairly easily and zoned accordingly to prevent unsafe new developments. Avalanche risk in some areas has also increased with deforestation and the creation of new ski runs. In areas prone to these events walls and fences can be placed above the starting zone for avalanches to prevent the accumulation of snow in critical areas while avalanche sheds can protect vulnerable stretches of roads and railway lines. Afforestation of the lower slopes may provide additional protection. In the runout zone at the base of the slopes banks can be constructed to deflect the course of debris. Probably the most effective way of preventing disasters such as those cited above is more rigorous planning and land-use zonation with the refusal of permission to construct buildings in areas where historical records suggest that there is a significant avalanche risk (Smith, K. 1992). More generally, Alpine countries have brought in more comprehensive land-use planning for tourist areas, which attempts to take environmental considerations on board and restrict resort growth.

Environmental degradation cannot be blamed entirely on tourism. The growth of population in the eighteenth century led to large-scale felling of Alpine woodlands, causing the compaction and waterlogging of soils and increased erosion, landslides and flooding. Since the last quarter of the nineteenth century in Switzerland and other parts of the region government and federal initiatives have encouraged replanting. At the same time major changes were occurring in agriculture. Many parts of the Alps had already moved from a mixed subsistence economy to commercial livestock rearing. In the nineteenth century the introduction of dairies led to the abandonment of many Alpine pastures and their recolonisation by woodland. The growing commercialisation of agriculture in surrounding lowland areas, however, and the collapse of local cottage industries under competition from outside manufacturers as communications improved, led in the late nineteenth and early twentieth centuries to large-scale depopulation. With the abandonment of high-level marginal land the upper limit of permanent settlement in parts of the Alps has fallen by 300m. (Lichtenburger 1975). Only careful management of the higher areas can prevent environmental degradation, but farmers are still leaving the land (Frey 1976).

Trees, Woodland and Identity in the British Landscape

The examples of environmental change and human response we have considered so far have mostly been examined in an objective manner. But we have also seen that subjective reactions to environmental change are important in influencing people's actions and decision-making, such as the essentially negative response of the Norse Greenlanders to a deteriorating climate. How people feel about their environments and the ways in which these have changed can be a powerful force, expressed through history, legend and myth. Particular environments have helped to shape the imaginations of individuals, communities and nations. Distinctive landscapes such as coasts, forests and mountains have been used to epitomise regional and national identities. When such environments come under threat they can become foci for group solidarity and nationalist sentiments.

On the other hand, nations can rewrite histories of environmental change to fit their own viewpoints. This is particularly evident when it comes to allocating blame for what are seen in retrospect as undesirable changes. Trees and woodland have been particularly influential in shaping national images of landscape within Europe: from the darker, more sombre Germanic and Scandinavian forests to the lighter ones of the Mediterranean. In this section we look at how images of trees and woodland in Britain have developed and changed over the centuries and how these images have helped to shape modern attitudes to the landscape. Until recently Britain had one of the most open, least forested countries in Europe. Yet paradoxically the very lack of extensive woodlands in the last few centuries has helped to highlight the symbolic character and importance of those that remain.

Trees with particular historical or literary associations can be powerful symbols of continuity. The Royal Oak at Boscobel, in which Charles II hid from his pursuers after the Battle of Worcester, still attracts large numbers of visitors even though the original tree was killed off long ago by over-enthusiastic souvenir hunters; the one on view today is merely a replacement, supposedly sprung from one of the acorns of the original tree (see Plate 14). The Major Oak in Sherwood Forest has a hollow trunk inside which Robin Hood is said to have hidden and is up to 1,000 years old. Even more venerable are some yew trees such as the one at Wraysbury in Berkshire under which Henry VIII is said to have courted Anne Boleyn and which was standing when King John signed the Magna Carta at nearby Runnymeade. With the 200th anniversary of the Battle of Trafalgar having fallen in 2005, it seems fitting that Nelson's flagship, HMS *Victory*, is being repaired using oak timber from the Forest of Dean, taken from trees planted shortly before the battle on Nelson's personal recommendation.

The Discovery of England's Ancient Woodlands

The English image of woodlands is not that of the Germanic peoples, so well expressed in the brooding treescapes of Caspar David Friedrich, and the children's stories of the Brothers Grimm (Schama 1995), or the even more spartan northern forests of Finland so evocatively captured by Sibelius in tone poems such as 'Tapiola'. In modern times woodland has become a powerful focus for the English imagination and sense of identity. This is brought out by modern fantasy fiction such as Robert Holdstock's *Mythago Wood* (1984), in which England's woodlands are seen as a repository of myth and legend, or J. R. R. Tolkien's *Lord of the Rings*, in which Fangorn, Mirkwood and the Old Forest are places isolated from mainstream life, scary, but inhabited by friends as well as foes. Fiction such as this has helped to give English woodlands an air of timelessness and mystery. These images also reflect a long tradition of seeing woodlands as distinctive environments inhabited by people who were in some ways 'different', isolated from mainstream society.

Trees and woodland were potent symbols for pre-Christian settlers and with the coming of Christianity their traditions merely became absorbed into a new set of beliefs. At Gosforth in Cumbria a striking Viking-period cross in the churchyard has a base which is round and carved to resemble the bark of a tree (see Plate 15). The four panels of the cross depict symbols both pagan and Christian, but the base of the cross represents Yggdrasil, the great ash tree which supported the world in Norse legend (Bailey 1980). Medieval churches throughout England have carvings in both wood and stone of heads disguised by foliage or actually disgorging it. The Green Man (also commemorated in a number of pub names) is a pre-Christian figure, linked to woodlands and fertility (Anderson 1990).

Woods offered shelter for outlaws and refugees from oppression. Ballads celebrating Robin Hood go back to the fourteenth century, though the historical Robin, if he indeed existed, remains elusive (Holt

1982). The greenwood of Robin Hood was a lighter, less sinister place than the forests of Germanic legends and tales, a place from which people could break free, if only temporarily, from the conventions of normal society. In the late eighteenth and early nineteenth centuries the New Forest was seen as a seat of English liberty and resistance to oppression by writers like William Gilpin who could identify the location of the tree from which, in 1100, an arrow had supposedly glanced off before killing William Rufus. Yet at the same time the contemporary inhabitants of the forest were seen as idle and shiftless, not fully integrated with the rest of rural society. One of the last remnants of an independent woodland society of this sort were the charcoal burners of south Lakeland, who continued to work into the 1920s and 1930s and were memorably described in Arthur Ransome's *Swallows and Amazons* (1930).

Continental forests may have remained genuine wilderness areas, inhabited by wild animals as well as wild people, until relatively modern times, but the smaller areas of England's woodlands made them less frightening places. Predators such as bears and wolves disappeared early compared with the Continent. Bears may have survived in Britain until Roman times, but were possibly wiped out even earlier. Wolves seem to have become extinct over most of England by the end of the thirteenth century (Rackham 1986). From early medieval times at least, woods were carefully managed, busy places with the pasturing of livestock, including pannage for pigs, the production of bark for tanning, the cutting of timber for construction, and coppicing for making wattle and daub panelling, tools and charcoal.

Yet different histories of England's woodlands have been written. The traditional one stressed their late survival then rapid demise since Tudor times. The landscape historian W. G. Hoskins (1955) believed that the extent of deforestation in prehistoric and even Roman times was quite limited. The Anglo-Saxon settlers moved into a country that was still largely a wilderness with huge areas retaining their original woodland cover, little affected by human activity. Even as late as the fifteenth century, he suggested, almost any part of the English lowlands, seen from rising ground, would have appeared as a great continuous forest. Much of this, he thought, was removed by a phase of immense destruction during the sixteenth and seventeenth centuries due to activities such as iron smelting and the great rebuilding of housing during Tudor times. Although more recent research indicates a very different story, elements of this older interpretation linger on and the ironmasters still often receive a bad press as entrepreneurs who shamelessly sacrificed England's woodlands to line their pockets.

By contrast, more recent views emphasise that both deforestation and careful woodland management began early in prehistoric times. The Sweet Track, named after its discoverer, Raymond Sweet, a timber walkway across the Somerset Levels built in 3806 BC, was made from a combination of planks, rails and pegs, which indicates that the woodlands in the immediate area were already being carefully coppiced some 6,000 years ago (Parker Pearson 1993). As estimates of the population in Britain during late prehistoric and Roman times have steadily been revised upwards and the density of settlement increased, so has the probable scale of pre-Saxon woodland clearance. It is now believed that only around 15 per cent of England was wooded when the great Domesday survey of 1086 was written.

A lot of damage to English woodlands occurred during the Civil War in the mid-seventeenth century, either by direct military action or by the depredations of local people who took advantage of the disruption of society and the relaxation of normal controls on the cutting and use of wood. It was in the aftermath of this, in 1664, that John Evelyn wrote *Silva or a Discourse of Forest Trees*, a book which originated in a request to the Royal Society from the Commissioners of the Navy to prepare a programme for replanting. Although influential in its day, Evelyn's book had even more impact during the eighteenth century.

From the middle of the eighteenth century the increasing demands of the navy for timber encouraged landowners to extend the plantations on their estates. As we saw in Chapter 6, the Royal Society for the Encouragement of Arts, Manufactures and Commerce offered prizes for planting trees, which was sometimes done on a heroic scale. Sturdy long-lived oaks symbolised the power and durability of the landed families who planted them and fitted in well with the contemporary ethos of stewardship – the idea that one might make improvements to one's estate in the knowledge that the full effects, aesthetic and economic, might be enjoyed only by one's son or even grandson. The timber provided landed estates with a valuable source of income as well as giving their owner the smug feeling that they were doing their patriotic duty – and it helped to provide sufficient home-grown oak-wood for the navy to see it through the Napoleonic wars.

The 'golden age' of tree planting in landscape parks occurred between about 1725 and 1830 and the designs of landscape planners such as 'Capability' Brown and Humphry Repton were not only widely imitated in England, but spread to Ireland and Scotland. Trees were one of the essential components of a Capability Brown landscape park, planted singly or in small clumps on artificial mounds or in larger wilderness areas threaded by paths and opening into glades decorated with statues, classical temples or grottoes. Brown is sometimes credited with having created 'perfect' landscapes. Research on modern people's 'ideal' landscape has demonstrated a distinct preference for parkland views with scattered trees. Orians (1986) has suggested that, since humans originated in savanna environments, landscapes of grassland with groups of trees should stir strong deep-seated emotions. Another theory (Appleton 1975) is that our European hunter-gatherer forebears preferred edge habitats where woodland gave way to more open country, providing hunters with locations from which they could see without being seen. Alternatively, Cosgrove (1984) believes that preferences for such landscapes are the result of modern cultural conditioning rather than subconscious instinct.

By the second half of the eighteenth century the felling of ancient timber was beginning to be condemned. When Greenwich Hospital, which had acquired land on the shores of Derwentwater in the Lake District, began wholesale felling they caused a public outcry. Both Robert Burns and William Wordsworth were scathingly critical of landowners who sacrificed amenity for profit in this way.

Progressively through the nineteenth century the idea developed that plantation forestry was the most efficient way of producing timber. Traditional skills of woodmanship declined and were lost first in northern England in the later nineteenth century under competition from coal and coke, which required less labour to produce than charcoal, and then in southern England in the early twentieth century. Only in recent times has this tradition been rediscovered both in terms of practical skills and in our ability to interpret the landscape of our ancient woodlands. The concept of 'Ancient Woodland', applying to areas which can be shown to have been continuously woodland since at least AD 1600, was first advanced by Oliver Rackham in 1971, though it took some time to catch on in certain circles, notably the Forestry Commission. The term is now in general use and surveys of the distribution and character of Ancient Woodlands have been undertaken throughout England (Rackham 1976). Ancient Woodlands are much richer in plant species than secondary woodlands created in recent times and are characterised by indicator species such as Dog's mercury (*Mercurialis perennis*), which spread only very slowly from their original habitats. Ancient Woodlands may have a species mix which preserves a hint of the original wildwood from which they are ultimately descended, but they have also been carefully managed by local communities, often for centuries, with a range of earthworks indicating former human activity such as charcoal-burning sites and banks dividing up sections of coppice (see Plate 16). Even remnants of high-level dwarf oakwoods, such as at Keskadale in the Lake District, show signs of former management (Pearsall and Pennington 1973). The survival of scattered pollards in areas like the Yorkshire Dales (Muir 2000) or charcoal pitsteads on what are now open hillsides are often clues to the former existence of areas of woodland.

The legacy of former woodlands in the English landscape is more extensive than has often been realised. Rather than having been deliberately planted, some ancient hedges appear to have been left as strips of relict woodland on the boundaries of estates. They can be distinguished by the richness of their species mix of woody shrubs and flowering plants. As recently as the nineteenth century there were thousands of

Ancient Woodlands throughout England which had barely changed for centuries in terms of their boundaries and composition, and which were managed using traditional techniques that exploited the woods in a sustainable fashion, using the power of deciduous trees to renew themselves from a cut stump or as suckers from their roots.

Ancient Woodlands were managed by coppicing, where, as already noted, the stump of a felled deciduous tree is left to send up a crop of shoots which can be harvested as poles every ten to twenty years on a sustainable basis. Coppice shoots had to be protected from damage by livestock, so areas of young coppice were enclosed by stockproof barriers. An alternative option, used when a combination of woodland and pasture was needed, is pollarding, where trees are cut down to between six and a dozen feet or more above the ground, producing crops of coppice poles out of reach of livestock, creating a mixture of open scattered woodland and grassland called wood-pasture.

The failure of economic historians to appreciate that woodlands could be managed sustainably by coppicing helped to perpetuate the myth that the sixteenth- and seventeenth-century iron industry in areas like the Weald 'destroyed' the woodlands through the insatiable demand for charcoal. In fact, what happened was that the iron industry expanded in particular regions until it reached limits set by the amount of charcoal that surrounding woodlands could produce. Further expansion could be achieved only by turning to new regions where coppice resources were not being fully exploited. The charcoal iron industry, rather than destroying woodlands, actually encouraged their expansion. In the southern Lake District in the eighteenth century the demand for charcoal was so great that any area of pasture on steeper ground was liable to be converted to coppice woodland (Bowden, M. 2000; Lowe, A. 1989).

Woodland, Myth and National Identity in Scotland: the 'Great Wood of Caledon'

Despite the influence of Oliver Rackham the traditional view of a thickly wooded medieval England has proved hard to dispel. In Scotland a similar myth has been equally tenacious in the popular imagination. The story of the Great Wood of Caledon runs as follows: the Scottish Highlands were thickly wooded, notably with forests of Scots or Caledonian pine, until relatively recent times. The woods were then rapidly destroyed by greedy clan chiefs, absentee landlords and ruthless English industrialists seeking fuel for the iron industry which had already devastated the English landscape, and to provide timber for shipbuilding. Wholesale deforestation in the seventeenth and eighteenth centuries produced the bare, denuded Highland landscapes which are so familiar today, a 'wet desert' where there had once been fertile ground. The extent of deforestation cannot be doubted; what has been debated is its chronology and causes. Particularly influential has been the idea that Highland forests remained largely intact in many areas until comparatively recently (Smout 2000).

There is no doubt about the distinctive appearance and atmospheric character of surviving Scottish pinewoods. Although they are a variant of the pinewoods that occur widely on heathlands in northern Europe, their particular species mix is unique. The flora of these native pinewoods is distinctive, if limited. As well as Scots pine, birch and rowan trees are common, holly and juniper more occasional. The ground cover beneath the trees is often dominated by heather and bilberry, with plants like cotton grass and bog myrtle in the wetter areas. The fauna include red and roe deer, otters, foxes, red squirrels and wildcats as well as birds such as the capercaillie (*Tetrao urogallus*), crested tit (*Parus cristatus*) and Scottish crossbill (*Loxia Scotica*).

Native pine forests have been seen as symbolising the traditional Scottish landscape – but how extensive were they? Modern palaeoecological research has shown that they did not cover anything like the whole of Scotland in the past. During mid-post-glacial times most of the Lowlands and the south-western Highlands were dominated by mixed deciduous woodlands with oak and hazel being prominent. The north east and north of Scotland had a cover of birch woods with hazel and some oak, shading off in Caithness, the Northern Isles and the Outer Hebrides into scrub communities. The Caledonian pinewoods dominated an area that extended from the Great Glen south to Rannoch Moor, east to the Cairngorms, north to the Black Isle and north west to Ullapool. Today only a few remnants of this once extensive woodland type survive, especially in the upper valleys of the Spey and the Dee. The area of surviving native pine forest is hard to calculate because so much of it is scattered in small, isolated remnants or is so open that its boundaries are hard to determine. But by whatever measure is used less than 1 per cent of the original area of pinewood remains (Atherden 1992).

But was the Great Wood of Caledon cleared out as late as the tradititional view suggests? Recent studies of environmental change from pollen deposits have presented a very different picture, pushing back the onset of major woodland clearance in Scotland from recent centuries into prehistory. They have shown that the scale of deforestation in Scotland, especially in the Lowlands, during the Bronze Age, Iron Age and early historic times, was far greater than had been previously supposed. When the Romans began to construct Hadrian's Wall they did not have to remove extensive areas of woodland to give their sentries a clear field of view. The landscape had already been opened out by the indigenous inhabitants and turned, at best, into a parkland landscape with only isolated stands of trees. The quantities of timber required to construct the large circular houses built by the Iron Age inhabitants of southern Scotland and, to an even greater degree, the palisades, timber facings and interlaced beams of the ramparts that defended them, must have been prodigious. A switch from timber construction to stone foundations and walls in the last few centuries before the Romans arrived hints at a timber shortage (Armit 1997). Woodland was probably still a good deal more extensive than this in the Highlands, but it had nevertheless been substantially reduced even here by both natural forces and human activity (Tipping 1994). Climatic shifts also played an important part in the shrinkage of the area under pinewoods. Over the last 4,000 years the extent of pine forests has been greatly reduced by the onset of wetter conditions and the spread of peat bogs. Unlike the conifer species introduced to Scotland in modern times, Scots pines are not particularly suited to wet environments.

If the Romans were not responsible for major deforestation in the Lowlands, their effects in the Highlands are likely to have been even less. The ancient Caledonian Forest may indeed have served the Picts as a refuge from the legions. In the post-Roman period, however, the woodlands were slowly, but relentlessly whittled away due to the depredations of livestock and demand for construction timber. Burning of woodlands associated with clan warfare and the activities of Cromwellian troops in the Highlands may have had some local effect, but probably much more important was the direct and indirect impact of the steady growth of Highland population between the sixteenth and the later eighteenth centuries, increasing the demand for construction timber. Early commercial charcoal-iron smelting sites in areas such as Strath Naver and Loch Maree may have made some inroads into the woodlands, but only at a local scale, for levels of production were modest and the lifespan of the industrial operations at particular locations short. Moreover, oak and birch wood was preferred to pine for making charcoal and these deciduous trees could be managed sustainably by coppicing.

It is clear that from medieval times the Lowlands, with their higher density of population, more extensive cultivation and strings of small burghs round the coastline, were deforested much more rapidly than the Highlands. By later medieval times timber shortages were being experienced there leading to growing imports of softwoods from Scandinavia. By 1500 somewhere between 10 and 15 per cent of Scotland may still have been wooded, the bulk of this being in the Highlands (Smout 2003). The Military Survey of 1747–55 shows that by this time the figure had dropped to around 4 per cent. By the end of the nineteenth century the proportion may have been as low as 3 per cent.

By the late eighteenth century there was very little old-established woodland left in the Lowlands. The lack of trees is emphasised by Samuel Johnson's comment, 'A tree in Scotland is as rare as a horse in Venice.' Having reached Inverness without, supposedly, having seen a tree that was any taller than himself, he warned his companion, James Boswell, that he was keeping a tight hold on his walking stick; 'imagine the price of such a piece of timber here'! Johnson was, however, like so many English travellers in Scotland during the seventeenth and eighteenth centuries, exaggerating to suit the preconceptions and prejudices of his (mainly English) audience. He must certainly have passed by a number of estates on which extensive plantations of trees had been created around country houses and castles.

There was undoubtedly an acceleration in the rate of woodland clearance in the Highlands during the eighteenth century, though not as rapid as was once believed. After the Jacobite rebellions of 1715 and 1745 a number of Highland estates were forfeited to the crown and more timber was felled for making charcoal to smelt iron and lead. Pine was also in growing demand as masts for the navy. Timber was floated down to the sea around Loch Arkaig and in Ardgour on the west coast. In 1728 a dubious bunch of speculators, the York Buildings Company, bought 60,000 pine trees in Abernethy Forest and began to float them down to the mouth of the Spey to be used for shipbuilding on Tyneside. The main phase of commercial exploitation of Glenmore Forest in the same area occurred after 1783 (Whyte and Whyte 1987). After 1745 a few new charcoal blast furnaces were established in the Highlands. Most were short-lived. The exception was one at Bonawe, on Loch Etive. It was established by Cumbrian ironmasters, the output of whose blast furnaces in the Lake District had reached the limits of their fuel supply. They looked to the West Highlands as a new source of charcoal. Bonawe operated between 1753 and 1876, but, because coppiced oak was the preferred source of charcoal, it preserved rather than destroyed the surrounding woodlands (Lindsay 1975).

During the nineteenth century a more widespread assault on the pinewoods occurred, with the increase first in sheep numbers and then the growing popularity of deer stalking and grouse shooting. Management of heather moorland by burning to increase grouse populations killed off seedling trees. Markedly increased grazing intensities in the surviving woods, caused by a rapid growth in deer numbers, also killed off young seedlings and prevented regeneration, a problem that continues to the present. As the area of pinewoods diminished, their fauna came under growing pressure. Capercaillies, the largest and most distinctive of the pinewood birds, became extinct in 1785. The present population is descended from reintroductions from Sweden in 1837. Red squirrels were also driven to the brink of extinction. The present population is again mainly derived from reintroductions. On the other hand, numbers of deer have increased to an extent where they now threaten the very survival of the pinewoods by browsing seedlings and damaging the bark of mature trees. Today in many areas deer numbers are three, five or even six times the levels needed to allow natural regeneration of the pinewoods to occur.

The appearance of the surviving pinewoods is by no means representative of their ancestors. Their age structure has been influenced by phases of felling followed by regeneration, so that often most of the trees in a wood are of similar age and size. On the Mar Lodge estate in the southern Cairngorms most of the surviving pine trees started growing at the end of the eighteenth century or the early years of the nineteenth, when deer numbers were lower. There has been little regeneration since then. Modern forestry has often changed the appearance of the pinewoods by planting introduced conifers such as Sitka spruce (*Pinaceae picea sitchensis*) and Lodgepole pine (*Pinus contorta*), though these are now being removed in many areas, while rhododendrons have aggressively invaded some woods.

The origins of the myth of the Great Wood of Caledon lie not in deforestation, but deep in the mists of nineteenth-century German romanticism. In part it developed from the romantic fantasies of the Sobieski Stuarts, two brothers of Anglo-German origin, who purported to be the grandchildren of Prince Charles Edward Stuart. They imported notions of the Germanic woodlands as the foundation of liberty, and transferred them to a Scottish context in their published collections of verse. The idea that the Germanic forests were a symbol of freedom and independence goes back to the defeat of the legions of Publius Quintilius Varus in AD 9 by the German leader Arminius in the

Teutoburgerwald (Schama 1995). In the early nineteenth century the brothers Grimm began publishing their collections of folk tales portraying the forests as places of mystery, magic and fear. Nineteenth-century Scottish writers and artists helped to foster the image of wild, shaggy Highland forests. Sir Walter Scott, in his poem *The Lady of the Lake* (1810), compares the chieftain Roderick Dhu with the sturdy pine tree that was the badge of his clan. The Highland paintings of Victorian artists such as Edwin Landseer and Horatio McCulloch continued the tradition (Whyte 2003).

This image of a distinctively Scottish type of woodland which survived until comparatively recently and was then destroyed at much the same time, and by the same forces, as Scotland's national identity has been perpetuated into modern times with books such as *The Great Wood of Caledon. The Story of the Ancient Scottish Pine Forest* by Hugh Miles and Brian Jackman (1991). The supposed loss of Highland pinewoods on a massive scale after the Jacobite defeat at the Battle of Culloden in 1746 has been seen by nationalists as part of Scotland's political and economic subjugation by Hanoverian England. Conversely, calls to 'reforest' Scotland, to create a new 'Wood of Caledon' in the Highlands and reorientate large areas towards a forest economy have also been linked to the modern resurgence of Scottish nationalism. Tied in with this have been campaigns for the reintroduction of former Scottish woodland animals such as elk, lynx, beaver and even wolves. Scottish Natural Heritage has voted in favour of reintroducing the beaver although final permission has been blocked recently by the Scottish Deputy Environment Minister. Lynx may already be breeding in the Highlands thanks to escapes. Attempts to reintroduce wolves, however, hardly seem likely to find much support from Highland sheep farmers!

Trees for Life, a Scottish conservation charity, is dedicated to the regeneration of the Caledonian Forest over an extensive area of the Highlands. Its focus lies west of the Great Glen in the Glen Affric area, where it is currently attempting to create linkages or corridors between surviving remnants of Scots pinewoods. Efforts to reforest land with native species and re-create something of the original wildwood have also been ongoing in the Lowlands. The Wildwood Group of the Scottish Borders Trust have purchased a steep 650ha upland catchment in the Carrifan valley at the head of Moffatdale. Their aim is to restore it to woodland using a species mix similar to the one that existed in the area before the advent of humans. To what extent such a goal is attainable given modern soil conditions may be questionable, especially if human access to the valley is to be allowed. On the Mar Lodge estate at the head of the River Dee, bought in 1995 by the National Trust for Scotland, measures have been introduced to halt the decline of the surviving pine forests and encourage regeneration. The estate has about 5 per cent of the surviving area of native pinewoods. Management has focused on reducing the deer population on the estate by around half to reach a grazing density of about five deer per 100ha in the valleys and sixteen per 100ha on the open moorlands. Large-scale regeneration has not yet begun, but previous experience suggests that this is a process likely to take considerable time.

Twentieth-century Afforestation in Britain and Landscape Perception

As we saw earlier in this section, in the later eighteenth and early nineteenth centuries there was a move towards large-scale plantation forestry by a number of landowners with estates in more marginal upland areas of Britain such as the Lake District and the Scottish Highlands. Introduced conifer species such as larch were well suited to the thin acid soils of such areas. In the Lake District in the early nineteenth century the large-scale plantation of larch trees by landowners such as John Christian Curwen and the Bishop of Llandaff attracted widespread approval, but was condemned by William Wordsworth as an alien visual intrusion (Pearsall and Pennington 1973). On the Atholl estates in Perthshire, however, the millions of conifers planted in the later eighteenth century were seen as a considerable ornament to an otherwise bare countryside. The fourth Duke of Atholl (1755–1830) undertook forestry on such a scale that he became known as 'Planter

John'. His ambitious goal was to be able to supply the entire British navy with larch timber from his estates (Smout 2003).

In the later nineteenth century plantation forestry was developed for other reasons. In 1877 Manchester Corporation applied to Parliament for permission to construct a reservoir at Thirlmere in the Lake District with the aim of raising the level of the existing lake substantially by means of a dam to provide the city's inhabitants with a supply of clean drinking water. Some 2,000 acres of the catchment were planted with conifers to stabilise the soil and reduce the amount of inwash into the new reservoir. Conifers were chosen in preference to deciduous trees as it was believed that the leaves of the latter would be more likely to pollute the water. The scheme was fought by a local amenity group, the Thirlmere Defence Association, but the corporation claimed that their alterations would improve the scenery rather than ruin it. Certainly the introduction of non-native species of conifers was not necessarily detrimental to the landscape. This is demonstrated by the Lake District beauty spot of Tarn Hows near Hawkshead where in the later nineteenth century the Marshall family of Monk Coniston Hall created an artificial lake and planted the surrounding slopes with spruces, larches and other conifers. Today Tarn Hows is visited by hundreds of thousands of people each year. Few of them realise the extent to which the landscape they walk around and photograph is both a recent and a man-made creation. The nineteenth century also witnessed the widespread introduction to British gardens and parks of a growing range of exotic conifers from the Americas and other distant parts of the world. Trees such as redwoods, cedars, Chile pines and Douglas firs have all made an important contribution to the British landscape.

During the First World War, with timber imports greatly reduced due to the German submarine threat, there was a timber shortage in Britain, especially of pit props for coal mines. Following a government report in 1917 the Forestry Commission was created by an act of Parliament in 1919 with the aim of establishing a strategic reserve of timber. The initial target was to plant 80,000 acres (32,000ha) of forest within ten years, but from the 1930s an additional aim was to provide badly needed rural employment. During the first twenty years of its existence the Forestry Commission planted 593,000 acres (240,000ha), mostly in upland areas where land was cheaper and options for alternative land uses fewer. Many private estates also followed the Commission's example.

By the 1930s, however, the Forestry Commission's work was starting to attract criticism on aesthetic grounds. The large, geometrical blocks of alien conifers, unvarying in age and colour, were seen by walkers and climbers as unattractive when they occupied an entire Lake District valley such as Ennerdale, where extensive afforestation began in 1933. Conifer plantations, with trees of the same species and age planted in regular rows, shading out most of the ground flora beneath, were seen as inappropriate and unattractive; 'rigid and monotonous ranks of spruce ... goose stepping on the fellsides' as one writer described them (Symonds 1936). The Forestry Commission's response, which was to claim that the addition of the conifers to valleys such as Ennerdale made the background of Lake District fells look more alpine in character, did not convince many people. In addition the loss of access caused by the need to fence off the young plantations to keep out animals and reduce the risk of fire also caused widespread objections from ramblers' organisations.

When the Commission began buying extensive areas in other western Lakeland valleys, such as Eskdale and Dunnerdale, in order to extend their plantations, opposition grew, leading to an agreement in 1938 with the Council for the Preservation of Rural England in which the Commission agreed not to undertake any further extensive block planting in 300 square miles (777sq. km) of the central mountain core of the Lake District, an agreement which still stands today and which marks an important step in integrated planning for British upland areas at a time when public and even government opinion was moving towards the creation of national parks. The debate over afforestation in the Lake District in the 1930s formed an important strand in the discussions which led to the setting up of national parks in England and Wales after the Second World War.

Most of the new conifer plantations were too young to be felled during the Second World War and, after 1945, the work of the Commission continued with extensive new forests being created in areas such as Galloway, the central Scottish Borders and Northumberland. During the same period the need for timber became less critical with the development of new materials and the decline of the mining industry. In the 1940s and 1950s the Forestry Commission had little interest in nature conservation, which they considered got in the way of commercial forestry, but they were more responsive to demands to provide greater access for recreation. The Commission had made some moves towards encouraging access and recreation in some of its forests with the creation of Forest Parks from 1955 onwards. The creation in 1948 of Glenmore Forest Park on the northern slopes of the Cairngorms was a visionary step and overnight stays in National Forest Park sites rose from 15,000 in 1948 to more than a million by 1978 (Lambert, R. A. 2001). From the late 1960s the provision of recreation facilities and amenities became a more central part of their remit, to which was added, from 1974, the protection of the environment, with a more sensitive approach to the conservation of habitats such as wetland sites within existing forests. Today the softening of the formerly sharp edges of plantations, the use of a mixture of conifer species to give more variety of colour and tone, and the addition of screens of deciduous trees along roadsides and trackways has helped to make plantations seem less artificial. Grizedale Forest in the Lake District with a visitor centre, theatre, woodland sculptures and nature trails is one of the most popular attractions in the region.

The debate over the visual character of conifer plantations and their ecological effects crystallised in the 1980s and early 1990s around the question of the afforestation of the Flow Country of Caithness and Sutherland. The area preserves a highly distinctive landscape of blanket peat bog up to five metres deep and lochans (small lakes) with occasional isolated hills. Much of it was once wooded, in mid-post-glacial times, with a mixture of birch, alder and pine. But the onset of wetter conditions caused the trees to be replaced by peat from around 7000

BC. Although not particularly rich in species, the flora and fauna are very distinctive with plants such as dwarf birch, crowberry and sundew, and breeding birds such as greenshank, golden plover, dunlin and curlew.

As a habitat the Flow Country is significant not just in European, but in world terms. The area had been grazed by livestock for centuries, but with only a moderate impact on the distinctive ecosystems. The development of deer stalking and grouse shooting in the mid-nineteenth century led to the 'improvement' of many areas of bog by drainage and burning. The Forestry Commission tried some small-scale, mainly unsuccessful, planting early in the twentieth century. It was not until the spread of private forestry during the late 1970s that the landscape began to be altered on a large scale as landowners exploited tax advantages and began to plant large plantations of Lodgepole pine and Sitka spruce. Soon a single firm was planting 9,880 acres (4,000ha) a year. By 1988 more than 148,000 acres (60,000ha) had been planted; part private, part Forestry Commission. The plantations required networks of drainage channels to dry out the surface peat – affecting peatlands well beyond the plantations. The drainage channels increased run-off to streams and rivers. The addition of fertilisers to the acid soils led to nutrient enrichment of the lakes, causing algal blooms, while the native bird species as well as the original vegetation cover were replaced. In a reaction against the damage being done to the landscape the Nature Conservancy Council scheduled extensive areas as Sites of Special Scientific Interest (SSSIs). In addition, in 1995 the Royal Society for the Protection of Birds (RSPB) bought 18,000 acres (7,200ha) of peatland at Forsinard in Sutherland as a wildlife refuge. Extensive areas of the surviving peat bogs have been preserved, but the halting of afforestation was due as much to changes in tax regulations after 1988 (Atherden 1992).

Today woodland covers some 11 per cent of Britain and around 23 per cent of the uplands. Landscapes in some areas have been drastically altered as a result; Britain, like other developed countries, has gone through a 'forest transition' in the twentieth century in which, after centuries of deforestation, the area under woodland has started to expand again (Mather 2004). Conifers are normally felled only when they are at least forty-five years old, so that there is a long time lag between policy changes and their visual effect on the landscape. As new generations grow up accustomed to conifer plantations as part of the view rather than an alien intrusion, however, perceptions of woodlands are likely to change again.

Drought on the American Great Plains

Between the Mississippi and the Rockies lie the Prairies, the grasslands of America, a vegetation type which is, to a certain extent, the result of lack of precipitation, but whose boundaries with the eastern forests seem to have been at least partly culturally determined by the use of fire. To the east of this area is the region known as the Mid West, associated with maize, pigs and fat cattle. To the west are the Great Plains, specialising in wheat. The western boundary of the Great Plains is formed by the Rocky Mountains, but the eastern boundary is much less clear.

The Great Plains contain a substantial proportion of the best arable land in the USA: fertile, flat and – for part of their area at least – with adequate rainfall in most years. But the higher parts of the Plains, increasingly in the rain shadow of the Rockies as one moves west, gradually become drier and in this area prospects for arable farming are less certain. The climate is a semi-arid one and a failure to recognise the reality of this lies at the root of the problems that the population of the area has experienced in the last 130 years. The Great Plains are an area where significant short-term fluctuations in precipitation are the rule rather than the exception, an area which has been perceived in markedly different ways at various times over the last two centuries. After more than a century of settlement, western society has not fully adapted to the harshness of the environment. The modern history and landscape of the Great Plains is as much the product of particular sets of perceptions and attitudes as of environmental changes.

Since the start of European settlement in the later nineteenth century

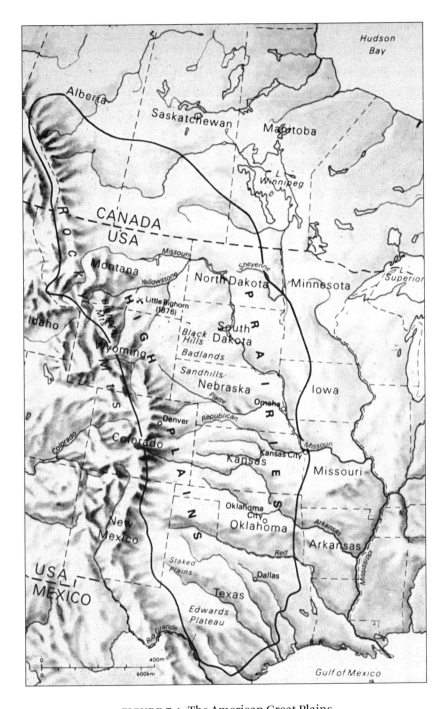

FIGURE 7.1 The American Great Plains

a number of droughts of varying intensity have occurred. Tree-ring evidence suggests the existence of a cycle, with droughts around every twenty-two years going back for several centuries. In the longer term the Great Plains have experienced many periods of severe drought over the past 2,000 years. A study of the diatom assemblages from Moon Lake, North Dakota, which are sensitive to changes in lake salinity and thus indirectly measure variations in precipitation, has shown that severe drought was more frequent and persistent before around AD 1200 than has been the case in recent centuries (Laird et al. 1996). After 1200 climate shifted quite abruptly into the modern mode, which – for all the problems Great Plains farmers have experienced – is a relatively wet one by comparison (Schubert et al. 2004). But within this modern, wetter regime, major droughts have still occurred. Dendrochronological data show that there was a particularly severe one in the south west between AD 1276 and AD 1299, which forced the Anasazi people to abandon their cliff settlements in places like Chaco Canyon. Other severe droughts occurred during the fifteenth and sixteenth centuries.

The seventeenth century, with the widespread introduction of the horse to native society in central North America, saw the development of the Plains Indian culture, which was well adapted to the environment. In the early nineteenth century the Great Plains were an area which European settlers simply had to get across in order to reach the west coast, rather than an objective in itself. Early explorers such as Lewis and Clark, who may have first penetrated the region during a particularly dry phase, coined the term 'Great American Desert' to describe it, an off-putting name which decorated maps of the USA for many decades. The name 'Great Plains' began to be used more widely after the Civil War, particularly in promotional material circulated by the railway companies, which were keen to boost traffic by bringing in settlers. Down to the 1890s there was a widespread belief among professional people as well as farmers that 'rain follows the plough' – that ploughing and cultivating the Prairie soils would somehow actually make the climate moister. The science involved in such a relationship was rather vague, but the concept was eagerly seized on by developers.

Some professionals working for the government seem to have had a more realistic appreciation of the severity of the drought hazard in this region, but their views did not gain widespread support (Bowden, M. J. 1976).

Settlement of the Prairies began in the late nineteenth century. Under the Homestead Act of 1862 a farmer had to live on his 160-acre (64ha) claim and cultivate it for five years before he could claim title to it. The eastern margins of the grasslands in Illinois, Wisconsin and Minnesota were settled down to around 1870 by Yankees from the north east, with a tradition of wheat farming; then, after 1870, by their children and by people born in Norway and Germany. In the late nineteenth century the northern part of the Plains was occupied by German-speaking Russian immigrants with experience of the steppes of southern Russia and a tradition of building sod houses by cutting up the tough prairie turf in blocks. Mennonite immigrants from the Ukrainian Steppes of south Russia also introduced hard winter wheat, a strain better suited to the Great Plains environment than the varieties of winter wheat previously in use. Between 1873 and 1883 some 18,000 of them settled in Kansas, Nebraska and the Dakotas (Conzen 1990). The central area of the grasslands, south of Chicago, which was settled by groups from the middle part of the east coast, contained some extensive areas of wet prairie which required artificial drainage, but yielded large grain crops. From the mid-1850s Kansas and Nebraska were opened up for settlement and, by the 1880s, were being vigorously promoted by the railway companies. After 1900 Chicago-based railway companies were encouraging settlement in western Oklahoma and Texas. The advertising campaigns mounted by the railway companies – aimed at attracting farmers from the eastern USA and from Europe – rivalled those of any modern 'hard sell' advertising with their exaggerated, over-optimistic claims.

Disease and the wholesale slaughter of the buffalo herds rapidly reduced the numbers of native North Americans on the Great Plains in the later nineteenth century. Initially the Plains were used for open range ranching; between 1867 and 1885, while the frontier of arable

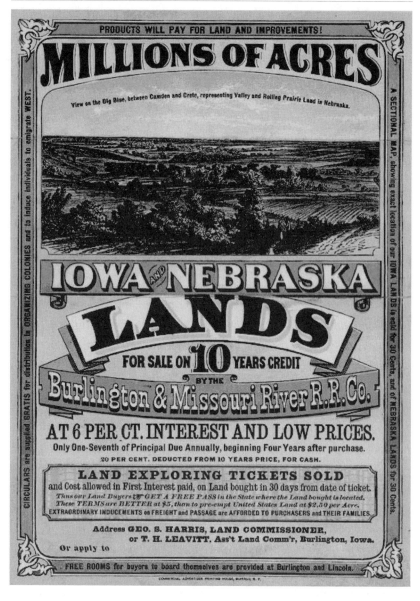

FIGURE 7.2 Railway company advertisement promoting Iowa and Nebraska

farming paused at the margins of the Plains, the legendary cattle drives from Texas to the railheads in Kansas occurred. In some areas ranchers grazed four times as many cattle as the grasslands could support, leading to lasting damage to vegetation and soils. Overgrazing and the bad winter of 1887–88, however, helped to bring about a collapse in the ranching economy and the farmers moved in. As the frontier of settlement pushed west there was little attempt to alter the scale or nature of enterprises to suit ever more marginal conditions. For instance, large cattle ranches were split up into the standard 160-acre (64ha) farm units under the Homestead Act of 1862 even where much larger units, worked less intensively, would have been far more suitable. The first wave of Plains settlers peaked in the mid-1870s before the onset of drier conditions in the late 1880s and early 1890s. By 1890 there were some six million settlers in the region. Between 1881 and 1904, out of twenty-four years, fifteen had below average rainfall. The drought was not accompanied by large-scale wind erosion, as happened in the 1930s, because so much of the area was still unploughed. With limited reserves and no federal or state assistance, many of the first settlers fared badly: some literally died of starvation; others, bankrupt and broken, gave up. Immigration to the area ceased and many people moved out. Some counties lost 30, 60 even 90 per cent of their population.

The early twentieth century brought above-average rainfall for a number of years and another speculative boom in land ensued. Any lessons from the 1890s were rapidly forgotten. Historians of the American frontier, such as Frederick Jackson Turner, had laid emphasis on the ability of settlers to conquer and control the environment. Even the language used by the settlers was aggressive and invasive: they talked of 'busting' or 'breaking' the land. The idea of nature placing restraints on what humans could do was not entertained. The crop failures of the 1890s began to be blamed not on drought, but on the inadequacy of the farmers. The 1910s saw the last big homesteading rush in the Dakotas and eastern Montana. Over 100,000 immigrants had settled in North Dakota between 1879 and 1886, but a further 250,000 arrived between 1898 and 1915. Many of them were homesteaders taking 160-acre plots, but in the Red River valley huge farms covering tens of thousands of acres were bought by investors from the east.

High wheat prices during and immediately after the First World

War, accompanied by favourable rainfall, led to the ploughing up of the Prairies on an unprecedented scale. In 1919 wheat prices were 2.5 times those of 1914. A depression in the cattle market made many ranchers sell their land to speculators, who paid $3–4 per acre for it and sold it to eastern farmers for $30–40 per acre. Equally, lower prices in the early 1920s and the Great Depression of the 1930s forced farmers to cultivate as much land as they could. The record harvest of 1926 allowed many farmers to buy tractors and put millions more acres under the plough. As the area under wheat increased, the remaining pasture areas were badly damaged by overgrazing. The availability of petrol-driven tractors and combine harvesters reduced farmers' labour inputs and costs, but to make the machinery pay they had to become more highly specialised, commercialised wheat producers, running highly mechanised factory farms, abandoning the more diversified, partly self-sufficient, but more flexible farming systems that their fathers had used. Inevitably, the enormous increase in grain surpluses from the region had a disastrous effect on prices when demand fell. Additionally, the recovery of European farming, in the aftermath of the First World War, reduced demand for American wheat and cut the prices that farmers were able to obtain. Faced with growing financial pressure, farmers responded in the only way open to them: by cultivating even more land.

Then came disaster. In 1930 the region was still seen as a prosperous one compared with the Depression-hit industrial east. Farmers were more cushioned than urban workers from the impact of the Depression. But weather conditions in 1930 sounded a warning with a shortage of rain affecting many parts of the Mid West. The year 1931 produced a bumper crop, although the resulting low prices forced some farmers to sell out. Many of the recently arrived farmers were only just beginning to pay off their debts when the drought struck. In 1931 drier conditions began to shift westwards to the Great Plains, affecting North and South Dakota and much of Montana; 1932 was an even drier year, 1933 was worse and during 1934–36 the drought was severe, affecting nineteen states.

The worst area – the classic 'Dust Bowl' – covered nearly 100 million acres (40m. ha), a third of the Great Plains. The drought was also accompanied by extreme temperature; in 1934 hundreds of people in Colorado, Kansas, Oklahoma and Texas died from the heat. There had been droughts before, but not as severe as those of the 1930s. A dust storm in May 1934 dropped a layer of Great Plains soil 1,500 miles away in Washington DC and beyond into the Atlantic. The winds carried 350 million tons of topsoil out of the region. It is no wonder that some farmers thought that the Second Coming was imminent. When the dust storms abated they left behind them an epidemic of respiratory infections. Drifting topsoil formed dunes and exposed an infertile, hard subsoil. Ten million acres (4m. ha) lost at least the upper five inches (12cm) of soil, and 13.5 million more (5.4m. ha) at least 2.5 inches (6cm). Loss of topsoil averaged over 400 tons per acre.

The threat of widespread malnutrition quickly led to the provision of government aid. In the worst year, 1936, 21 per cent of all rural families on the Great Plains were receiving relief, a figure that rose to 90 per cent in the worst-affected counties. By 1936 more than two million farmers were being paid relief. Over 3.5 million people gave up farming and left the area, loading their possessions on to trucks and, abandoning their farms, slipping away to avoid creditors, many of them heading for the west coast, an exodus memorably described by John Steinbeck in *The Grapes of Wrath* (1939) (Yancey 2004). So severe and widespread was the agricultural crisis caused by the drought that it prolonged the Depression and had worldwide impacts. The drought of the 1930s was seen by many as a short-term problem, though: wheat yields had been good in the 1920s and favourable years returned during the 1940s. Others, more far-sighted, realised that the basic problem was that farmers were trying to impose on the Great Plains an agricultural system that ignored environmental constraints under a climatic regime where annual rainfall fluctuated wildly around an average which itself was barely adequate to give good crops.

Attitudes and values, then, were as much a cause of the Dust Bowl era as the environment. Gradually, as a result of the disaster, ideas began to change. The Great Plains Committee, established in 1936, made considerable efforts to alter the mind-sets of farmers. Nevertheless, deep-seated attitudes were hard to overcome: the idea that the family farm was the source of good human values, as demonstrated in so many American films and television series, was so deeply embedded in the national psyche that it was hard to challenge. The assumption that such farms were inherently environmentally friendly compared with large commercial ones was also deeply ingrained, along with the belief that farmers should be able to do whatever they liked on their own property. Following the 1930s droughts a range of soil and moisture conservation measures, such as deep ploughing (leaving alternate strips of land in fallow to conserve moisture), contour ploughing and the planting of shelter belts, were advocated by agricultural colleges and were widely adopted (Conzen 1990).

The boom-and-bust/moist-and-drought cycle repeated itself with price-depressing surpluses followed by drought in the 1950s, though with less severe effects than in the 1930s. Drought began in the south-western Plains in 1950 then spread to Oklahoma, Kansas and Nebraska by 1953, affecting ten states by the time it peaked in 1956. Extensive areas were declared Federal Drought Disaster Areas. Drought struck again in the 1970s, particularly in 1977 when severe wind erosion affected millions of acres. In 1987–89 the most widespread and persistent drought since the 1950s affected the region. In economic terms it proved to be the most expensive drought in US history, with losses amounting to some 39 billion dollars, and it demonstrated that despite soil conservation measures the Great Plains still remained vulnerable to rainfall variability. Blowing topsoil in drier than average years has remained a problem, affecting states such as South Dakota in 1995–96. At the turn of the twenty-first century drought has recently affected many parts of the region yet again. Between 1999 and 2001 on the northern Great Plains most weather stations recorded record low precipitation. There are concerns that global warming could expose a larger area of the plains to the impacts of drought (Sauchin et al. 2003).

In the post-Second World War period the provision of irrigation water seemed to offer the prospect of assisting farmers in drier years.

Water from the west slope of the Front Range of the Rockies was transported eastwards under the watershed in a 33km-long tunnel, while the potential of other, more local, sources of surface water was maximised. Even more dramatic was the discovery and exploitation of a huge underground water source in the Oglala Aquifer underlying some 250,000sq. km of Colorado, Nebraska and Texas. But the water in the aquifer is 'fossil' water, which accumulated over a million years ago and is not being recharged under present climatic conditions. So it is a finite resource, which is being used up at an increasing rate.

It seems that a failure to accurately appreciate the extent of the threat posed by the drought hazard has been a perennial problem on the Great Plains since the 1890s, when farmers from the wetter east began to settle the region. In a classic early study of behavioural geography, published in 1966, Thomas Saarinen considered how Great Plains farmers perceived the drought hazard. He found that farmers were well aware of the threat of drought, but they nevertheless consistently tended to underestimate its frequency and, correspondingly, to exaggerate the number of really good years. Lacking accurate climatic data, they often fitted the cycles into preconceived, often biblical, time frameworks, such as the seven good and the seven lean years of Joseph's Egypt. The more arid the area, however, the closer were the farmers' estimates to reality; older, more experienced farmers tended to have better perceptions than younger ones

The problems of early settlers on the Great Plains were due in part to the speed at which immigration and development occurred. Farmers did not have sufficient time to adjust to the new conditions before the first serious drought occurred. Following this, market forces helped to force some adjustments, such as an increase in average farm size to more viable levels. Nevertheless, a streak of stubbornness – call it dogged determination or a reluctance to face reality – together with an urge to maximise income during short-term boom periods without sufficient thought to the long-term consequences, has reduced the rate at which farmers have adapted.

The Dust Bowl has been identified by George Borgstrom (1973) as one of the three worst ecological blunders in human history. The other two were the deforestation of the Chinese uplands around 3000 BC and the destruction of the Mediterranean forests (Chapter 5). It was not a uniquely American phenomenon, however. Between 1954 and 1965 President Khrushchev authorised the ploughing of 40 million hectares of virgin land in southern Russia, Kazakhstan and Siberia. Drought in the 1960s led to damage by wind erosion to some 17 million hectares. A similar pattern of underestimating the severity of the environment and overestimating the capacity for modern technology to overcome problems led to another huge ecological disaster with major social and economic dimensions.

CHAPTER 8

The Modern Less Developed World

Sea Level Change and Vulnerable Coastal Areas

There is a growing consensus that global warming has occurred during the last century, with a rise in mean global air temperatures of about 0.7°c. The problems of calculating such a figure, and of distinguishing any real long-term trend from the background noise of short-term global, regional and local variations, are considerable, but need not concern us here. But if the existence of a warming trend is accepted for the moment (and by no means all climatologists agree that it has occurred), it is still uncertain whether such a rise is the result of human modification of the climate system, principally through an increase in the amount of greenhouse gases such as carbon dioxide and methane in the atmosphere, or whether the trend is a purely natural one. In Europe, for example, the level of recent warming has barely taken us back to the temperatures of the twelfth and thirteenth centuries AD; we are still within the range of natural variation of the climate.

One of the most publicised side effects of global warming is a rise in mean sea level due principally to the thermal expansion of the oceans and the melting of land-based glaciers and ice caps. The Intergovernmental Panel on Climatic Change (IPCC) has claimed that over the last century world sea levels have risen by 18cm (7in.), at an average rate of 1.8mm per year and that the rise is likely to accelerate to 50cm (19.5in.) during the twenty-first century, or about 5mm a year (Warrick et al. 1993). In some parts of the world a rise on this scale will cause inconvenience and expense, but for some small island states in tropical areas like the Caribbean, the Indian Ocean and the Pacific, a rise of sea level on the scale predicted will threaten their very survival. The south and central Pacific Ocean is scattered with thousands of coral atolls, many of which are inhabited only along narrow coastal strips. These coral atolls are geologically recent features, with elevations generally less than five metres above mean sea level. Such island states are already vulnerable to short-term weather phenomena such as hurricanes, which regularly cause damage and devastation to property, infrastructure and agricultural land. Between 1958 and 1994 the southern Pacific experienced more than twenty major cyclones and, since 1990, cyclones in this area have caused more than 6,000 deaths. In many small island states high population densities and rapid population growth at rates of up to 4 per cent per annum are putting an increasingly severe strain on existing resources. Rising sea levels pose yet another potentially serious problem.

In this section we look, first, at the threats posed to island groups, in particular the Maldives and Tuvalu. But many larger countries with extensive coastal lowlands would also be threatened by a sea level rise linked to global warming. In Bangladesh a one-metre rise could displace 60 per cent of the population. In China it would threaten seventy million people and in Japan half of the country's industry. Other states, such as the Philippines and Indonesia, would also be at serious risk. In the second part of this section we consider Bangladesh in more detail.

Small Island States

It is in the smaller island groups that the problem seems most pressing. In countries like the Maldives in the Indian Ocean and Tuvalu in the Pacific, the main islands are less than four metres above mean sea level and much of the area is less than two metres. In addition to the threat of sea level rise there is a concern that more frequent and more violent tropical cyclones and higher storm surges could totally overwhelm them. Even islands away from the main tropical storm tracks could be affected by the higher seas and swells associated with cyclones. In some groups the main islands are protected from the worst of tropical cyclones by outer coral reef barriers. Small rises in mean sea level could submerge these and expose the islands behind them to increased erosion. And although coral reefs do grow in response to sea level rises, some marine experts fear that the speed of change may be too rapid for them to respond to. Others point to the danger that higher sea temperatures may bleach the coral and kill it off entirely.

Small island groups are especially vulnerable to sea level rise for a wide range of reasons in addition to their lack of altitude. Their areas and their resources are limited. Their economies are often weak due to their isolation and their distance from markets. Their economic options are limited. Some countries, such as the Maldives, have developed successful tourist industries. In fact, in the Maldives tourism accounts for 95 per cent of GNP. But industries like tourism are vulnerable, not only to changes of fashion, but to environmental fluctuations. Most of the infrastructure of such island groups, as well as their population, is concentrated close to the sea. Their population densities are high and, in some cases, total numbers are growing steadily. Small island states lack the resources either to protect themselves from sea level rise or to adapt to it. And although mangrove systems in Pacific states like Fiji provide valuable protection for coastal areas, they are under pressure from a range of influences such as reclamation for sugar cultivation and for construction projects.

Tuvalu is a string of coral atolls whose highest point is only 4.6m. above sea level and where most of the area does not reach more than 2m. above sea level. Formerly a British possession known as the Ellice Islands, they lie some 1050km (650 miles) north of Fiji. The area of Tuvalu is a mere 26sq. km, making it the world's fourth smallest state, and 40 per cent of this is already uninhabitable due to the removal of coral and the creation of an airstrip dug out of the coral by the Americans during the Second World War. Because of its small area and low altitude Tuvalu has been described as the world's first victim of global warming. In 1997 Bikenibeu Paeniu, the Prime Minister of Tuvalu, told Greenpeace that sea level change was an urgent and critical issue for his country. The previous month a severe cyclone had devastated one of the outer islands of the group. Tidal flooding has been increasingly common in recent years, with salt water seeping into the limited areas of arable land. The government of Tuvalu has asked both Australia and New Zealand to accept their 11,000 inhabitants as 'climate refugees' if future sea level rise should force an emergency evacuation: both countries have refused, despite the offer of the government of Tuvalu to purchase two uninhabited islands in the Torres Strait to rehouse their population. New Zealand, however, already takes seventy-five Tuvaluans a year and offers all the islanders a three-month visa-free visit in order to help them find work. The Australian government has promised help in the event of the islands being swamped in the future, but there is a worry among leaders in Tuvalu that such belated assistance may be too slow. This has led to debate over whether more developed nations should accept refugees from such countries, based on the size of their populations or their calculated contribution to greenhouse gas emissions. Small island states contribute less than 1 per cent of global greenhouse gas emissions, yet seem to be most at risk from the atmospheric pollution generated by larger, wealthier nations.

But never mind global figures for a moment: how much has sea level risen specifically in relation to Tuvalu? It is difficult to answer this question. A run of measurements for at least twenty years and preferably for between fifty and eighty years is needed to establish clear trends in mean sea level at any location. Yet here, as for so much of the southern hemisphere, tide gauge information for more than a short run of years does not exist. An analysis of data from 1978 onwards, combining readings collected by the University of Hawaii Sea Level Centre and the Australian National Tidal Facility, has been interpreted to show that there is a 68 per cent probability that an annual rise of between 1.1 and 2.77mm/year has occurred, a magnitude similar to that of the IPCC's global estimates. By no means all scientists, however, are agreed that such trends have actually occurred at Tuvalu (Eschenbach 2004).

There is no doubt about the environmental problems currently being faced in Tuvalu, though. Groundwater resources are becoming undrinkable due to contamination by sea water. Pits, used for growing the root crop taro, are also being flooded. In addition, increased variability in weather conditions is causing more frequent periods of drought. Coastal erosion, claimed by some to be due to increased cyclonic activity, has been eating away at the coral. Other people have blamed the extraction of sand for construction, leading to eroded beaches, as a major cause of the increased flooding. In addition long-term changes in hydrology may have resulted from Second World War construction activity (Connell 2003).

The Maldives are a larger island group than Tuvalu, with some 1,196 islands, again mostly below 2m. in altitude but supporting a much larger population of 311,000. Their potential situation in the event of sea level rise is just as serious as that of Tuvalu, however. In 1987 and 1991 storm surges flooded a number of the islands including the airport and a third of the capital. Nearly a third of the 200 inhabited islands are currently threatened by beach erosion. Under the IPCC's scenario most of the country is set to be flooded in the next fifty to one hundred years. The problems of the islands, however, have undoubtedly been worsened by the quarrying of coral offshore for construction work linked to the rapidly developing tourist industry. The cost of protecting the Maldives from projected sea level rise has been estimated at 34 per cent of the country's GDP. The comparable figure for the United Kingdom is 0.02 per cent (Warrick et al. 1993).

Construction projects such as hotels, roads and airports depend on the dredging of coral as a source of aggregates. This may weaken reefs directly. It may also weaken them indirectly, through pollution killing off the coral or by increasing the depth of water offshore, which allows larger waves to attack the reefs. The health of reefs and their ability to keep up with sea level rise may be damaged by over-intensive fishing causing damage to the coral. Coral bleaching episodes occur especially during El Niño events, when warmer water affects the health of the reefs. It is not clear how reef and beach systems will respond to sea level rise; more understanding of the dynamics of reef systems is needed.

In the Maldives coral reefs have the capacity to grow in response to sea level rise and mangroves play an important part in coastal protection. So it is important to understand the dynamic response of coral and mangroves to sea level rise. Retreat from the coast is not a feasible option for the populations of small island states and careful management and planning is needed to address the threats of possible sea level rise (Morner 2001).

Flooding in Bangladesh

Bangladesh is situated between the north Indian Ocean and the Himalayas. This location gives the country its monsoons, vital for agriculture, but also exposes it to periodic catastrophic disasters, which include tropical cyclones, storm surges and floods, bringing loss of life on a massive scale. With its low topography and high population density, Bangladesh is already one of the world's poorest and most vulnerable countries as far as natural disasters are concerned, particularly in its coastal areas, but it is under threat of even greater disasters if predicted sea level rises actually occur.

Bangladesh is a deltaic plain of three huge rivers, the Ganges, Brahmaputra and Meghna, bringing huge amounts of sediment into the Bay of Bengal. Bangladesh has 24,000km of rivers, covering 7 per cent of the area. The coastal zone has important fisheries, the major ports of Chittagong and Mongla, many industrial complexes, prospects for oil and gas, and the area is especially fertile for rice production. With an area of 147,570 square kilometres and a population of 130 million there is an average density of 874 persons per square kilometre. About a tenth of the country is less than a metre above mean sea level. Over much of the delta when flooding occurs it is by fresh water ponded back by high tides in the Bay of Bengal. Settlement can cover 40 per cent of the land in the most densely populated areas (Warrick et al. 1993).

A rise in mean sea level of only 10cm would submerge 2 per cent of the country. A 30cm rise would affect 5 per cent and a one-metre rise 10 per cent. Some of this flooding would be due to the direct impacts of sea level rise, but some of it to the effects of higher sea levels in backing up flood waters from the rivers, especially the Meghna, causing the inundation of agricultural lands on either side well inland from the coast, an effect which could be increased by monsoon winds and storm surges. If the strength of the monsoons were to increase due to global warming, as some climatologists have suggested, this could worsen flood effects.

The Bay of Bengal is a notorious source area for tropical cyclones and Bangladesh has a particularly bad record for suffering from their effects. More than half the world's tropical cyclones with a fatality rate of over 5,000 people have occurred in Bangladesh. There seems, so far, to be no long-term trend for the frequency of cyclones in this area to increase, but predictions are that the intensity, if not the number, of cyclones may rise in the future due to global warming. Casualties during cyclones are due mainly to storm surges, which can reach heights of ten metres or more above mean sea level. Storm surges have, in the past, penetrated as much as 100km inland. A rise of sea surface temperatures of 2°C is predicted to increase storm surge heights by 21 per cent with increased penetration of flood waters inland of 13 per cent. The 1970 storm surge killed over 250,000 people. In 1991 a cyclone caused a death toll of at least 138,000 people. In 1998 a flood, the worst in at least a hundred years, lasted for seventy-eight days. Sea level rise will increase the intrusion of saline water inland, contaminating groundwater resources and affecting agriculture, particularly rice production.

Sea level rise also threatens the area known as the Sundarbans, the largest single mangrove forest in the world, and puts at risk the wide range of mammals and birds that inhabit it. The forests also protect densely populated areas inland from storm surges.

For Bangladesh a simple superimposition of a higher sea level on the existing coastline is not enough for future emergency planning purposes, as the complicated dynamic processes involved are not taken into account. The most likely adverse effect of sea level rise is inland flooding due to higher river bed levels and levees relative to the surrounding countryside.

Measuring Sea Level Change

Variations in sea level are nothing new. During the last interglacial, some 120,000 years ago, when mean temperatures were a little greater than now, sea level was some 5–6m. higher than today, possibly due in part to the melting of substantial volumes of Antarctic ice. At the height of the last glaciation, around 18,000 years ago, when mean temperatures were some 5°C colder than they are now, sea levels were around 140m. lower due to the massive amounts of water locked up in land-based ice sheets. Following the break-up of the North American ice sheet, around 8,000 years ago, sea level rose by nearly half a metre a year for short periods and continued to rise by about 6–12mm a year until about 6,000 years ago (Tooley and Jelgersma 1992). Within historic times, however, the rise had slowed to around 0.1–0.2mm a year. Estimates of sea level rise during the last century are ten times the recorded rate of rise over the last few hundred years.

Worldwide or *eustatic* sea level changes are usually what is referred to in predictions of the likely impacts of global warming. Measurements of mean sea level are made more difficult by the effects of atmospheric pressure: sea level can rise 1cm for every millibar fall in pressure. El Niño events can change sea level by 20–30cm along the Pacific coast of South America.

Some scientists, such as Gornitz (1993), believe that an upward trend in mean sea level can be detected from existing data after the careful extraction of background 'noise', but others do not. Gornitz has suggested that the rise over the last century has been of the order of 1–2mm per year, but with no acceleration in recent decades, a rise which is an order of magnitude higher than in previous centuries (Warrick and Farmer 1990).

But not all scientists agree with the IPCC's claim that global sea levels have in fact risen substantially during the last century and are set to rise at an accelerated rate in the future. Sea level can be measured directly by hourly readings of tide gauges and indirectly from satellite altimetry. Tide gauge data in western Europe go back to 1700 for Amsterdam and 1805 for Brest, but most records of sea level variation around the coasts of the North Atlantic area are far shorter than this. Runs of data extending back beyond recent times are much rarer in the southern hemisphere. Nearly 90 per cent of tide gauge stations are north of twenty-three degrees north – although some 70 per cent of the world's coastlines also lie in this area. A long time series is required to remove the effects not just of short-term tidal cycles, but also the 18.6-

year cycle related to the moon's orbit. When the trends of many long data sets from tide gauges in the northern hemisphere are examined they do tend to suggest that a rise of sea level relative to the land has occurred. At Brest this has been of the order of 200mm since 1805, a change of over 1mm per year. At Aberdeen there appears to have been a rise of only 7cm from 1862.

But is it the sea that is rising or the land that is falling? Many tide gauges, especially those with long runs of data, tend to be located in long-established major ports. Urbanisation, with the increasing weight of brick, stone and concrete pressing on the underlying rocks, tends to cause the subsidence of the land surface relative to sea level in coastal locations, so producing a rise in sea level relative to the land. One of the most extreme cases is Venice, which is steadily sinking on its medieval wooden piles. Venice has sunk by 30cm during the last century, due substantially to subsidence under its own weight. The removal of groundwater from strata under major port cities can increase this effect, something which has been demonstrated for cities such as Adelaide and Bangkok, where there has been a relative sea level rise of a metre in thirty years (Bird 1993). Land subsidence can be caused by other factors, too. Parts of the English Fenlands have been lowered by 2.3m. since the mid-nineteenth century due to the drying and shrinkage of the reclaimed peat surface (Darby 1956). Tide gauges can also be affected by more local sources of subsidence, as they are often fixed to docks and buildings, and by changes in coastal configuration and tidal patterns, as seems to have happened at Amsterdam with the reclamation of the Zuider Zee.

Other forces that influence relative sea level include tectonic activity. Many tide gauges around the Pacific Rim in areas such as California, Japan and New Zealand, are affected by uplift or subsidence of this nature. Areas that were glaciated during the last Ice Age – principally in the northern hemisphere – are still being affected by isostatic recovery, as the land surface slowly rebounds after being depressed by the weight of ice during the last glaciation. This is a particularly important influence on relative sea levels in northern Europe. At Stockholm, for

192 · World Without End?

example, sea level relative to the land has actually fallen by some 40cm since about 1880 as a result of the land rising. In Britain the north and west of Scotland are still rising by up to 6mm a year. In the Gulf of Bothnia, at the head of the Baltic Sea, the land is still rising as much as 1cm each year; and Finland acquires up to 1,000sq. km of new land each century (Jones, M. 1977). To compensate for such rises, areas just beyond the maximum extent of the former ice sheets – such as south-east England, the Netherlands and parts of the eastern USA – are subsiding. All this means that some tide gauge records may show trends that are the result of a range of local and regional forces totally unconnected with the volume of water in the oceans. In the case of data from areas of isostatic uplift, correction factors are applied to make allowance for the effect of the rebounding land surface. All this means that the IPCC's preferred value of an 18cm rise in mean global sea levels during the twentieth century is not a simple measured value, but the product of the complex manipulation of huge data sets. The accuracy of both the data and the manipulations has been questioned.

Predictions for sea level change in the twenty-first century are based on assessments of the thermal expansion of the oceans due to global warming, and the contribution of melting glaciers, the Greenland ice cap and permafrost. The melting of small glaciers and ice caps, excluding Antarctica and Greenland would, it has been calculated, add another 0.5m. of water to the oceans (Kuhn 1993). Greenland and Antarctica contain around 99 per cent of the world's land ice, but their response to temperature change is very slow (though the ice sheets on the Antarctic peninsula are more sensitive to climatic change). Mountain glaciers and small ice caps, while accounting for only 1 per cent of the world's land ice, are much more sensitive to change than the large ice caps.

Other changes that may affect sea levels include the abstraction of groundwater from underground aquifers which are not recharged under present climatic conditions, representing a new addition to the seas and losses from inland water bodies such as the Caspian and Aral Seas. Adding water to the oceans from landlocked seas may be balanced by increases in the amount of water stored on land in reservoirs. Sea level rise due to the deposition of suspended sediment from rivers is equivalent to 0.004–0.02mm/year of a rise. Additionally, a good deal of moisture is locked up in the permafrost which underlies a quarter of the land area of the northern hemisphere. If air temperatures continue to rise then large areas of this could melt, and though the surplus water would not necessarily all find its way to the sea it has been suggested that this might add another 5cm to global sea level rise by 2100. Figures for each of these sources, however, are estimates with wide margins of error. Mass balance data are available for only a small proportion of the world's glaciers. Most glaciers are retreating, but some, in New Zealand and southern Scandinavia, are actually advancing due to regional-scale changes in climate.

Antarctica's likely contribution to sea level rise, by contrast, has been estimated to be a negative one. Warmer global temperatures are likely to lead to more precipitation falling as snow over the southern continent. In particular it has been claimed that the measured recent rate of increase of carbon dioxide in the atmosphere – around 1.5ppm/year – is substantially less than the figures used in some calculations on which estimates of future sea level rise have been based. Some scientists feel that the computer modelling involved is not sufficiently accurate to provide meaningful results and that the IPCC's predictions are misleading. They point to examples of records from tide gauges in tectonically stable areas of the southern hemisphere, where isostatic recovery is not a problem. Data from stations such as Montevideo in South America, East London in South Africa, and Newcastle in New South Wales, some of them extending back to the 1930s, demonstrate no measurable sea level rise relative to the land. An analysis of Australian tide gauges for stations with reasonable lengths of records has shown that in eleven out of twenty-seven cases sea level appears to have fallen rather than risen. When an overall mean figure is calculated it indicates a rise of only about 0.3mm/year, a sixth of the IPCC's figure.

So, mean sea level remains an elusive concept and both its past trends and predicted future changes are in dispute. Recent satellite measurements of mean sea level have indicated that considerable variation can exist across an ocean such as the Pacific at any one time, with differences of up to 2m. resulting from contrasts in tides, wind and pressure patterns. They can also be interpreted as suggesting that mean sea levels in areas such as the Pacific have actually fallen slightly in recent years rather than risen.

It has been argued that neither the Maldives or Tuvalu are suffering from the effects of sea level rise due to global warming and that relative sea levels have fallen rather than risen during the last twenty to thirty years. Instead it has been claimed that their problems are the result of more localised environmental threats, which are killing off the coral and causing erosion, such as pollution and unsuitable construction projects associated with tourism, which can disrupt the circulation of nutrient-rich waters to the coral polyps and kill them. On this view the governments of small island states need to put their own houses in order before blaming their problems on the world at large. Even if there is disagreement about the trend of global mean sea level, however, there is no doubt that such island states are particularly vulnerable to environmental change, a vulnerability that may well increase in the future and that, without outside financial and technical assistance, their ability to cope will be very limited. The Mississippi delta was in a state of balance, or slowly growing, for thousands of years, but due to human interference, including levee construction and damming of distributaries, wetlands have been starved of sediment and fresh water. Relative sea level in this area is now rising by around a metre a century and up to 1,000sq. km of wetlands are being lost each year. Levee construction and dams reflect a narrow-minded preference for hard engineering solutions to flood problems. Without a broader-based and more flexible strategy, problems caused by rising sea levels are likely to increase substantially within the next few decades.

The Desiccation of the Aral Sea

The drying up of the Aral Sea, the world's fourth largest inland sea after the Caspian Sea, Lake Superior and Lake Victoria, has been

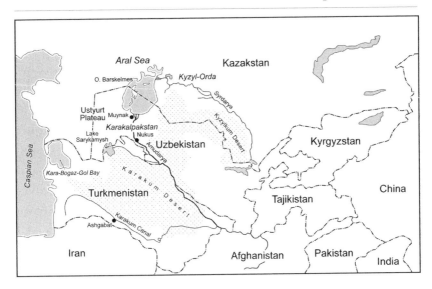

FIGURE 8.1 Location of the Aral Sea

described as one of the most serious environmental disasters of the twentieth century (United Nations 1992; Glantz 1999). The Aral Sea is situated in the semi-desert area on the borders of Kazakhstan and Uzbekistan in Central Asia. In the 1950s it had a surface area of 66,000sq. km, a volume of c.1,090 cubic kilometres, and a maximum depth of 68m. Within four decades the Aral Sea basin has become a world-class environmental disaster. Since the 1960s its area and volume have been shrinking steadily, but the process has accelerated in recent decades. Between 1960 and 1987 its level dropped by nearly 13m., while its area was reduced by 40 per cent. By the opening of the twenty-first century there had been a 53 per cent decrease in surface area and a more than 70 per cent drop in volume (Micklin 1998). The level of the sea's surface has fallen from fifty-three metres to only twenty-eight.

The reduction in the extent of the sea has been due to a reduction in the amount of inflow, caused mainly by the abstraction of water for irrigation. The annual inflow to the sea in 1960 was 63–5 cubic km. Now it is only around 1.5, even though a minimum of 10 cubic km is needed to prevent further shrinkage. As a result of the drying up of the sea severe environmental problems have been experienced.

Major changes in the volume of the sea are not a new phenomenon – abandoned former shorelines and fossils show that there have been major rises and falls of its surface throughout the Holocene, with a range of at least 20m. and possibly over 40m. In the earlier part of the Holocene such changes were purely natural in character, the result of variations in climate and alterations in the courses of the rivers flowing in to the sea. Within the last 3,000 years human societies have played an increasing role through the diversion of water for irrigation and other purposes. Between the late eighteenth century and the first half of the twentieth century, however, the amount of fluctuation was quite small. In the early years of the twentieth century the level of the lake was relatively high and this resulted in a time lag in the late 1950s and early 1960s before the full impact of the new irrigation systems on the sea's hydrology started to become apparent. Nevertheless, the loss of volume since the 1960s has represented the fastest and most marked rate of decline in more than 1,000 years. If shrinkage continues at the present rate only a small saline remnant of the sea will survive within a decade or two.

The recession of the lake shorelines has caused economic, social and health problems as well as environmental ones. For a start the shrinkage of the Aral Sea has had a significant impact on the regional climate in a belt up to 2–300km wide. It was unfortunate that from the mid-1960s until the end of the 1970s a drier climatic phase set in, seemingly naturally, but as the area of the sea was reduced, anthropogenic influences began to push the climate further in the direction of aridity. The climate has shifted to a more continental regime. The waters of the sea at its 1950s level exerted a moderating effect, reducing cold conditions in winter and keeping temperatures down in summer. As a result of the shrinkage of the sea, winters have become longer, colder but snowless, summers shorter, hotter and rainless. One spin-off from this has been a reduction in the length of the growing season, which is putting the future of cotton production at risk in the surrounding irrigated areas: some farmers have been forced to switch from cotton production to rice growing. Ironically, it was in order to expand cotton production that water was diverted from the sea in the first place.

Because the sea is located on a powerful west-to-east airstream the salt crystals from the seabed have been widely scattered – they have been detected in Belorus, more than 1,000km away, and even in snow layers on the Greenland ice cap. The salt has had another unlooked-for effect: its deposition on the surfaces of glaciers in the Himalayas, Pamirs and Altay mountains has enhanced the melting of the glaciers there.

Part of the recent changes in the volume of the sea have been due to climatic shifts: a run of dry years in the 1970s cut discharge into the lake from the Syr Dar'ya and Amu Dar'ya rivers. Dry years continued into the 1980s, but the key factor in causing continued shrinkage has been the abstraction of water for irrigation. The amount of irrigated land in the Aral Sea basin rose from around three million hectares in 1900 to five million by 1960, 6.5 million by 1980 and 7.6 million by 1987. The Kara-Kum Canal, constructed from the mid-1950s, the longest irrigation canal in the old Soviet Union, running for 1,300km from the Amu Dar'ya into the Kara-Kum desert, has been the most significant user of water which would otherwise have gone into the Aral Sea, withdrawing up to 13 cubic km of water a year (Glantz 1999). The irrigation systems were badly designed, unlined, inefficient and poorly maintained. Some 50–60 per cent of the water that they carried never even reached the fields, being lost by seepage and evaporation. Seepage losses from the Kara-Kum Canal in the first five years of its operation were estimated at c.25 cubic km. The cotton crop required around half the available water resources of the two river basins and, other environmental considerations aside, the over-dependence of the region on a single crop, requiring so much irrigation water, was in itself dangerous. Cotton production in the area has trebled since the 1940s (ibid.). Over-intensive cropping of the irrigated soils led to a fall in fertility, which was tackled by an increase in the use of fertilisers, herbicides and pesticides. When these were flushed into the rivers and the Aral Sea itself they caused additional ecological complications.

Some reduction in the size of the sea due to the use of irrigation water had been expected in the original plan, but the possible impacts on local climate and ecosystems had been dismissed as negligible. Few scientists had foreseen that damagingly large amounts of salt would be blown from the dried-out lake bed on to nearby agricultural land, causing serious salinity and loss of productivity. Between 1960 and 1987 around 27,000sq. km of lake bed became exposed. Windblow has spread some of this salt on to land hundreds of kilometres away. It has been estimated that forty-three million metric tons of salt have been blown off the exposed lake bed each year and deposited across an area of up to 200,000sq. km, damaging crops and harming the soil. The dust storms were so serious that Soviet cosmonauts were able to identify them from space. By the end of the 1990s over 2m. ha of agricultural land in the Amu Dar'ya delta were suffering from desertification and the unique forest ecosystem of the area had been largely destroyed.

Within the sea itself fish stocks have been devastated. By the early 1980s, out of twenty-four species of fish, twenty had been killed off; an influx of pesticides from surrounding land used for growing cotton as well as the increasing salinity of the shrunken lake were major causes. Commercial fisheries had declined from an annual catch of 48,000 metric tons in 1957 to zero. By 1982 all commercial fishing had ceased. Local canning plants had closed and fishing villages were abandoned, their boats stranded increasingly far from water by the retreating sea. Damage has been especially severe in the delta areas, where the main rivers flow into the sea. Not only did they once have a rich flora and fauna, they were also a vital source of grazing for livestock, a spawning area for fish, and a major supplier of reeds for industrial uses. As the inflow from the rivers has decreased, the delta areas have dried out, water tables have fallen, and distinctive ecosystems have been devastated; only thirty-eight out of a former 173 animal species had survived by the end of the 1980s and 160 of 319 species of birds. The decline of vegetation has promoted desertification around the sea and a major decline in livestock numbers.

The Aral Sea is not just an environmental disaster. It is a human and a health tragedy, too. The exposure of over 36,000sq. km of former seabed has greatly increased the incidence of dust storms in the region. This is likely to be a factor behind the high incidence of respiratory illness that has been reported from the region, though recent research has shown that in this area, which has suffered from general desiccation of the climate, the Aral Sea is by no means the only source of dust (Wiggs et al. 2003). The region has the highest levels of infant and maternal mortality in the former Soviet Union. Infant mortality is around seventy-five for every 1,000 children born, while in excess of 120 women die per 10,000 births. More than 70 per cent of young women aged between thirteen and nineteen have kidney diseases, 23 per cent have thyroid problems and over 80 per cent of all women are anaemic (Small et al. 2001).

In addition, as desiccation has intensified and the regional economy has collapsed, water supply systems from the Soviet era have begun to break down through inadequate maintenance. As a result supplies of good-quality drinking water have become more and more scarce, forcing many people to take drinking water directly from the irrigation canals, water contaminated with salts, bacteria and pesticides. There have been severe water-borne outbreaks of typhoid and viral hepatitis as a result. Diseases such as anaemia, cancer and tuberculosis are frequent and many children are born with physical defects. Many of these problems can be attributed directly to the drying up of the sea, the spread of dust from the seabed and the impact of the associated changes in climate on agriculture. As a result at least 100,000 people are thought to have fled the region. So severe has the problem of supplying clean drinking water become in the delta of the Amu Dar'ya that a 200km pipeline has had to be built to bring water in from a reservoir upstream. A drop in the quality of drinking water has also been linked to the spread of intestinal diseases and throat cancer.

The economic impact of the shrinkage of the Aral Sea has, inevitably, been severe, affecting as it has agriculture, livestock farming, the fishing industry, transport and living conditions. River inflow by the later 1980s had dwindled to almost nothing and the break-up of the Soviet Union has meant that even those aid schemes that might realistically have been implemented have been cancelled due to lack of resources. The cotton crops remain the main source of revenue for the new independent republics that have been created.

Shrinkage seems set to continue; soon the sea is likely to consist of a main lake in the south, as saline as the ocean, and a series of smaller brine lakes in the north. Continued reduction of the sea's volume could be halted, but irrigation water is vital for the wider economy of people living within the basin of the Aral Sea, where some 90 per cent of the harvest depends on it. The more efficient use of irrigation water (reducing losses by evaporation) would undoubtedly be a help, but this would also be expensive. Partitioning the Aral Sea using embankments to preserve at least a portion of the water in conditions of low salinity has been tried. More drastic are suggestions such as diverting water from rivers such as the Ob and Irtysh, which flow north to the Arctic towards the Aral Sea via a major canal. The ecological implications of such a massive undertaking, however, are far from clear.

Plans to tackle the problem in the 1990s involved the construction of a 14km-long dam to separate the smaller northern part of the sea from the larger southern one, to try to maintain at least part of the sea with a reasonable depth. The dyke was not sufficiently strong, however, and in 1999 it was breached, with a major release of water into the southern part of the sea.

In the Soviet era the various republics had a tradition of non-co-operation when it came to the management of water resources. The fact that several countries were using the water which would once have flowed into the sea undoubtedly exacerbated the problem. There are some signs of greater co-operation today, but this may be too late. There are currently fears that other large inland lakes, like Lake Balkhash, some forty times the size of Lake Geneva and the next largest lake in Central Asia, may be the next to face total extinction.

There have been many studies and evaluations of the problems facing the Aral Sea area – indeed there is a local saying that if every visiting expert brought with them a bucket of water the sea would long since have been replenished! Dramatic images of rusting fishing vessels stranded scores of kilometres from the present shoreline have featured in the *National Geographic* magazine and Sunday colour supplements as an icon and a warning of just how badly things can go wrong when changes in the environment are implemented without sufficient thought. But the actual amount of direct aid that has gone to the people of this area has been comparatively limited. The area still supports some five million people, whose quality of life is deteriorating in step with their surroundings.

The case of the Aral Sea provides an excellent example of how different elements of an environmental system are inter-related and interdependent. You cannot change one element within an environmental system without having an effect on others. By drastically altering the area and volume of the sea the whole system has become destabilised. Arguably, the impact of taking so much irrigation water away from the sea's inflow was foreseeable, and indeed ought to have been foreseen. There is evidence that economic planners did expect a reduction in the volume of the Aral Sea, though presumably not on the scale that actually occurred. But the expansion of the irrigated area in Central Asia with the aim of achieving self-sufficiency in cotton production as part of President Khrushchev's 'virgin lands' scheme, was linked to the need, under the Soviet system, to meet short-term performance targets with no consideration of potential long-term impacts. Economic imperatives prevailed over environmental concerns (Glantz 1999).

This same approach produced some appalling examples of industrial pollution in eastern Europe and contamination of the Barents Sea with nuclear waste (Goldman 1972). And in a post-Soviet climate, matters are scarcely any better; in many respects even worse. Less money is available for projects which might help to ameliorate the situation, such as reducing the loss of irrigation water. Without central control, competition and mutual suspicion between different autonomous republics flourishes. It is easy to criticise the environmental record of the former Soviet Union, whose command economy tried to solve twentieth-century problems with what was essentially a nineteenth-century planning approach. As the example of the Dust Bowl of the

American Great Plains shows, however, the USSR was far from having a monopoly of environmental short-sightedness.

The nature of the environmental changes around the Aral Sea in recent decades – slow-onset, long-term and cumulative – is characteristic of what has been called a creeping environmental problem. Because of their nature, such problems do not attract attention or remedial measures until the scale of the disaster is too great. Various stages of awareness of creeping environmental problems have been identified:

1   Early warnings about a problem
2   Threshold 1 – awareness of change
3   Threshold 2 – awareness of a problem
4   Threshold 3 – awareness of a crisis
5   Threshold 4 – awareness of a need for action
6   Threshold 5 – action

Sadly, while the problem of the Aral Sea has gone through stages 1–5, little has so far been achieved with regard to stage 6. In some recent years the inflow into the Aral Sea has approached zero (Glantz 1999).

Hard Engineering: the Three Gorges Dam in China

In recent decades large dam schemes have had a unique hold on human imagination, symbolising the technological progress of humanity, 'taming' its 'wild' rivers whose waters would otherwise be 'wasted'. Large dams are more than a means of generating electricity – they express the domination of the technological age over nature, they are icons of scientific progress and economic development, major status symbols for both developing and developed nations. On the less positive side, large dams have also been described as being to a nation's development what nuclear bombs are to its military arsenal – they are both weapons of mass destruction. In this section we look at some of the problems arising from the macro-scale human interference with river systems resulting from the construction of such dams, focusing on a particular example from China.

The World Commission for Dams, in its final report in 2000, has shown that there are some 40,000 large dams worldwide, all but 5,000 of them constructed since 1950. The term 'large dam' is usually taken to mean one at least fifteen metres high. China had eight dams of this size in 1949 but more than 19,000 in 2000. In the year 2000 the USA had 6,575 and India had 4,291. Between 1996 and 2001 around one thousand new large dams were built worldwide. The rate of construction of new dams peaked in the 1980s and has been falling steadily since, partly because many of the best sites have already been exploited, but also as a result of growing opposition, regionally and internationally, to the impact of such schemes. There is increasing concern that large dams often have massive negative impacts on nature and society in areas both upstream and downstream from them, and that the objectives of such schemes could often have been achieved in less grandiose, less expensive and less destructive ways (McCully 2001; Scudder 2001).

The World Bank – the largest funding body of this kind of project – is cutting back on the number of schemes it supports. One reason is the poor economic performance of such projects. The technical and economic record of big dam and irrigation schemes has been described as appalling. At best many large dams are only marginally viable economically. Multi-purpose projects tend to fare worse than more specialist schemes. Although around half the world's large dams have been built primarily for irrigation, they have, at most, contributed to only 12–16 per cent of world food production.

The two main functions of large dams are, first, to store water – either to compensate for fluctuations in river flow or to meet the demand for hydroelectric power. Second, they raise water levels to enable it to be diverted to a canal for navigation and irrigation or to generate power (a fifth of the world's electricity comes from hydroelectric sources), providing water for agriculture and industry, controlling floods and aiding navigation. Power generation capacity is a function of the volume of flow and the head of water.

As a result of poor planning, poor construction standards or fraudulent diversion of funds, the overrun of construction costs on large dam projects is often massive. Large dam schemes have often been poorly designed with major unexpected technical problems and long delays. In addition they have often failed to generate the expected power output. Geological data and hydrological information have often been inadequate or, where available, ignored. The very scale of such projects can also have unforeseen results: large dams can, for example, trigger earthquakes as a result of water under pressure being forced into cracks and lubricating geological faults already under stress. Attempts to control flooding by damming rivers may only increase the damage that is done: average floods may be eradicated, but the impact of major floods can be disastrously increased (McCully 2001).

Dams may be constructed to supply irrigation water to increase crop yields over a wide area, but they also destroy cultivated land by flooding, with some of the best-quality soils being affected. Around the world an estimated 400,000sq. km or more of land has been lost to reservoir flooding, much of it fertile alluvial land. Once a dam is built, the character of the river channel downstream can change rapidly. Sediment below the dam is removed, and is not replaced from upstream as the reservoir becomes a gigantic sediment trap. The river bed below the dam becomes an 'armoured' one of bare rock, which may wipe out spawning grounds for fish. Without a supply of sediment the river bed below a major dam may quickly become deepened. In the case of the High Dam at Aswan on the Nile, around 98 per cent of the sediment formerly deposited each year at flood time on the alluvial valley floor is now trapped by the Nasser Reservoir. The lack of fertilising silt, the traditional 'gift of the river' in ancient times, has resulted in the greatly increased use of artificial fertilisers to maintain soil fertility. Apart from the cost, this causes problems with pollution as chemicals are washed into the river. Reduced sediment supply can lead to erosion not just in the valley below a dam, but also at the coast. The Nile delta, which has some two-thirds of Egypt's arable land, is being eroded by the sea at a rate of up to 240m. a year because the river is no longer supplying sediment to the delta.

The sedimentation of reservoirs is another major problem. By 1987 it was estimated that c.50 cubic km of sediment was being trapped in the reservoirs of large dams each year. Major reservoirs may lose more than 2 per cent of their capacity due to sediment infill every year – with a far higher proportion on dams on rivers such as the Yellow River in China, where sediment concentrations are especially high. The Sanmenxia dam on the Yellow River, built from 1987, has lost 40 per cent of its capacity to sedimentation. The Yangouxia dam, higher on the same river, lost a third of its capacity even before it started generating power.

The flooding of fields and settlements is not the only problem. There can also be a reduction in the quality of the water in them, due to the long time that the water is retained there; algal blooms in enriched waters can deprive fish and other aquatic life of oxygen and make the water unfit for either domestic or industrial use. In addition, in the early years of a reservoir the amount of rotting vegetation from the flooded land surface can greatly deplete oxygen levels. Dams in hot climates can increase markedly the amount of water lost by evaporation; about a third of the river flow of the Colorado is lost in this way. Dams also cause problems for migratory fish such as salmon, which may be barred from their spawning grounds unless adequate fish ladders are provided. River and floodplain ecosystems are closely adapted to an annual cycle of flooding and drying – many species cannot survive if this cycle is broken.

Dams cause major damage to fresh-water ecosystems. Traditional fishing communities are destroyed. Far from being environmentally friendly, hydroelectric power schemes are not as 'clean' as is often suggested, due to the release of greenhouse gases, especially carbon dioxide and methane from flooded vegetation. Reservoirs may also be significant sources of greenhouse gases due to emissions from algae in the water. Climatic change is rendering obsolete the ideas that are the basis for dam planning and design: that past hydrological conditions provide the key to the future. Flood severity may become greater than has been planned for in dam construction, should a greater frequency of extreme meteorological events occur. Conversely the generation of hydroelectricity could be severely reduced by an increased incidence of drought and higher than expected levels of evaporation.

Dams are also a physical danger if they collapse due to poor design or the effects of earthquakes, or if they prove incapable of accommodating flood waters and are overtopped. Some 200 dams outside China have failed for such reasons and more than 13,500 people have been drowned in these incidents. In China the scale of disaster has been an order of magnitude worse, due largely to a catastrophic series of dam bursts in Henan province in 1975, which may have drowned around 230,000 people. A whole series of dams which had been built to be capable of withstanding a once-in-a-1,000-years flood had to face a once-in-2,000-years event, and failed. News of this disaster was long suppressed by the Chinese government.

On a scarcely less catastrophic note is the large-scale human misery caused by dams – the failure of resettlement programmes, with community hardship and economic disintegration and an increase in health problems. In India an estimated 75 per cent of people displaced in this way have received no alternative land or housing. As many as eighty million people around the world have lost their land and homes without compensation. Dams in the Yangtze basin alone are thought to have displaced more than ten million people. People around large dams are driven from their land in a variety of ways other than simply by flooding. Some may lose it right at the start due to the need to provide accommodation for the thousands of construction workers required on such projects. They may have their land expropriated by the state in order to make way for wildlife reserves or afforestation designed to mitigate the effects of the dam. Fishermen and boatmen both upstream and downstream may lose their livelihoods. Farmers, and graziers downstream, will also be affected by changes in the river regime. The influx of large numbers of construction workers from outside may cause social disruption, while people in an area which is expected to be flooded can suffer from long-term planning blight and loss of government funds, which can begin years before construction of the dam is even started. Even where resettlement schemes have been implemented, they have often been badly planned and executed.

While a series of smaller dams would not necessarily generate as much power as one large scheme, it would cost a lot less and would have a more limited effect on the rural population. A number of community-scale projects in countries such as India have demonstrated that more low-key, sustainable projects can deliver many of the benefits of large dam schemes without as many severe disadvantages. Such programmes tend to find little favour with engineers, bureaucrats and politicians, however, whose mind-sets are locked into the perceived need for major hard-engineering schemes.

These problems can be better appreciated by looking in more detail at such a project – for example, the building of the Three Gorges Dam in China. With a population of *c*.1.3 billion in 2003, China's recent economic growth has been impressive: between 1978 and 1991 its GNP increased by 8.6 per cent per annum, making China's economy the fastest-growing in the world. Inevitably this has attracted large amounts of foreign investment in development projects. When it is appreciated that China feeds 22 per cent of the world's population on 8 per cent of global water resources, the attraction of big dam schemes can be understood. China, however, also has a poor environmental record, with one of the world's most serious soil erosion problems, affecting as much as a third of its arable land. This is a long-established feature of China: not for nothing is one of its great rivers named the Yellow River. But this in turn emphasises the dangers of trying to modify the environment at a macro scale without a full understanding of the likely effects. Major schemes such as the Three Gorges Dam have been described as long-term irreversible environmental experiments (Heming et al. 2001).

The Yangtze River, at 3,700 miles long, is the third longest river in the world, with millions of people living along its banks. The Three Gorges Dam, a scheme described by one author as 'monstrous' (McCully 2001), is the biggest hydroelectric dam in the world. It has also been called the most environmentally and socially destructive project of its kind. The project was begun in 1993 and was completed in 2006. The dam is more than 600 feet high. A 600km lake has been created, flooding 632sq. km of land. It has displaced an estimated 1.3 million people

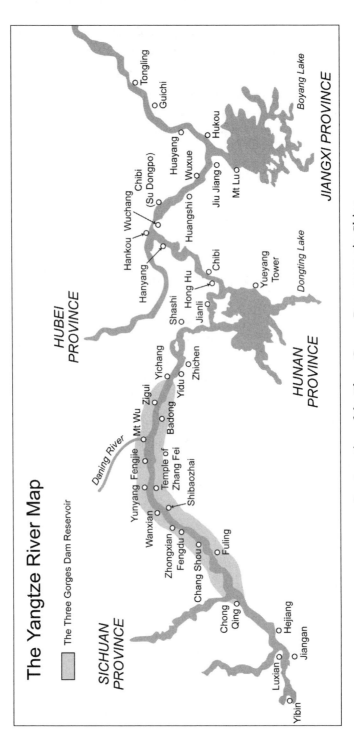

FIGURE 8.2 Location of the Three Gorges Dam reservoir, China

from land which is among the most fertile in China. The turbines, if they operate as projected, will produce over 18m. kw – up to a ninth of China's electricity output. An estimated 250,000 workers have been involved in the project (Barber and Ryder 1993).

Ideas for a dam on this part of the Yangtze River go back to the early twentieth century, but neither the political nor the economic conditions were favourable at that time. From the late 1950s, with the active support of Chairman Mao Zedong, serious plans began to take shape, but were then shelved as a result of the economic depression resulting from Mao's Great Leap Forward. Only in 1979 did the State Council finally approve the plan, leading to a feasibility study in 1982–83 to try to calm fears that the project did not adequately address technical, social or environmental issues (Luk and Whitney 1993). The study nevertheless seems to have underestimated both the technical difficulties and environmental impacts of the planned scheme. There was serious concern by archaeologists at the loss of some 1,300 known sites beneath the reservoir, and by the tourist industry that the scenery of the famous gorges would be ruined. An engineer, Dai Qing, published a book which was highly critical of the project. He was imprisoned in 1989 after the Tiananmen Square protests and the scheme was pushed through regardless. The alternative of a series of smaller dams was rejected. Resettlement of the people whose homes and livelihoods would be flooded by the rising waters began soon after, while construction started in 1994. The project, however, was plagued by scandals over corruption: money was embezzled on a grand scale, while the construction standards of much of the infrastructure were so substandard that work was halted in 1999 in order that various elements could be rebuilt. Not surprisingly, costs escalated rapidly so that the project has now broken all records as the most expensive in history, estimated at $75 billion or more. At the same time there are doubts about whether there will be sufficient market for the electricity that the dam will generate (Qing et al. 1998; Shapiro 2001).

Meanwhile, many of the people who have been resettled have been crowded on to poor land with unsatisfactory living conditions and few job opportunities. Supporters of the project counter this by emphasising the benefits to the people living downstream – from a reduction in flood hazards as well as the availability of power. Environmentalists have been concerned that there will be an increase in pollution as the Yangtze will no longer be able to flush out as many pollutants as before. There are worries that a project on this scale will have major ecological impacts, threatening species of fish, birds and animals. Extensive logging associated with the project is a potential source of increased soil erosion.

The plan was for a dam that would help control flooding, generate power and improve navigation. A series of locks would increase the volume of river shipping from ten million tonnes a year to fifty million. Ocean-going vessels of 10,000 tons would be able to sail for 1,500 miles (2,413km), directly into the heart of China, opening up the region's economy. In terms of power, the scheme is planned to generate as much energy as eighteen nuclear power stations. But can China's unsophisticated electrical system actually cope with the power? In terms of flood control the 22.1 billion cubic metres capacity of the reservoirs lessens the risk of major floods downstream from once in every ten years to once a century; and the river's floods have claimed more than a million lives during the past century. But there are concerns that the Yangtze will dump 530 million tons of silt into the reservoir each year, rapidly reducing its effectiveness. As many contaminated industrial sites will be flooded by the reservoir there are worries that pollutants will seep into the water and create a health hazard. There are also concerns about the dumping of untreated human waste into the reservoir, potentially creating an open sewer the length of Lake Superior. And there are further fears that an earthquake might cause the dam to burst. Environmentalists have suggested that the real source of flooding is the loss of forest cover in the Yangtze basin. There were objections that the dam would result in the flooding of at least a hundred towns as well as fertile agricultural land. It was also feared that the upstream Sichuan province would incur much of the cost while the downstream Hubei province would receive most of the benefits

Given these concerns, many people have wondered why the Chinese government has continued to back the project. The kudos of bringing to fruition such a huge scheme, and the need to avoid the loss of face that would occur if the scheme were to be abandoned, seem to be involved. The dam can be seen as a symbol of China's vitality and economic growth in a new century. Unfortunately, China has chosen to launch the project and then tackle the problems it creates along the way instead of thinking them out in advance and altering the project to accommodate them. In September 2004 the scheme was put to the test for the first time when the dam was put on high alert as flood water from the Yangtze poured into the reservoir. Navigation through the dam's locks was suspended for the first time since they were opened. It remains to be seen whether the elements of success in the project outweigh the damage and environmental degradation which a project of this scale can generate. That the Chinese government is still firmly wedded to the idea of large dam schemes is shown by recent plans to construct an even higher dam in the Tiger Leaping Gorge, much higher up the Yangtze where it emerges from the Tibetan plateau. The 130-mile- (209km) long reservoir would be located in a UNESCO World Heritage Site where the gorge walls soar to snow-capped, 15,000-foot (4,600m.) peaks. If the scheme goes ahead it will displace at least 100,000 people. There have been violent protests, however, by tens of thousands of farmers over plans to build another dam in Hanyuan county, particularly over the inadequate nature of the compensation. So widespread has been the opposition that the project has been halted, at least temporarily. As pressures for development increase the control and management of water, resources will become more and more important over huge areas of the world, leading to international tensions as well as internal disturbances (Amery 2002).

CHAPTER 9

Postscript: Environmental Change and the Future

In the last few chapters we have ranged through 12,000 years, from the Palaeolithic hunters of North America to one of the world's largest (and undoubtedly most expensive) contemporary construction projects. In the course of this journey we have seen a gradual shift from societies that were capable of modifying their environments to only a modest degree, to ones which have had the temerity, and possibly short-sightedness, to make modifications to their surroundings which have the potential to impact at a global scale (whether the modifications be deliberate or accidental).

Four features stand out in particular. First is that during the Holocene environmental change has been the rule rather than the exception. There can have been few places and few periods in which people did not perceive some natural and man-made changes occurring to their surroundings in the course of a normal human lifespan. For the most part, however, these changes were gradual and did not threaten totally to undermine the basis of the societies that experienced them. Dramatic, rapid change of the kind we have seen associated with events such as volcanic eruptions or other natural catastrophes (such as the drought, which may have led to the collapse of the Maya civilisation) were the exception rather than the rule. And as we have seen, human societies were often remarkably resilient in the face of adversity: adaptation rather than adversity has been the norm. Instances where environmental change caused complete social collapse have, mercifully, been rare.

Second: it is clear that humans have been able to modify their environments even from very early times. It may seem incredible that a few thousand Stone Age hunters could so dramatically alter the fauna of an entire continent as to wipe out many large animal species in North America at the end of the last Ice Age. Not all scientists believe that this is the explanation for the megafauna extinction, but the theory is nevertheless taken seriously by many specialists.

Third, while the nature of environmental change can often be established, the causes and timing of change are often known much less precisely. The precise role of human agency is often in doubt and many of the case studies we have looked at are amenable to being interpreted from a range of standpoints, not all of which are completely unbiased and objective. Environmental history and palaeo-environmental studies may employ an increasingly impressive battery of scientific techniques, but they cannot always guarantee the levels of precision that we might wish for.

Fourth, the pace of environmental change has undoubtedly accelerated dramatically in many parts of the world since the beginning of the twentieth century. The great English landscape historian W. G. Hoskins wrote, in his *Making of the English Landscape* (1955), that since the start of the Industrial Revolution, and particularly from 1914: 'every single change in the English landscape has either uglified it or destroyed its meaning'. Hoskins's view was an extremely pessimistic one, but it does give voice to the feeling, widely held in Britain today, that environmental change, whether purely natural or human-induced, is becoming an ever more prominent feature in our lives, none of it for the good.

We have seen examples of human interaction with the environment that have been thoughtless or heavy-handed. In other cases the societies concerned, lacking the ability to identify, far less control, rising population trends, were unwitting perpetrators of disaster. On the other hand it is worth remembering examples where, arguably, human intervention has worked with nature rather than against it, to produce intricate and complex landscapes that are highly cherished. In 1810 William Wordsworth, in the first edition of his *Guide to the Lakes*, produced a detailed analysis of the way in which such processes had shaped the landscapes of the Lake District, an area currently being put forward for consideration as a World Heritage cultural landscape. Since his day, the landscape of this much-cherished area has been exposed to some insensitive treatment – e.g. heavy overgrazing in recent decades

– but even the scars of former mining and quarrying have faded, while the spread of bracken, to the detriment of the grazing, adds a superb element of colour in autumn. And to set against such treatment we must consider the sensitive management policies of the National Park Authority and, on a smaller scale, of landowners such as the National Trust, as well as the impact of conservation groups such as the Friends of the Lake District. Similar claims regarding the uniqueness of particular combinations of human and physical influences could be made for many areas with distinctive landscape in other parts of Europe where there has been human settlement and activity for thousands of years, whether the *pays* of France or the landscapes of the Mediterranean. The key feature of the inter-relationships that have produced such landscapes has been gradual evolution rather than rapid change.

The pace of environmental change does seem to be accelerating. As a boy in the 1950s and early 1960s, interested in geography, I was aware of debates about the rate of clearance of tropical rainforests or the speed at which we were consuming fossil fuels. Today such issues loom larger in popular consciousness. As a young academic in the 1970s, lecturing on climatic change, theories about the human-enhanced greenhouse effect were fascinating but still seemed largely speculative. Severe winters in Britain, notably that of 1962–63, seemed to be suggesting that we were heading for colder rather than warmer conditions. And if we did have the power to alter global climate it seemed, during the Cold War, more likely to come through a 'nuclear winter' scenario in the aftermath of atomic warfare. Now hardly a week goes by without further evidence appearing in the media in support of continuing, and indeed accelerating, global warming and associated environmental change. The reality of global warming is becoming much more difficult to deny than it was even a decade ago.

I am writing this postscript in a year in which the Caribbean has seen more hurricanes than in any other in the twentieth century. The rate of rise of atmospheric carbon dioxide levels, measured at Mauna Loa in Hawaii, has suddenly jumped some 25 per cent. In the Philippines at least 1,100 people have been killed in flash floods and mudslides resulting from typhoons. It has been an above-average year for typhoons in this part of the Pacific. By definition, above-average years are likely to occur with reasonable frequency but, more worryingly, the number of typhoons occurring annually has been rising since 1945. The usual suspect is, of course, global warming, whether human-induced or otherwise. The authorities in the Philippines, however, have strongly expressed the view that the disaster was greatly exacerbated by large-scale illegal logging, which had increased the rate of runoff and slope instability, leading to more severe flooding and more widespread mud-slides. The moral is an obvious one, but doing something about it in practical terms is more difficult.

Thus the problems caused by environmental change and how societies respond to them seem particularly relevant at the present time. Some of the apparent changes may be due more to better communications, more detailed reporting and heightened awareness of environmental issues: but only a certain amount. There is still a tendency to caricature environmental specialists as bearded eco-freaks. Yet our need for specialists who can monitor and explain environmental change is becoming ever greater. If there is a message to be drawn from the examples we have considered in this book it is this: that we need to think very carefully about the implications and possible side effects of the changes we make to our environment, as well as monitoring more closely the operation of natural processes, both to increase our understanding of what is going on and to be able to predict more accurately what is likely to occur in the future. Where we do, consciously or otherwise, interfere with our surroundings we need to try to ensure that we do so gradually, so that if undesirable side effects begin to emerge we can reverse the trends, or at least deal with them in a considered, measured way rather than through a panic response. If this book has perhaps over-emphasised the down side of environmental change, then it is worth remembering that while our technology undoubtedly gives us the power to destroy habitats it also allows us to remake them. Environmental change is not bad in itself if we respond to it in the right kinds of way.

BIBLIOGRAPHY

Adams, R. M. (1966) *The Evolution of Urban Society: Early Mesopotamia and Prehispanic Mexico*, London.

— (1981) *Heartland of Cities: Surveys of Ancient Settlement and Land Use on the Central Flood Plain of the Euphrates*, Chicago.

Affleck, T. L., K. J. Edwards and A. Clarke (1988) 'Archaeological and palynological studies at the Mesolithic pitchstone and flint site of Auchareoch, Isle of Arran', *Proceedings of the Society of Antiquaries of Scotland*, 118, pp. 37–59.

Amery, H. A. (2002) 'Water wars in the Middle East: a looming threat', *Geographical Journal*, 168, pp. 313–23.

Amorosi, J., P. Buckland, A. Dugmore, J. H. Ingimundarson and T. H. McGovern (1997) 'Raiding the landscape: human impact in the Scandinavian North Atlantic', *Human Ecology*, 25, pp. 491–518.

Anderson, W. (1990) *The Green Man*, London.

Appleton, J. (1975) *The Experience of Landscape*, London.

Armit, I. (1997) *Celtic Scotland*, Edinburgh.

Arneborg, J. (1990) 'The Roman Church in Norse Greenland. The Norse of the North Atlantic', *Acta Archaeologica*, 61, pp. 142–50.

Atherden, M. (1992) *Upland Britain. A Natural History*, Manchester.

Bailey, R. N. (1980) *Viking Age Sculpture in Northern England*, London.

Baillie, M. (1989) 'Do Irish bog oaks date the Shang Dynasty?', *Current Archaeology*, 117, pp. 310–13.

— (1995) *A Slice Through Time. Dendrochronology and Precision Dating*, Oxford.

Baillie, M. and M. A. R. Munro (1988) 'Irish tree rings, Santorini and volcanic dust veils', *Nature*, 332, pp. 344–6.

Ballantyne, C. K. and G. Whittington (1999) 'Late Holocene floodplain erosion and alluvial fan formation in the central Grampian Highlands', *Journal of Quaternary Science*, 14, pp. 651–71.

Barber, M. and G. Ryder (1993) *Damming the Three Gorges*, London.

Barlow, L. E., J. P. Sadler, A. E. J. Ogilvie, P. C. Buckland, T. Amorosi, J. H. Ingimundarson, P. Skidmore, A. J. Dugmore and T. T. McGovern (1997) 'Interdisciplinary investigations of the end of the Norse Western settlement in Greenland', *The Holocene*, 7, pp. 489–99.

Barnatt, J. (1999) 'Taming the land: peak district farming and ritual in the Bronze Age', *Derbyshire Archaeological Journal*, 119, pp. 19–78.

Barton, G. A. (2002) *Empire Forestry and the Origins of Environmentalism*, Cambridge.

Bar-Yosef, O. and D. H. Meadow (1995) 'The origins of agriculture in the Near East', in T. P. Price and A. B. Gebauer (eds), *New Perspectives on the Prehistoric Transition to Agriculture*, Santa Fe, pp. 39–54.

Beaumont, P. (1993) *Drylands: Environmental Management and Development*, London.

Beck, M. W. (1996) 'On discerning the cause of late Pleistocene megafaunal extinctions', *Palaeobiology*, 22, pp. 91–103.

Behringer, A. (1999) 'Climatic change and witch hunting: the impact of the Little Ice Age on mentalities', *Climatic Change*, 43, pp. 335–51.

Bell, M. and J. C. Walker (1992) *Late Quaternary Environmental Change: Physical and Human Perspectives*, Harlow.

Beresford, G. (1981) 'Climatic change and its effects upon the settlement and the desertion of medieval villages in Britain', in C. Delano Smith and M. Parry (eds), *Consequences of Climatic Change*, Nottingham, pp. 30–39.

Binford, L. R. (1968) 'Post-Pleistocene adaptations', in S. R. Binford and L. R. Binford (eds), *New Perspectives in Archaeology*, Chicago, IL, pp. 313–41.

Bird, E. (1993) *Submerging Coasts: The Effects of Rising Sea Levels on Coastal Environments*, Chichester.

Borgstrom, G. (1973) *World Food Resources*, New York.

Boserup, E. (1965) *The Conditions of Agricultural Growth*, London.

Bottema, S. and A. Sarpaki (2003) 'Environmental change in Crete: a 9,000-year record of Holocene vegetation history', *The Holocene*, 13, pp. 233–49.

Bowden, M. (2000) *Furness Iron*, London.

Bowden, M. J. (1976) 'The Great American Desert in the American mind: the historiography of a geographical notion', in D. Lowenthal and M. J. Bowden, *Geographies of the Mind*, New York, pp. 119–47.

Bradley, R. S. (1985) *Quaternary Palaeoecology*, London.

Braidwood, R. J. and B. Howe (1961) *Prehistoric Investigations in Iraqi Kurdistan*, Chicago.

Brandt, C. J. and J. B. Thornes (eds) (1996) *Mediterranean Desertification and Land Use*, London.

Braudel, F. (1972) *The Mediterranean and the Mediterranean World in the Age of Philip II*, London.

Bryans, R. (1959) *Madeira, Pearl of the Atlantic*, London.

Buckland, P., A. J. Dugmore and K. J. Edwards (1997) 'Bronze Age myths? Volcanic activity and human responses in the Mediterranean and North Atlantic regions', *Antiquity*, 71, pp. 581–93.

Buckland, P., T. Amorosi, L. Barlow, A. J. Dugmore, P. A. Mayewski, T. H. McGovern, A. E. J. Ogilvie, J. P. Sadler and P. Skidmore (1996) 'Bioarchaeological and climatological evidence for the fate of Norse farmers in medieval Greenland', *Antiquity* 70, pp. 88–96.

Burgess, C. (1985) 'Population, climate and upland settlement', in D. Spratt and C. Burgess (eds), *Upland Settlement in Britain: The Second Millennium BC and After*, British Archaeological Reports, British Series, 143, Oxford, pp. 195–219.

— (1989) 'Volcanoes, catastrophe and the global crisis of the late second millennium BC', *Current Archaeology*, 117, pp. 325–9.

Burton, I. R., W. Kates and G. F. White (1993) *The Environment as Hazard*, New York.

Byock, J. (2002) *Viking Age Iceland*, London.

Caseldine, C. and D. Maguire (1986) 'Late glacial and early Flandrian vegetation changes on northern Dartmoor, SW England', *Journal of Biogeography*, 13, pp. 255–64.

Cavali-Sforza, L. L., P. Menozzi and N. Piazza (1994) *The History and Geography of Human Genes*, New York.

Champion, T. (1999) 'The Later Bronze Age', in J. Hunter and I. Ralston (eds), *The Archaeology of Britain*, London, pp. 95–112.

Chester, D. K. and P. A. James (1991) 'Holocene alluviation in the Algarve, southern Portugal: the case for an anthropogenic cause', *Journal of Agricultural Science*, 18, pp. 73–87.

Chetham, D. (2002) *Before the Deluge: The Vanishing World of the Yangtse's Three Gorges*, New York.

Childe, V. G. (1954) *What Happened in History*, London.

Chorley, R. J., R. D. Beckinsale and A. J. Dunn (1964) *The History of the Study of Landforms, or the Development of Geomorphology*, Volume 1, London.

Claris, P. and J. Quartermaine (1989) 'The Neolithic quarries and axe factory sites in Great Langdale and Scafell: a new survey', *Proceedings of the Prehistoric Society*, 55, pp. 1–25.

Coe, M. D. (2000) *The Maya*, London.

Connell, J. (2003) 'Losing ground? Tuvalu, the greenhouse effect and the garbage can', *Asia Pacific Viewpoint*, 44, pp. 89–107.

Conzen, M. (ed.) (1990) *The Making of the American Landscape*, Boston, MA.

Cosgrove, D. (1984) *Social Formation and Symbolic Landscapes*, London.

Cowley, D. C. (1998) 'Identifying marginality in the first and second millennia BC in the Strath of Kildonan, Sutherland', in C. M. Mills and G. Coles (eds), *Life on the Edge. Human Settlement and Marginality*, Oxford, pp. 165–71.

Crosby, A. W. (1986) *Ecological Imperialism. The Biological Expansion of Europe 900–1900*, Cambridge.

Crutzen, P. J. (2002) 'Geology of mankind', *Nature*, 415, p. 23.

Culbert, T. (1973) *The Classic Maya Collapse*, Albuquerque, NM.

— (1988) 'The collapse of classic Maya civilization', in N. Yoffee and G. L. Cowgill (eds), *The Collapse of Ancient States and Civilizations*, Arizona, pp. 69–101.

Cunliffe, B. (2001) *Facing the Ocean. The Atlantic and Its Peoples 8,000BC–AD1500*, Oxford.

Curry, A. M. (2000) 'Holocene reworking of drift-mantled hillslopes in the Scottish Highlands', *Journal of Quaternary Science*, 15, pp. 529–41.

Dansgaard, W., J. W. C. White and S. J. Johnsen (1989) 'The abrupt termination of the Younger Dryas climate event', *Nature*, 339, pp. 532–4.

Darby, H. C. (1956) *The Draining of the Fens*, Cambridge.

Delano-Smith, C. (1979) *Western Mediterranean Europe. An Historical Geography of Italy, Spain and Southern France Since the Neolithic Period*, London.

Dodgshon, R. A. (1981) *Land and Society in Early Scotland*, Oxford.

— (1998) *From Chiefs to Landlords*.

Social and Economic Change in the Western Highlands and Islands c1493–1820, Edinburgh.

— (2004) 'Researching Britain's remote spaces: some themes in the history of upland landscape', in A. R. H. Baker (ed.), *Home and Colonial. Essays on Landscape, Ireland, Environment and Empire in Celebration of Robin Butlin's Contribution to Geography*, London, pp. 29–38.

Doumas, C. (1974) 'The Minoan eruption of the Santorini volcano', *Antiquity*, 48, pp. 101–15.

— (1978) *Thera and the Aegean World*, London.

Dugmore, A. and P. Buckland (1991) 'Tephrochronology and Late Holocene Soil erosion in south Iceland', in J. K. Maizels and C. Caseldine (eds), *Environmental Change in Iceland: Past and Present*, Dordrecht, pp. 147–59.

Dugmore, A. J., A. J. Newton, G. Larsen and G. T. Cook (2000) 'Tephrochronology, environmental change and the Norse settlement of Iceland', *Environmental Archaeology*, 5, pp. 21–34.

Eastwood, W. J., J. Tibby, N. Roberts, H. J. B. Birks and H. E. Lamb (2002) 'The environmental impact of the Minoan eruption of Santorini (Thera); statistical analysis of palaeoecological data from Golhisad, southwest Turkey', *The Holocene*, 12, pp. 431–49.

Edwards, K. J. and I. B. M. Ralston (eds) (1997) *Scotland: Environment and Archaeology 8000BC–1000AD*, Chichester.

Elsasser, H. and P. Messerli (2001) 'The vulnerability of the snow industry in the Swiss Alps', *Mountain Research and Development*, 4, pp. 335–9.

Eschenbach, W. (2004) 'Tuvalu not experiencing increased sea level rise', *Energy and Environment*, 15, pp. 527–44.

Evans, J. G. (1975) *The Environment of Early Man in the British Isles*, London.

Evans, K. and I. Ralston (1984) 'Postglacial hunter-gatherers and vegetation history in Scotland', *Proceedings of the Society of Antiquaries of Scotland*, 114, pp. 15–33.

Fagan, B. (2000) *The Little Ice Age*, New York.

Fagan, B. N. (1987) *The Great Journey*, London.

Fairhurst, H. and D. B. Taylor (1974) 'A hut circle settlement at Kilphedir, Sutherland', *Proceedings of the Society of Antiquaries of Scotland*, 103, pp. 65–99.

Fernandez-Arnesto, F. (1982) *The Canary Islands after the Conquest; the Making of a Colonial Society in the Early Sixteenth Century*, Oxford.

Fleming, A. (1987) 'The co-axial field system: some questions of time and space', *Antiquity*, 61, pp. 188–202.

— (1988) *The Dartmoor Reaves*, London.

— (1998) *Swakedale. Valley of the Wild River*, Edinburgh.

Flinn, M. W. (1976) *Scottish Population History*, Cambridge.

Frey, V. H. (1976) *The Impact of Mass Tourism on a Rural Community in the Swiss Alps*, Ann Arbor, MN.

Gerrard, J. (1991) 'An assessment of some of the factors involved in recent landscape change in

Iceland', in J. K. Maizels and C. Caseldine (eds), *Environmental Change in Iceland: Past and Present*, Dordrecht, pp. 237–53.

Gibson, A. and T. C. Smout (1989) 'Scottish food and Scottish history 1500–1800', in R. A. Houston and I. D. Whyte (eds), *Scottish Society 1500–1800*, Cambridge, pp. 59–84.

Gill, R. (2001) *The Great Maya Droughts: Water, Life and Death*, Albuquerque, NM.

Gillespie, R., D. R. Horton, P. Ladd, P. G. Macumber, R. Thorne and R. V. S. Wright (1978) 'Lancefield Swamp and the extinction of the Australian Megafauna', *Science*, 200, pp. 1044–8.

Glantz, M. H. (ed.) (1999) *Creeping Environmental Problems and Sustainable Development in the Aral Sea Basin*, Cambridge.

Goldman, M. L. (1972) *Environmental Pollution in the Soviet Union*, Cambridge, MA.

Gornitz, V. (1993) 'Mean sea level changes in the recent past', in R. Warrick, E. M. Barrow and T. M. Wigley (eds), *Climate and Sea Level Change*, Cambridge, pp. 25–44.

Grattan, J. (1998) 'The response of marginal societies and economies in Britain to Icelandic volcanic eruptions', in C. M. Mills and G. Coles (eds), *Life on the Edge. Human Settlement and Marginality*, Oxford, pp. 22–30.

Grattan, J. P. and D. D. Gilbertson (1994) 'Acid loading from Icelandic tephra falling on acidified ecosystems as a key to understanding archaeological and environmental stress in northern and western Britain', *Journal of Archaeological Science*, 21, pp. 851–9.

Grove, A. T. and O. Rackham (2001) *The Nature of Mediterranean Europe. An Ecological History*, London and New Haven, CT.

Grove, J. M. (1988) *The Little Ice Age*, London.

Grove, J. M. and A. Conterio (1995) 'The climate of Crete in the sixteenth and seventeenth centuries', *Climatic Change*, 30, pp. 1–25.

Grove, R. (1995) *Green Imperialism: Colonial Responses, Tropical Island Edens and the Origins of Environmentalism 1600–1850*, Cambridge.

— (1997) 'The island and the history of environmentalism: the case of St. Vincent', in M. Teich, R. Porter and B. Gustaffson (eds), *Nature and Society in Historical Context*, Cambridge, pp. 148–62.

Hammer, C. U., H. B. Clausen, W. L. Friedrich and H. Tauber (1987) 'The Minoan eruption of Santorini in Greece dated to 1645BC', *Nature*, 328, pp. 517–19.

Harris, D. R. (ed.) (1996) *The Origin and Spread of Agriculture and Pastoralism in Eurasia*, London.

Harris, D. R. and G. C. Hillman (eds) (1989) *Foraging and Faring: The Evolution of Land Exploitation*, London.

Harrison, P., C. Renfrew and J. A. Sabloff (2000) *The Lords of Tikal: Rulers of an Ancient Maya City*, London.

Hastrup, K. (1985) *Culture and History in Medieval Iceland*, Oxford.

Haynes, C. V. (1991) 'Geoarchaeological and palaeohydrological evidence for Clovis-age drought in North America and its bearing on extinction', *Quaternary Research*, 35, pp. 438–50.

Heming, L., P. Waley and P. Rees (2001) 'Reservoir settlement in China: past experience and the Three Gorges Dam', *Geographical Journal*, 167, pp. 195–212.

Henry, D. O. (1989) *From Foraging to Agriculture, the Levant at the end of the Ice Age*, Philadelphia, PA.

Hey, D. (2000) 'Moorlands', in J. Thirsk (ed.) *The English Rural Landscape*, Oxford, pp. 188–209.

Hodell, D., J. H. Curtis and M. Brenner (1995) 'Possible role of climate in the collapse of the Classic Maya civilisation', *Nature*, 375, pp. 391–4.

Hodell, D., R. M. Brenner, J. H. Curtis and T. Guilderson (2001) 'Solar forcing of drought frequency in the Maya lowlands', *Science*, 292, pp. 1367–70.

Holt, J. C. (1982) *Robin Hood*, London.

Horne, P. and D. MacLeod (2001) 'Unravelling the Wharfedale landscape: a case study in field enhanced aerial survey', *Landscapes*, 2, pp. 65–82.

Hoskins, W. G. (1955) *The Making of the English Landscape*, London.

Hosler, D. H., J. A. Sabloff and D. Runge (1977) 'Simulation model development: a case study of the Classic Maya collapse', in N. Hammond (ed.), *Social Processes in Maya Prehistory*, London, pp. 553–90.

Houghton, J. T. (ed.) (2001) *Climate Change 2001*, Cambridge.

Hughen, K. A., J. T. Overpeck, L. C. Peterson and S. Trumbore (1996) 'Rapid climatic changes in the tropical Atlantic region during the last deglaciation', *Nature*, 380, pp. 51–4.

Ingstad, H. (1969) *Westwards to Vinland*, New York.

Jacobsen, T. and R. M. Adams (1958) 'Salt and silt in Ancient Mesopotamia', *Agricultural Science*, 128, pp. 1251–8.

Johnston, R. (2000) 'Dying, becoming and being the field: prehistoric cairnfields in Northumberland', in J. Harding and R. Johnston (eds), *Northern Parts: Interpretation of the Later Prehistoric of Northern England and Southern Scotland*, British Archaeological Reports, 302, Oxford, pp. 57–70.

Jomelli, V. and P. Pech (2004) 'Effects of the Little Ice Age on avalanche boulder tongues in the French Alps (Massif des Ecrins)', *Earth Surface Processes and Landforms*, 29, pp. 553–64.

Jones, C. W. (1994) *Scotland's First Settlers*, Edinburgh.

Jones, G. (1986) *The Norse Atlantic Saga*, Oxford.

Jones, M. (1977) *Finland, Daughter of the Sea*, Folkestone.

Jones, R. L. (1976) 'The activities of Mesolithic man: further palaeobotanical evidence from north east Yorkshire', in D. A. Davidson and M. Shackley (eds), *Geoarchaeology: Earth Sciences and the Past*, London, pp. 355–67.

Kahn, T. M. A., D. A. Quadir, K. A. Murty and M. A. Sarker (2003) 'Relative sea level changes in the Maldives and vulnerability of land due to abnormal coastal inundations', *Marine Geodesy*, 25, pp. 133–43.

Kariel, H. G. and P. E. Kariel (1982) 'Socio-cultural impacts of tourism:

an example from the Austrian Alps', *Geografiska Annaler*, series B 64, pp. 1–16.

Kenyon, K. (1956) 'Jericho and Its Setting in Near Eastern History', *Antiquity*, 30, pp. 184–97.

Kuhn, M. (1993) 'Possible contributions to sea level change from small glaciers', in R. Warrick, E. M. Barrow and T. M. Wigley (eds), *Climate and Sea Level Change*, Cambridge, pp. 131–43.

Ladurie, E. Le Roy (1971) *Times of Feast, Times of Famine. A History of Climate Since the Year 1000*, London.

Laird, K. D., S. C. Fritz, K. A. Maasch and B. F. Cumming (1996) 'Greater drought intensity and frequency before AD 1200 in the northern Great Plains, USA', *Nature*, 384, pp. 552–84.

Lamb, H. H. (1982) *Climate, History and the Modern World*, London.

Lambert, J. (1996) *Transect Through Times. The Archaeological Landscape of the Shell North Western Ethylene Pipeline*, Lancaster.

Lambert, R. A. (2001) *Contested Mountains. Nature, Development and Environment in the Cairngorms Region of Scotland, 1880–1980*, Cambridge.

Lawson, M. P. and M. E. Baker (eds) (1981) *The Great Plains. Perspectives and Prospects*, Lincoln, NE.

Leech, R. H. (1983) 'Settlements and groups of small cairns on Birkby and Birker Fells, Eskdale, Cumbria', *Transactions of the Cumberland and Westmorland Antiquarian and Archaeological Society*, 83, pp. 15–24.

Lewin, J., M. G. Macklin and J. C. Woodward (eds) (1995) *Mediter-* ranean *Quarternary River Environments*, Rotterdam.

Lichtenberger, E. (1975) *The Eastern Alps*, Oxford.

Lindsay, J. M. (1975) 'Charcoal iron smelting and its fuel supply: the example of Lorn furnace, Argyllshire 1753–1876', *Journal of Historical Geography*, 1, pp. 283–98.

Lowe, A. (1989) 'The industrial landscape', in W. Rollinson (ed.), *The Lake District. Landscape Heritage*, Newton Abbott, pp. 101–29.

Lowe, J. J. and M. J. C. Walker (1984) *Reconstructing Quaternary Environments*, Harlow.

Lowe, J. W. G. (1985) *The Dynamics of Apocalypse. A Systems Simulation of the Classic Maya Collapse*, Albuquerque, NM.

Luk, S. and J. B. Whitney (1993) *Megaproject: A Case Study of China's Three Gorges Project*, New York.

McCully, P. (2001) *Silenced Rivers: The Ecology and Politics of Large Dams*, New York.

McFarlane, A. (1992) *The British in America 1480–1815*, London.

McGovern, T. H. (1981) 'The economics of extinction in Norse Greenland', in T. M. L. Wigley, M. J. Ingram and G. Farmer (eds), *Climate and History*, Cambridge, pp. 404–30.

— (1983) 'Contributions to the palaeoeconomy of Norse Greenland', *Acta Archaeologica*, 54, pp. 73–122.

McNeill, J. R. (1992) *The Mountains of the Mediterranean*, Cambridge.

MacPhee, R. D. and D. A. Marx (1997) 'The 40,000 year plague: humans, hyperdisease and first contact extinction', in S. M. Goodman and B. D. Paterson (eds), *Natural Change and Human Impact in Madagascar*, Washington, DC, pp. 169–217.

Macklin, M. G., D. G. Passmore and B. J. Rumsby (1992) 'Climatic and cultural signals in Holocene alluvial sequences: the Tyne basin, northern England', in S. Needham and M. G. Macklin (eds), *Alluvial Archaeology in Britain*, Oxford, pp. 123–40.

Maisels, C. K. (1990) *The Emergence of Civilization: From Hunting and Gathering to Agriculture, Cities and the State in the Near East*, London.

Malone, C. (1989) *Avebury*, London.

Manley, G. (1974) 'Central England temperatures: monthly means 1659–1973', *Quarterly Journal of the Royal Meteorological Society*, 100, pp. 389–405.

Manning, S. W. (1999) *A Test of Time: The Volcano of Thera and the Chronology and History of the Aegean and East Mediterranean in the Mid Second Millennium BC*, Oxford.

Marinatos, S. (1939) 'The volcanic destruction of Minoan Crete', *Antiquity*, 48, pp. 425–39.

Martin, P. S. (1973) 'The discovery of America', *Science*, 179, pp. 969–72.

Martin, P. S. and R. Klein (eds) (1984) *Quaternary Extinctions: A Prehistoric Revolution*, Tucson, AZ.

Martin, P. S. and H. E. Wright (eds) (1967) *Pleistocene Extinctions: The Search for a Cause*, New Haven, CT.

Martin, S. (2000) *Chronicle of the Maya Kings and Queens*, London.

Mather, A. S. (2004) 'Forest transition theory and the reforestation of Scotland', *Scottish Geographical Journal*, 120, pp. 83–98.

Mellars, P. A. and P. Dark (1998) *Starr Carr in Context*, Cambridge.

Mellars, P. A. and M. R. Wilkinson (1980) 'Fish otoliths as evidence of seasonality in prehistoric shell middens: the evidence from Oronsay (Inner Hebrides)', *Proceedings of the Prehistoric Society*, 46, pp. 19–44.

Micklin, P. (1988) 'Desiccation of the Aral Sea: a water management disaster in the Soviet Union', *Science*, 241, pp. 1170–76.

— (1998) 'Regional and international responses to the Aral crisis', *Post-Soviet Geography*, 39, pp. 399–416.

— (2000) *Managing Water in Central Asia*, London.

Miles, H. and A. Jackman (1991) *The Great Wood of Caledon. The Story of the Ancient Scottish Pine Forest*, Lanark.

Miller, G. H. (1999) 'Pleistocene extinction of Genyodnis newtoni. Human impact on Australian megafauns', *Science*, 283, pp. 205–8.

Mills, C. M. and G. Coles (1998) 'Clinging on for grim life: an introduction to marginality as an archaeological issue', in C. M. Mills and G. Coles (eds), *Life on the Edge. Human Settlement and Marginality*, Oxford, pp. vii–xii.

Morner, N.-A. (2001) 'The Maldives project: a future free from sea level flooding', *Contemporary South Asia*, 13, pp. 149–55.

Muir, R. (1982) *The Lost Villages of Britain*, London.

— (2000) 'Pollards in Nidderdale: a landscape history', *Rural History*, 11, pp. 26–38.

Netting, R. M. (1981) *Balancing on an Alp: Ecological Change and*

Continuity in a Swiss Mountain Community, Cambridge.

Olafsdottir, R. and H. J. Gudmundsson (2002) 'Holocene land degradation and climatic change in North East Iceland', *The Holocene*, 12, pp. 159–68.

Orians, G. H. (1986) 'An ecological and evolutionary approach to landscape Aesthetics', in E. C. Penning-Rowsell and D. Lowenthal (eds), *Landscape Meaning and Value*, London, pp. 3–25.

Owen-Smith, N. (1987) 'Pleistocene extinctions: the pivotal role of megaherbivores', *Palaeobiology*, 13, pp. 351–63.

Park, C. C. (1997) *The Environment. Principles and Approaches*, London.

Parker Pearson, M. (1993) *Bronze Age Britain*, London.

Parry, M. L. (1975) 'Secular climatic change and marginal agriculture', *Transactions of the Institute of British Geographers*, 64, pp. 1–14.

— (1978) *Climatic Change, Agriculture and Settlement*, Folkestone.

Parsons, J. J. (1981) 'Human influences on the pine and laurel forests of the Canary Islands', *Geographical Review*, 71, pp. 260–64.

Pearsall, W. H. and W. Pennington (1973) *The Lake District. A Landscape History*, London.

Perera, J. (1993) 'A sea turns to dust', *New Scientist*, 140, no. 1896, pp. 24–7.

Phillips, G. (1998) *Act of God*, London.

— (2002) *The Moses Legacy*, London.

Piggott, S. (1962) *The Prehistoric Peoples of Scotland*, Edinburgh.

Pollard, S. (1997) *Marginal Europe: The Contribution of Marginal Lands Since the Middle Ages*, Oxford.

Post, J. D. (1977) *The Last Great Subsistence Crisis in the Western World*, Baltimore, MD.

Postgate, J. N. (1992) *Early Mesopotamia: Society and Economy at the Dawn of History*, London.

Price, T. D. and A. B. Gerbauer (eds) (1995) *Last Hunters – First Farmers*, Santa Fe, NM.

Qing, D., J. Thorbeau and P. B. Williams (1998) *The River Dragon Has Come! The Three Gorges Dam and the Fate of China's Yangtse River and Its People*, New York.

Rackham, O. (1976) *Trees and Woodland in the British Landscape*, London.

— (1986) *The History of the Countryside*, London.

— (2000) 'The prospects for landscape history and historical ecology', *Landscapes*, 1, pp. 3–15.

Rackham, O. and J. Moody (1996) *The Making of the Cretan Landscape*, Manchester.

Ransome, A. (1930) *Swallows and Amazons*, London.

Renfrew, C. (1973) *Before Civilization*, London.

Richards, M. P. and P. A. Mellars (1998) 'Stable isotopes and the seasonality of the Oronsay middens', *Antiquity*, 72, pp. 178–84.

Ring, J. (2000) *How the English Made the Alps*, London.

Roberts, B. K. (1993) 'Some relict landscapes in Westmorland: a reconstruction', *Archaeological Journal*, 150, pp. 435–55.

Roberts, N. (1989) *The Holocene. An Environmental History*, Oxford.

Royal Commission on the Ancient and Historical Monuments of Scotland (1993) *Strath of Kildonan. An Archaeological Survey*, Edinburgh.

— (1997) *Eastern Dumfriesshire: An Archaeological Landscape*, Edinburgh.

— (2001) *'Well Sheltered and Watered'. Menstrie Glen: A Farming Landscape Near Stirling*, Edinburgh.

Saarinen, T. (1966) *Perception of the Drought Hazard on the Great Plains*, Chicago, IL.

Sauchin, D. J., J. Stroich and A. Beriault (2003) 'A palaeoecological context for the drought of 1999–2001 in the northern Great Plains of North America', *Geographical Journal*, 169, pp. 158–67.

Schama, S. (1995) *Landscape and Memory*, London.

Schubert, D., M. J. Suarez, D. T. Pegion, R. P. Koster and J. Bacmeister (2004) 'Causes of long-term drought in the US Great Plains', *Journal of Climate*, 17, pp. 485–503.

Scudder, T. (2001) 'The World Commission on Dams and the need for a new development paradigm', *International Journal of Water Resources Development*, 17, pp. 329–41.

Shapiro, J. (2001) *Mao's War Against Nature: Politics and the Environment on Revolutionary China*, Cambridge.

Shaw, B. D. (1981) 'Climate, erosion and history: the case of Roman North Africa', in T. M. L. Wigley, M. J. Ingram and G. Farmer (eds), *Climate and History*, London, pp. 379–403.

Sherratt, A. (1980) 'Water, soil and seasonality in early cereal cultivation', *World Archaeology*, 11, pp. 313–29.

Shipley, G. and J. Salmon (eds) (1996) *Human Landscapes in Classical Antiquity: Environment and Culture*, London.

Simmons, I. A. (1996) *The Environmental Impact of Later Mesolithic Cultures. The Creation of Moorland Landscape in England and Wales*, Edinburgh.

— (2001) *An Environmental History of Great Britain*, Edinburgh.

Simmons, I. A. and M. J. Tooley (1981) *The Environment in British Prehistory*, London.

Simmons, I. G. (2003) *The Moorlands of England and Wales. An Environmental History 900BC–AD2000*, Edinburgh.

Small, I., J. Van der Meer and R. E. G. Upshur (2001) 'Acting on an environmental health disaster: the case of the Aral Sea', *Environmental Health Perspectives*, 109, pp. 547–9.

Smith, B. D. (1995) *The Emergence of Agriculture*, New York.

Smith, J. (1997) *Environmental Hazards*, London.

Smith, K. (1992) *Environmental Hazards*, London.

Smout, T. C. (2000) *Nature Contested. Environmental History in Scotland and Northern England Since 1600*, Edinburgh.

— (ed.) (2003) *People and Woods in Scotland*, Edinburgh.

Stone, R. (1999) 'Coming to grips with the Aral Sea's grim legacy', *Science*, 284, pp. 30–33.

Sveinbjarnardottir, G. (1991) 'A study of farm abandonment in two regions of Iceland', in J. Maizels and C. Caseldine (eds), *Environmental Change in Iceland: Past and Present*, Dordrecht, pp. 167–88.

Symonds, H. H. (1936) *Afforestation in the Lake District*, London.

Tainter, J. A. (1988) *The Collapse of Complex Societies*, Cambridge.

Tallis, J. H. (1991) 'Forest and moorland in the south Pennine uplands in the mid-Flandrian period. III: The spread of woodland', *Journal of Ecology*, 79, pp. 401–24.

Tallis, J. H. and V. R. Switsur (1990) 'Forest and moorland in the south Pennine uplands in the mid-Flandrian period. II: The hillslope forests', *Journal of Ecology*, 78, pp. 857–83.

Taylor, J. A. (1980) 'Environmental Changes in Wales During the Holocene Period', in J. A. Taylor (ed.), *Culture and Environment in Prehistoric Wales*, British Archaeological Reports, 76, Oxford, pp. 25–37.

Thorarinsson, S. (1961) 'Population changes in Iceland', *Geographical Review*, 51, pp. 519–32.

Thornes, J. B. and D. Brunsden (1977) *Geomorphology and Time*, London.

Tipping, R. (1994) 'The form and fate of Scotland's woodlands', *Proceedings of the Society of Antiquaries of Scotland*, 124, pp. 1–54.

— (1998) 'Cereal cultivation on the Anglo-Scottish border during the "Little Ice Age"', in C. M. Mills and G. Coles (eds), *Life on the Edge. Human Settlement and Marginality*, Oxford, pp. 1–12.

— (2002) 'Climatic variability and "marginal" settlement in upland British landscapes: a re-evaluation', *Landscapes*, 3, pp. 10–29.

— (2005) 'Palaeoecology and political history: evaluating driving forces in historic landscape change in southern Scotland', in I. D. Whyte and A. J. L. Winchester (eds), *Landscape, Environment and Society in Upland Britain*, Society for Landscape Studies special publication No. 2, Birmingham.

Tooley, M. J. (1978) *Sea Level Change. North West England During the Flandrian Stage*, Oxford.

Tooley, M. J. and S. Jelgersma (1992) *Impacts of Sea Level Rise on European Coastal Lowlands*, Oxford.

Turner, J. (1981) 'The Iron Age', in I. G. Simmons and M. Tooley (eds), *The Environment in British Prehistory*, London, pp. 250–81.

United Nations Environmental Programme (1992) *The Aral Sea: Diagnostic Study for the Development of an Action Plan for the Conservation of the Aral Sea*, Nairobi.

Viazzo, P. (1989) *Upland Communities. Environment, Population and Social Change in the Alps Since the Sixteenth Century*, Cambridge.

Vita-Finzi, C. (1969) *The Mediterranean Valleys. Geological Changes in Historical Times*, Cambridge.

Warrick, R. A. and G. Farmer (1990) 'The Greenhouse Effect, climatic change and rising sea levels: implications for development', *Transactions of the Institute of British Geographers*, new series 15, pp. 5–20.

Warrick, R. A., E. M. Barrow and T. M. L. Wigley (1993) *Climatic Change and Sea Level Change*, Cambridge.

Watkins, C. (1998) *European Woods and Forests. Studies in Cultural History*, London.

Watson, A. (1991) 'Increase of people on Cairm Gorm plateau following easier access', *Scottish Geographical Magazine*, 207, pp. 99–105.

Watts, D. W. (1987) *The West Indies. Patterns of Development, Culture and Environmental Change Since 1492*, Cambridge.

— (1995) 'Ecological responses to ecosystem shock in the island Caribbean. The aftermath of Columbus 1492–1992', in R. A. Butlin and N. Roberts (eds), *Ecological Relations in Historical Time. Human Impact and Adaptation*, Oxford, pp. 267–79.

Whitehouse, R. (1977) *The First Cities*, Oxford.

Whittle, A. (2002) 'The coming of agriculture', in P. Slack and R. Ward (eds), *The Peopling of Britain. The Shaping of a Human Landscape*, Oxford, pp. 77–109.

Wickham-Jones, C. (2001) *The Landscape of Scotland. A Hidden History*, Stroud.

Whyte, I. D. (2003) *Landscape and History Since 1500*, London.

Whyte, I. D. and K. A. Whyte (1987) *Exploring Scotland's Historic Landscapes*, Edinburgh.

Wiggs, G. F. S., S. L. O'Hara, J. Van Der Meeds, I. Small and R. Hubbard (2003) 'The dynamics and characteristics of aeolian dust in dryland Central Asia: possible impacts on human exposure and respiratory health in the Aral Sea basin', *Geographical Journal*, 169, pp. 142–57.

Williams, L. D. (1978) 'The Little Ice Age glaciation level on Baffin Island, Arctic Canada', *Palaeogeography, Palaeoclimatology, Palaeoecology*, 25, pp. 199–207.

Williams, M. (1989) *North Americans and Their Forests: A Historical Geography*, Cambridge.

Williams, M., D. Dunkerley, P. De Deckker, P. Kershaw and J. Chappell (eds) (1998) *Quaternary Environments*, London.

Worster, D. (1979) *Dust Bowl. The Southern Plains in the 1930s*, Oxford.

Wrigley, E. A. and R. S. Schofield (1989) *The Population History of England 1541–1871. A Reconstruction*, Cambridge.

Yancey, D. (2004) *Life During the Dust Bowl*, San Diego, CA.

Yoffee, N. (1988) 'The collapse of ancient Mesopotamian states and civilizations', in N. Yoffee and G. L. Cowgill (eds), *The Collapse of Ancient States and Civilizations*, Tucson, AZ, pp. 44–68.

Zohary, D. and M. Hopf (1994) *Domestication of Plants in the Old World*, Oxford.

INDEX